Law, Economics
and Public Policy

POLITICAL ECONOMY AND PUBLIC POLICY, VOLUME 3

Editors: William Breit, *Department of Economics, Trinity University, San Antonio*
Kenneth G. Elzinga, *Department of Economics, University of Virginia*

POLITICAL ECONOMY AND PUBLIC POLICY

An International Series of Monographs
in Law and Economics, History of Economic Thought
and Public Finance

Edited by William Breit, Department of Economics, Trinity College and
Kenneth G. Elzinga, Department of Economics, University of Virginia

Volume 1. **CONTEMPORARY ECONOMISTS IN PERSPECTIVE**
Henry W. Spiegel, Catholic University of America
and Warren J. Samuels, Michigan State University

Volume 2. **METHODOLOGICAL CONTROVERSY IN ECONOMICS:**
Historical Essays in Honor of T.W. Hutchison
Edited by A.W. Coats, The University of Nottingham

Volume 3. **LAW, ECONOMICS AND PUBLIC POLICY**
Nicholas Mercuro and Timothy P. Ryan
University of New Orleans

To Louise

Law, Economics
and Public Policy

NICHOLAS MERCURO
TIMOTHY P. RYAN
*Department of Economics
and Finance
University of New Orleans*

JAI PRESS INC.

Greenwich, Connecticut   *London, England*

Library of Congress Cataloging in Publication Data
Main entry under title:

Law, economics and public policy.

    (Political economy and public policy; v. 3)
    Includes bibliographical references and index.
    1. Law—Economic aspects. 2. Economics. 3. Public
policy (Law)   I. Ryan, Timothy. II. Mercuro, Nicholas.
III. Series.
  K487.E3L4   1984   340'.11   84-4406
  ISBN 0-89232-396-5

62,942

CONTENTS

Preface   ix

I. **Introduction to Law and Economics**   1
    The Conventional Wisdom of Neoclassical
    Economics   2
    Welfare Economics   4
    Values, Law and Economics   9

II. **Law and Economics—A Descriptive Model**   13
    The Descriptive Model: Institutions and Legal
    Relations   15
    The Economic Impact Stage of Choice: The
    Interface Between Law and Economics   22
      The Market Sector   22
      Public Sector   29
      Communal Sector   30
      The Complex Legal-Economic Arena   31
    The Necessity of Choice   35

III. **The Problem of Externalities**   43
    A Formal Presentation of the Market Sector   44
    Market Failure   47
    Traditional Solutions to the Problem of
    Externalities   53
    Law and Economics and the Problem of Externality   56

IV. **The Economic Compensation Principle: Liability
    Rules and the Taking Issue**   69
    The Compensation Principle in Economics   70
    Tort Law and Liability Rules   76
      The Role of Liability Rules in Law and Economics   82

Liability Rules   87
Specific Liability Rules   92
The Taking Issue   99
The Taking Issue: The Legal Setting   100
Justice Holmes, the Taking Issue and Legal Rules   103

V. Economics and the Law   **117**
The New Law and Economics   117
Efficiency and the Common Law   119
Wealth Maximization   123
Criticisms of Wealth Maximization   130
Public Choice Theory   137
Public Choice Theory—An Overview   138
Contractarian Approach to Public Choice Theory   146

VI. Summary   **165**

Acknowledgments   **173**

Author Index   **177**

Subject Index   **181**

Preface

The purpose of this book is to provide an introductory exploration into the theory of Law and Economics. Throughout the book we use Law and Economics (higher case L and E) to include the new law and economics, the economics of property rights, old law and economics, public choice theory, neoinstitutionalist economic theory, and critical legal studies. The descriptive model of Law and Economics presented in the book encompasses these various schools of thought under an umbrella framework that identifies their commonalities as well as their differences.

The book presumes some understanding of economics, but not beyond the intermediate level. The attempt has been to identify and explicate some of the predominant legal economic theories contained in these schools of thought. We would hope that the level of the integrative treatment of law and economics provided in the book will allow both legal and economic scholars to better understand the interrelationships that exist between the two disciplines.

It should be noted that we use the word law in the broadest possible sense to include the prevailing and potential legal institutions. These institutions include: the judiciary, the executive branch, the legislature, government commissions and agencies, and custom. Largely employing the analytical apparatus of economics, typically that of welfare economics, our model of Law and Economics analyzes the systematic relationships that exist between the legal institutions and the character of economic life, utilizing what may be termed a comparative institutional approach. We believe that this approach logically emanates from a careful reading of those who have contributed to the field of Law and Economics. We have relied heavily on direct quotes from contributors to the literature together with our own interpretation and analysis in order to build a case for a comparative institutional approach to the study of the interrelations between law and economics.

We have proceeded to accomplish this task in the following manner: Chapter I provides an introduction to the interrelationships between Law and Economics. Chapter II develops our descriptive model of Law and Economics that provides the foundation for a comparative institutional approach to legal-economic analysis. Chapter III explores the concept of externalities inasmuch as it occupies a rather important niche in the literature. This discussion is expanded on in Chapter IV. This Chapter outlines the compensation principle in economics, analyzes liability rules in tort law, and describes the taking issue in constitutional law as it relates to the compensation principle. Chapter V proceeds to a description of much of the recent literature of the new law and economics including the concept of wealth maximization. It also provides a brief review of public choice theory before delving into a discussion of the contractarian approach to public choice theory. The book ends with Chapter VI that attempts to recast these theories within the context of the model of Law and Economics developed in Chapter II.

We would like to thank Professors William Breit and Kenneth Elzinga for comments, suggestions, and continuing encouragement throughout the development of the book. Any errors which remain, of course, are ours.

Nicholas Mercuro
Timothy P. Ryan

Chapter I

Introduction to Law and Economics

Economics and law considered as static phenomena are related as content and form; but both are subject to change—the one continuously, the other from time to time. . . . In reality law and economics are ever and everywhere complementary and mutually determinative. . . . Economics comprises both institutions and intellectual movements. It is somewhat surprising that so conspicuous a truth as the interaction of economics and law should have waited so long for recognition—a recognition by no means universal. Some of those who question it maintain the independence and self-sufficiency of law, while others maintain that of economics.[1] (Berolzheimer, 1912)

In the past two decades several schools of thought have taken up the task of describing and analyzing the systematic relationships between law and economics.[2] The schools of thought that make up what we will refer to here as Law and Economics include the new law and economics, the economics of property rights, old law and economics, public choice theory, neoinstitutionalist economic theory, and critical legal studies.

The subject matter of the new law and economics and the economics of property rights is typified by the contributions of Richard A. Posner, Guido Calabresi, Ronald H. Coase, Eirik G. Furubotn and Svetozar Pejovich among many, many others. The contributions to both the *Journal of Law and Economics* and the *Journal of Legal Studies* can serve to exemplify the past and present ongoing work in this area. By "old" law and economics we are referring to the traditional areas of economics such as antitrust, regulated industries and labor economics which because of their intrinsic features have historically concentrated on the interrelationships between laws and economic activity.[3] Public choice theory refers to the work of James M. Buchanan and Gordon Tullock among others and the past and present contributions from the Center for the Study of Public Choice. Contributions to a journal entitled *Public Choice*

1

serve well to exemplify the general thrust of this school of thought. Neoinstitutionalist economic theory incorporates the work of a variety of diverse contributors including the work of Clarence E. Ayers, Gunner Myrdal, Warren J. Samuels, A. Allan Schmid and H. H. Liebhafsky and many others. *The Journal of Economic Issues* includes many of the contributions that typify the recent direction of this school of thought. Finally, we have incorporated some of the work of the participants of the Conference on Critical Legal Studies, a national organization of law practioners and professors, social scientists and others committed to the development of a critical theoretical perspective on law, legal practice, and legal education. Some of its contributors include Duncan Kennedy, Mark Kelman, Karl Klare, and Mark Tushnet.[4] Their publications appear in various journals and law reviews. It should be noted that there are a variety of journals that also have a bearing on the general scope of the discipline of Law and Economics, some of which include *Law and Society Review, Research in Law and Economics, International Review of Law and Economics,* as well as many law reviews which have published contributions to the field.

While these schools of thought have a common interest in understanding and describing relationships between law and economic activity in society, they also differ in a variety of ways. The purpose of this work is to bring these schools of thought together under an umbrella framework that emphasizes the commonalities among the schools of thought, thereby providing a better understanding of what the discipline of Law and Economics, as defined here, is all about. As we integrate the various facets of Law and Economics into one model, we will proceed in a critical manner in an attempt to highlight some of the differences that exist. In order to understand the scope and content of Law and Economics, it is important to understand certain methodological conventions in neoclassical economics and welfare economics. The remainder of this chapter is intended to accomplish this task.

A. THE CONVENTIONAL WISDOM OF NEOCLASSICAL ECONOMICS

There is a general convention in neoclassical economics that is not well understood by some and hence leads to the feeling that economic theories are vague and divorced from the real world. This perception stems from the process of abstraction in formulating economic theories. In order to understand fundamental systematic relationships observed in the real world, economic theories are set forth as generalized propositions purporting to explain observed events. Economic effects are brought on by a variety of causes, and the process of abstraction enables the economist to set aside noneconomic variables and, conceptually, hold constant (i.e., take as given) less important economic variables that might be at work.[5] Through the use of theoretical models which incorporate the important endogenous economic variables (to the exclusion of certain exogenous variables) the economist can begin to investigate the precise nature of the relationship between the economic variables deemed relevant. Once these abstract theoretical models have been formulated, the testing of their generalized propositions against actual observed phenomena will in fact determine whether or not the theory has explanatory and predictive content, that is, whether it is useful or whether it is divorced from real world phenomena and hence irrelevant.[6] As models that can withstand the test of predictive content are developed the causes and effects of economic activity become better understood. Thus, the process of abstraction is a necessary activity inasmuch as it is only through such a process that an understanding of a very complex real world can begin to emerge. What today is characterized as neoclassical economics must be understood to be a collection of those theoretical models which purport to describe and explain what is transpiring in the economy. In Law and Economics, it is the microeconomic theoretical models which are most often applicable.

The quest of neoclassical microeconomics is to attempt to generate efficient solutions in the descriptive analytical sense, given or conceptually holding constant some conditions (i.e., exogenous variables)—conditions which are usually taken to be fashioned in the social, political, or legal arenas.[7] The economic analysis that generates efficient solutions is perceived as being positive, in that it attempts to determine "what is" in any social, political or legal environment. The concern is with statements and hypotheses that could conceivably be shown to be right or wrong based on an appeal to the facts. For example, the assertions that "policy X will reduce inflation" and "policy Y will reduce unemployment" are typical examples of positive statements. This is quite distinct from normative statements which assert "what ought to be." Disagreements over normative statements cannot be settled by an appeal to facts but are based on value judgments. For example, the assertion that "since unemployment is a more important problem than inflation, we should adopt policy Y" is a normative statement. The bulk of neoclassical microeconomics is positive in nature as opposed to normative. The neoclassical economist retains a positive stance in his analysis by not advocating any particular set of given conditions (conditions socially, politically or legally determined) within which efficient solutions can be sought, or so the conventional wisdom goes.

B. WELFARE ECONOMICS

To a limited extent, changes in certain exogenous variables (usually loosely referred to as institutional changes) can be analyzed by what has come to be known as welfare economics.[8] In practice, when welfare economists refer to an exogenous institutional change they are usually referring to a policy instrument (e.g., a new tax or tariff, or a new government program requiring a change in expenditures). The objective of welfare economics is to evaluate the social desirability of changes in certain, heretofore, exogenous institutional variables which result in alternative economic states, where each economic state is characterized by both a different allocation of resources and a different distribution of costs and benefits of economic activity.[9] There are two important characteristics of welfare economics to note at this point that subsequently can serve as a basis for better understanding Law and Economics.

First, in the development of its theories, welfare economics has traditionally focused attention on analyzing certain exogenous institutional variables while showing some reluctance to delve into others, leaving them as given. As J. de V. Graaff stated:

> We shall instead regard a person's choices, or general welfare, as determined by a large number of variables, some of which have traditionally interested economists and some of which have not. Those which have we shall call *economic variables*. Welfare economics then proceeds on the assumptions that the non-economic ones all remain unchanged. They can be thought of as exogenous—that is, as influencing the economic variables without being influenced by them. . . . A difficulty emerges when a variable which has not traditionally interested economists cannot be regarded as exogenous in this sense. For instance, it might be argued that there is a mutual interaction between forms of social organization . . . and economic variables.[10]

The essential point here is that certain exogenous institutional variables have been given attention by welfare economists while others have been neglected.

The second point to note (not unrelated to the first) is that those institutional changes or policies which have been analyzed by welfare economists are often brought on by or emerge via government actions, where the government is conceptually viewed as an exogenous force outside of the economic system and relied on to come to our aid to correct or rectify the occasionally misguided endogenously working market forces.[11] The essential methodological point here is that, in welfare economics, the government is treated as an exogenous variable.

An important facet of welfare economics that distinguishes it from neoclassical economics should also be emphasized at this point. Neoclassical economic analysis attempts to describe economic activity—the positive aspect of economics—whereas welfare economics is concerned with providing a guide for distinguishing between desirable and undesirable states of the economy—the normative aspect of economics.[12] James Quirk and Rubin Saposnik differentiate the two in the following manner:

> The fundamental distinction between positive economics and welfare economics is that positive economics is, or pretends to be, a science. Its assumptions as well as its conclusions, at least under ideal circumstances, can be subjected to empirical and/or logical tests to determine their truth or falsity, for example, as in testing the truth of the postulate that producers are profit maximizers. The basic assumptions underlying welfare economics, on the other hand, are value judgments that any economist is free to accept or reject; there is no conceivable manner in which the truth or falsity of these axioms could be tested. Welfare economics is scientific only insofar as its conclusions are based upon results of positive economics; thus, given value judgments sufficient to define what is meant by a 'desirable' state of the economy, positive economics can be employed to determine whether such a state is possible of achievement under a certain method of organizing the economy. . . . Because of the diversity of opinion, even among 'reasonable' men, as to the meaning of these terms, the ultimate validity of much of welfare economics must remain a matter of personal opinion.[13]

This combined positive and normative endeavor of welfare economics has provided the cornerstone upon which much of Law and Economics rests (*much*, not all). That cornerstone is the notion of Pareto optimality.[14] At this point, the reader should be aware that notwithstanding the position quoted above, prolonged philosophical debates have raged over how much normative content (if any) is contained in welfare economics in general and the Pareto principle in particular. Most welfare economists have attempted to retain a positive or "objective" stance. This has been observed by both S. K. Nath and Mark Blaug in their independent reviews of welfare economics. As Nath observed:

> Though value judgments are unavoidable in welfare economics, it is possible to try to pretend that any particular value judgments adopted are so 'widely acceptable', 'general', or 'minimal' that the welfare propositions based on them would be quite general, noncontroversial, or 'more-or-less objective'. This indeed has been the usual procedure in the literature of welfare economics.[15]

Similarly, Blaug stated:

> Welfare economics, whether pure or applied, obviously involves value judgments, and . . . the idea of value-free welfare economics is simply a contradiction in terms. This question would never have arisen in the first place if the new Paretian welfare economics had not adopted the extraordinary argument that a consensus on certain value judgments renders these judgments 'objective'.[16]

Much confusion over the positive and normative content of economics, welfare economics and therefore, ultimately, Law and Economics persists. An appreciation of this fact is essential in order to understand the literature of the various schools of thought that comprise Law and Economics. The following is a conceptual framework that may help to distinguish positive analysis from normative work as one proceeds through the remaining chapters and the literature contained therein.

First, economic analysis which attempts to describe "what is" is positive. Second, economic analysis which asserts "what ought to be" is strictly normative. While the latter proposition is hardly refuted by anyone, the former is still qualified, typically as follows:

> A related issue is whether economics is value-free. In a broad sense it is not, for clearly our values determine to some extent the type of research that we choose to do, what questions we view as important. Economists are, of course, human beings, and as such must be alert to the possibility that personal values may creep into their analysis. The point is to be on guard to distinguish between positive and normative elements in analysis rather than taking the view that technical analysis, as such, is value-loaded, and hence useless. Even recognition that we may never succeed in fully distinguishing between positive and normative elements is not to our minds a reason to abandon the attempt at positive analysis and conclude that because all analysis includes value judgments, any opinion on technical issues is as good as the next. Rather, in an imperfect world, we should strive to approach the ideal of full distinction between positive and normative elements as closely as possible and be on guard for biases that exist in analysis. The view that all analysis is value-loaded leads one to ignore a broad body of useful knowledge. In a reasonably open advocacy process, the competition of ideas should aid in bringing biases and value judgments to the surface.[17]

Third, and most important, economic analysis which attempts to describe and prescribe changes in the system in the context of economic efficiency (the domain of welfare economics) has both positive and normative content. This statement is, in fact, a simple restatement of Quirk and Saposnick's previous quote and deserves some elaboration. Welfare economics is positive to the extent that it investigates the following question: Does a change in the system result in an outcome which is more efficient than the outcome which prevailed before the change? Welfare economics is normative to the extent that it prescriptively asserts that the change that resulted in the more efficient solution should be undertaken, that is, it ought to be implemented. Steven N. S. Cheung described the shift from positive to normative as follows:

> To accept or to deny the desirability of a public policy necessarily involves 'normative' value judgments on whether it *should* (or should not) be adopted. Economic efficiency, on the other hand, can be defined in 'positive' terms concerned with

whether a certain activity *is* (or is not) efficient. The transition from positive analysis to normative argument on policy requires only the inference that efficient allocation of resources is desirable to society. This inference is easy to draw and, to most economists, easy to accept.[18]

This inference, drawn from the Pareto principle, has been accepted by many economists. It has been used extensively in welfare economics in an attempt to preserve "objectivity" in what are, in fact, the normative endeavors of welfare economics. Given the hold that the Pareto principle has over many of those who contribute to the discipline of Law and Economics, it is essential to understand it and its role in welfare economics.

A Pareto optimum is defined as the economy being in a state from which it is impossible to improve anyone's welfare (i.e., a movement to a higher level of utility) by realigning the use of resources or modifying consumption of commodities without impairing someone else's welfare. An outcome is recognized as Pareto superior as compared to another outcome only if at least one person believes himself better off under the former than under the latter outcome and no one believes himself worse off. The assumptions underlying, or subsumed in, the Pareto optimal (re)allocations of resources are: (1) methodological individualism; only data revealed through the choice behavior of the individual is relevant, i.e., no social values exist apart from individual values; (2) that the social welfare is defined only in terms of the welfare of individuals where social welfare is taken to be the collective welfare or utility (ordinally measured) of the individuals who comprise the society under consideration; and (3) that the welfare of individuals within the society may not be compared, i.e., interpersonal comparisons of utility are not valid.[19] These assumptions, together with the unanimous consent requirement directly incorporated into the Pareto optimal criterion, are said to generate "efficient" solutions that are often asserted to be value-free in the sense described above. That is, policies that realign resource use or consumption of commodities and satisfy the Pareto criteria are asserted to be neutral with respect to ideological or normative content.

For example, the Pareto principle states that a change in economic policy is judged to be Pareto optimal or efficient if the change leaves at least one individual better off and no individual worse off. Such a change carries with it the notion that if it acquires unanimous consent among the parties, then the policy will garner value-free recommendatory status inasmuch as it was shown to have unambiguously increased social welfare.

However, notwithstanding these claims, many still believe that assertions of the value neutrality of the Pareto optimal criterion are unfounded. In commenting on the proposition that the underlying assumptions of Pareto optimality are believed to be void of normative content inasmuch as these command wide, perhaps even universal, consent, Blaug stated, "Even a perfect consensus on value judgments [on these underlying assumptions] does not render them 'objective': they nevertheless remain value judgments."[20] Furthermore, since the Pareto principle directly incorporates the unanimous consent requirement, A. Radomysler, writing on policies prescribed on this basis, stated, "In recent contributions to welfare economics, this [cause versus prescription] has been obscured. It was overlooked . . . that all prescription is normative . . . even if it were universally agreed."[21]

Beyond the value judgments brought on by adherence to the unanimous consent requirement, Pareto optimality incorporates an additional normative element. Every different initial distribution of resources is associated with a unique Pareto optimal solution. Inasmuch as the Pareto principle does not speak to any specific initial distribution of resources, this omission has been interpreted by some as yet another normative facet of the application of the Pareto principle. This will be fully explored in Chapter II.

Additionally, because a change in a policy almost always redistributes welfare to the advantage of some while to the detriment of others and will therefore not garner unanimous consent, welfare economists developed the compensation principle. The body of literature that ultimately yielded what today is referred to as the economic compensation principle emerged as a response to the work of Lionel C. Robbins. In his classic work, Robbins denied the scientific comparability of different individuals' preferences for a particular policy because of the impossibility of interpersonal comparisons of utility.[22] The consequence of Robbins' assertion was that since there was no scientific way for aggregating individual preference orderings, economists would have no basis for solving practical economic problems beyond advocating their own ethical solutions (i.e., strictly a normative endeavor).

In an effort to remove the stigma of introducing value judgments into the "positive science of economic analysis," economists tried to find a way around Robbins' criticism. It was in this environment that the so called compensation test emerged as a variant to the principle of Pareto optimality. The compensation test is variously referred to throughout the literature as the Kaldor-Hicks criterion, potential Pareto superiority, and the Pareto-Wicksellian criterion. Whereas, a full discussion of this literature will be deferred until Chapter IV, Section A, the thrust of it simply states that a policy or legal change should be sanctioned if and only if those who gain could use part of their gains to compensate the losers and still remain gainers.[23] Thus, the logic of the compensation principle suggests that a legal change should be undertaken as long as the payment of compensation to those who are made worse off could be made by those who are made better off, as long as the latter remain better off than in the initial position. Not to allow the change would be to refuse to generate a surplus of value sufficient to compensate those harmed by the change and still have an increase in social welfare.

It should be underscored that, inasmuch as the underlying logic of the compensation principle is Paretian in origin, the compensation test is also proffered by some as a positive, i.e., value-neutral, criterion for evaluating legal change in society. From society's standpoint, since such a legal change has unambiguously increased social welfare, it garners value-free recommendatory status.

C. VALUES, LAW AND ECONOMICS

As stated earlier, the notions of Pareto optimality and the compensation test are used extensively by many who contribute to the literature of Law and Economics. It should be made clear that from the perspective of our model, that segment of Law and Economics which advances recommendations on the Pareto principle or the compensation principle is engaged in a normative endeavor. This is not intended in any way to denigrate normative work—in fact, normative work is to be encouraged in the marketplace of ideas pertaining to Law and Economics. In Law and Economics, pretenses to value-neutrality (and there are many) are just that—pretenses. As we develop our descriptive model we will try to point out the continuing necessity of choice, that is, the explicit, though very often subtle, introduction of values involved in the discipline of Law and Economics.

As we embark upon building a descriptive framework of Law and Economics the reader will be well served by reflecting on Bruce A. Ackerman's introductory statements in his book concerning Law and Economics. He stated:

> An even deeper difficulty is posed by the way in which value judgments are treated in the economist's approach. The orthodox economist prides himself on his 'value-neutrality,' on his insistence that he is simply concerned with the 'efficient' allocation of resources to achieve societal objectives, whatever they may be. Even on its own terms, this claim to neutrality is vulnerable to many kinds of philosophical attack; when the economist's methods are deployed in a law school classroom, however, all pretenses to value-neutrality must necessarily be discarded. Thus, the greatest danger involved in the use of these materials is the encouragement they may give to a naive belief that the economist's notion of 'efficiency' is sufficiently embracing so as to provide a comprehensive touchstone for policy judgments. *Nothing* could be further from the truth than this. . . . So long as economics is not mistaken as the sole

repository of principles of evaluation, its intelligent use can enable the student to pierce the veil of rhetoric and come to grips with the real normative issues that lie beneath the surface of a legal problem.[24]

NOTES AND REFERENCES

1. Fritz Berolzheimer, *The World's Legal Philosophers* (Boston: Boston Book Co., 1912. Reprinted by Rothman Reprints, Inc., 1968), pp. 22–23.

2. For a variety of perspectives as to what constitutes the field of Law and Economics see: Bruce A. Ackerman, "Introduction: On the Role of Economic Analysis in Property Law," in Bruce A. Ackerman, Ed., *Economic Foundations of Property Law* (Boston: Little, Brown and Co., 1975), pp. vii–xvi; Paul Burrows and Cento G. Veljanovski, "Introduction: The Economic Approach to Law," in Paul Burrows and Cento G. Veljanovski, Eds., *The Economic Approach to Law* (London: Butterworths, 1981), pp. 1–34; Ronald H. Coase, "Economics and Contiguous Disciplines," *The Journal of Legal Studies*, Vol. 7, No. 2 (June 1978), pp. 201–211; Allan G. Gruchy, "Law, Politics and Institutional Economics," *Journal of Economic Issues*, Vol. 7, No. 4 (December 1973), pp. 623–643; Werner Z. Hirsch, "Preface" and "Introduction" in Werner Z. Hirsch, *Law and Economics: An Introductory Analysis* (New York: Academic Press, 1979), pp. xi–xv, 1–15; Morton J. Horowitz, "Law and Economics: Science or Politics," *Hofstra Law Review*, Vol. 8, No. 4 (Summer 1980), pp. 905–912; Alvin K. Klevorick, "Law and Economic Theory: An Economist's View," *American Economic Review*, Vol. 65, No. 2 (May 1975), pp. 237–243; Robert Lekachman, "Law and Economics," *Journal of Economic Issues*, Vol. 4, No. 1 (March 1970), pp. 25–39; William A. Lovett, "Economic Analysis and It's Role in Legal Education," *Journal of Legal Education*, Vol. 26, No. 4 (1974), pp. 385–421; Henry G. Manne, "Preface" and "Introduction" in Henry G. Manne, Ed., *The Economics of Legal Relationships* (St. Paul: West Publishing Co., 1975), pp. vii–x, 1–3; Henry G. Manne, "The Marriage Between Law and Economics," *Emory Lawyer*, Vol. 4, No. 1 (December 1981), pp. 10–13; Richard A. Posner, *The Economic Approach to Law*, Law and Economics Center, University of Miami School of Law, No. 1 (1976), pp. 1–16; Warren J. Samuels, "Law and Economics: Introduction," *Journal of Economic Issues*, Vol. 7, No. 4 (December 1973), pp. 535–541; Warren J. Samuels, "Legal-Economic Policy: A Bibliographical Survey," *Law Library Journal*, Vol. 58, No. 3 (August 1965), pp. 230–252; Warren J. Samuels, "Law and Economics: A Bibliographical Survey," *Law Library Journal*, Vol. 66, No. 1 (February 1973), pp. 96–110; Bernard H. Siegan, "Preface," in Bernard H. Siegan, Ed., *The Interaction of Economics and the Law* (Lexington: Lexington Books, 1977), pp. vii–xiii; George J. Stigler, "The Law and Economics of Public Policy: A Plea to the Scholars," *Journal of Legal Studies*, Vol. 1, No. 1 (1972), pp. 1–12; W. Allen Wallis, "Law and the Economy," in Siegan, Ed., *The Interaction of Economics and the Law*, pp. 1–11; Allan Williams, "Collaboration Between Economists and Lawyers in Policy Research," *The Journal of the Society of Public Teachers of Law*, Vol. 13, No. 3 (January 1975), pp. 212–218. The brief characterizations of the various schools of thought which follow in the text are very general. Broad areas of overlap among the various schools of thought indeed exist.

3. For this definition see Posner, "The Economic Approach to Law," p. 1.

4. Additional contributors to the Critical Legal Studies include Richard A. Abel, Isaac D. Balbus, and Paul Brest. Other contributors are identified in a bibliography of the Critical Legal Studies literature distributed by Duncan Kennedy of the Harvard Law School. A brief description of the ongoing work in Critical Legal Studies is set forth in Karl Klare, "Law-Making as Praxis," *Telos*, No. 40 (Summer 1979), pp. 123–135 at 123–125.

5. For a description of this process see Ryan C. Amacher, Robert D. Tollison, and Thomas D. Willet, "The Economic Approach to Social Policy Questions: Some Meth-

odological Perspectives," in Ryan C. Amacher, et al., Eds., *The Economic Approach to Public Policy* (Ithaca: Cornell University Press, 1976), pp. 18–37; Oskar Morgenstern, "Descriptive, Predictive and Normative Theory," *Kyklos*, Vol. 25, No. 4 (1972), pp. 699–714 at 702; Nicholas Kaldor, "The Irrelevance of Equilibrium Economics," *The Economic Journal*, Vol. 82, No. 328 (December 1972), pp. 1237–1255 at 1244–1246; James Quirk and Rubin Saposnik, *Introduction to General Equilibrium Theory and Welfare Economics* (New York: McGraw Hill Book Co., 1968), pp. 76–77.

6. Milton Friedman, "The Methodology of Positive Economics," in Milton Friedman, *Essays in Positive Economics* (Chicago: University of Chicago Press, 1957), pp. 3–43. See also Kurt Klappholz, "Value Judgements and Economics," *British Journal for the Philosophy of Science*, Vol. 15, No. 58 (August 1964), pp. 97–114. Compare these to Kendall P. Cochran, "Economics as a Moral Science," *Review of Social Economy*, Vol. 32, No. 2 (October 1974), pp. 186–195; Morgenstern, "Descriptive, Predictive and Normative Theory," pp. 710–713; Duncan K. Foley, "Problems vs. Conflicts: Economic Theory and Ideology," *American Economic Review*, Vol. 65, No. 2 (May 1975), pp. 231–236.

7. Morgenstern, "Descriptive, Predictive and Normative Theory," p. 707.

8. As described by Tibor Scitovsky: "The aim of welfare economics is to test the efficiency of economic institutions in making use of the productive resources of the community." Tibor Scitovsky, "A Note on Welfare Propositions in Economics," *The Review of Economic Studies*, Vol. 9, No. 1 (1941–1942), pp. 77–88 at 77. S. K. Nath quoting J. Rothenberg wrote: "The welfare economist's competence is called on only to help reconstruct institutions in accordance with the newly formed values or to evaluate how well newly fashioned institutions accord with the new values." S. K. Nath, *A Reappraisal of Welfare Economics* (London: Routledge and Kegan Paul, 1969), p. 130. For an overview of the theory of welfare economics see Ezra J. Mishan, "A Survey of Welfare Economics," *The Economic Journal*, Vol. 70, No. 278 (June 1960), pp. 197–265. See also I. M. D. Little, *A Critique of Welfare Economics* (London: Oxford University Press, 1960). Charles K. Rowley and Alan T. Peacock, *Welfare Economics: A Liberal Restatement* (New York: John Wiley and Sons, 1975). J. de V. Graaff, *Theoretical Welfare Economics* (London: Cambridge University Press, 1975). Nath, *A Reappraisal of Welfare Economics*.

9. James M. Henderson and Richard E. Quandt, *Microeconomic Theory* (New York: McGraw Hill, 1971), pp. 254–255.

10. J. de V. Graaff, *Theoretical Welfare Economics*, pp. 5–6. The fact that many important institutional variables are excluded from the analysis of welfare economics was commented on by James M. Buchanan. With reference to those institutional variables he stated: "They constitute, so to speak, the 'rules of the game' within which individuals of the group make decisions and organize activity. . . . It is this set that has been largely neglected by welfare economists who have used the Pareto criterion, with the result that much of the analysis has been empty of content." James M. Buchanan, "The Relevance of Pareto Optimality," *Journal of Conflict Resolution*, Vol. 6, No. 4 (1962), pp. 341–354 at 342. See also Ragnar Frisch, "On Welfare Theory and Pareto Regions," *International Economic Papers*, No. 9 (1959), pp. 39–92, and Tjalling C. Koopmans, *Three Essays on the State of Economic Science* (New York: McGraw Hill Book Co., 1957), pp. 41–66.

11. Carl J. Dahlman, "The Problem of Externality," *The Journal of Law and Economics*, Vol. 22, No. 1 (April 1979), pp. 141–162 at 162. See also Harold H. Hochman and James D. Rodgers, "Pareto Optimal Redistribution," *American Economic Review*, Vol. 59, No. 4 (September 1969), pp. 542–557 at 542.

12. Henderson and Quandt, *Microeconomic Theory*, p. 255 and Quirk and Saposnik, *Introduction to General Equilibrium Theory and Welfare Economics*, pp. 103–104.

13. Ibid., pp. 103–104. J. de V. Graaff stated the distinction between positive and normative economics in a different way: "Whereas the normal way of testing a theory in

positive economics is to test its conclusions, the normal way of testing a welfare proposition is to test its assumptions. The significance of this should not be overlooked." He goes on to say: "It is in practice, if not in principle, exceedingly difficult to test a welfare proposition." J. de V. Graaff, *Theoretical Welfare Economics*, pp. 2, 3. Compare to Friedman, "The Methodology of Positive Economics," pp. 3–43.

14. Vilfredo Pareto, *Manuel d'Economie Politique* (Paris, 1906).

15. Nath, *A Reappraisal of Welfare Economics*, p. 2.

16. Mark Blaug, *Economic Theory in Retrospect*, 3rd ed., (Cambridge: Cambridge University Press, 1978), p. 709.

17. Amacher, et al., "The Economic Approach to Social Policy Questions," p. 20.

18. Steven N. S. Cheung, "The Myth of Social Cost," Cato Paper No. 16, (San Francisco: The Cato Institute, 1980), pp. 1–52 at 3.

19. This section borrows heavily from Blaug, *Economic Theory in Retrospect*, pp. 626, 707–710.

20. Ibid., p. 626.

21. A. Radomsyler, "Welfare Economics and Economic Policy," in Kenneth J. Arrow and Tibor Scitovsky, Eds., *A.E.R. Readings in Welfare Economics* (Homewood: Richard D. Irwin, 1969), p. 90. Commenting on both the underlying assumptions of and the Pareto principle itself, S. K. Nath states: "Thus there are serious objections to the procedure of *a priori* welfare economics, even if it is argued that the welfare criteria and the Pareto-type welfare function are *not deduced* from some alleged facts describing the wide acceptance of certain value judgments but are formulated to incorporate apparently 'widely acceptable value judgments' on practical grounds. However, welfare criteria and the Paretian optimum conditions aspire to be the guiding principles of social action about certain aspects of welfare called economic (which it may or may not be possible to delimit); therefore, irrespective of whether they are or are not based on 'widely acceptable value judgments,' any such principles cannot be above politics, because they constitute a social policy, and any social policy is a matter of politics. Moreover, starting with the 'most widely acceptable value judgments' or the 'prevailing values' and building a system of *a priori* welfare evaluations and recommendations runs a high risk of introducing a bias in favor of things as they are into the customary evaluations of economic policies." Nath, *A Reappraisal of Welfare Economics*, pp. 128–129. For a critique of the use of Pareto optimality in economics, see the following: Oskar Morgenstern, "Pareto Optimum and Economic Organization," in Norbert Kloten, et al., Eds., *Systeme und Methoden in den Wirtschafts und Sozialwissenschaften* (Tubingen: J. C. Mohr (Paul Siebeck), 1964), pp. 573–586. See also Warren J. Samuels, "Welfare Economics, Power, and Property," in Gene Wunderlich and W. L. Gibson, Jr., Eds., *Perspectives of Property* (University Park: Institute for Research on Land and Water Resources, Pennsylvania State University, 1972), pp. 61–148 at 68–103. Richard S. Markovits, "Causes and Policy Significance of Pareto Resource Misallocation: A Checklist for Microeconomic Policy Analysis," *Stanford Law Review*, Vol. 28, No. 1 (1975), pp. 1–43. Ezra J. Mishan, "Pareto Optimality and the Law," *Oxford Economic Papers*, Vol. 19, No. 3 (1967), pp. 255–287.

22. Lionel Robbins, *An Essay on the Nature and Significance of Economic Science* (London: Macmillan, 1932).

23. Mark Blaug states as follows: "A change that favors some people but harms others can now be pronounced a unanimous improvement in welfare if the gainers can compensate the losers so that they will accept the change; after the compensation payments are made, the gainers are better off and the losers are none the worse off." Blaug, *Economic Theory in Retrospect*, p. 621.

24. Ackerman, *Economic Foundations of Property Law*, pp. xi, xiv.

Chapter II

Law and Economics— A Descriptive Model

A society is a more or less self-sufficient association of persons who in their relations to one another recognize certain rules of conduct as binding and who for the most part act in accordance with them. Suppose further that these rules specify a system of cooperation designed to advance the good of those taking part in it. Then, although a society is a cooperative venture for mutual advantage, it is typically marked by a conflict as well as by an identity of interests. There is an identity of interests since social cooperation makes possible a better life for all than any would have if each were to live solely by his own efforts. There is a conflict of interests since persons are not indifferent as to how the greater benefits produced by their collaboration are distributed, for in order to pursue their ends they each prefer a larger to a lesser share. A set of principles is required for choosing among the various social arrangements which determine this division of advantages and for underwriting an agreement on the proper distributive shares. . . . [The principles] provide a way of assigning rights and duties in the basic institutions of society and they define the appropriate distribution of the benefits and the burdens of social cooperation.[1] (Rawls, 1971)

As suggested in Chapter I, much of what today constitutes Law and Economics borrows heavily from economics in general and welfare economics in particular. That is, largely utilizing the analytical apparatus of economics, Law and Economics, broadly conceived, attempts to look at the manner in which both the prevailing and potential legal institutions affect the character of economic life.[2] Based on the belief that systematic relationships exist between legal institutions and the character of economic life, the scope of Law and Economics is then to describe and analyze these relationships. One method of accomplishing this task is to undertake a comparative institutional approach. This approach allows us to investigate the systematic relationships between (1) the structure of legal institutions, focusing on the rights and rules by which they operate;

13

(2) the conduct or observed behavior in light of the incentives (penalties and rewards) created by the structure of the legal institutions; and (3) the consequent economic performance, i.e., the allocation and distribution of resources that determine the character of economic life under those institutions. The fact that Law and Economics encompasses both allocation *and* distribution is generally accepted. Werner Z. Hirsh, in his introductory text entitled *Law and Economics*, stated the following:

> Our task would be so much easier if efficiency could be rigorously defended as the only and ultimate objective. Instead we face two all-too-often opposing objectives—efficiency and equity. It must be remembered that the ultimate goal is what economists like to call *social efficiency*, which requires trading off resource-allocation efficiency against distribution of income. Unfortunately, as all will agree, what is the most desirable distribution of income is a highly subjective decision. Nevertheless, legal rules must be concerned about both efficiency and income distribution. . . . Guidelines given by economic theory require two successive steps—first, income should be redistributed in the most desirable manner; second, resources should be allocated in the most efficient manner, preferably in response to competitive forces. An effort must thus be made to agree on a subjectively preferred income distribution and it must be followed by an effort to attain allocative efficiency. The formulation of prudent legal rules would have to proceed by considering both goals, not just allocative efficiency—a formidable task.[3]

In order to better understand the comparative institutional approach described above, a brief digression will be provided in order to define several terms that are employed throughout our discussion of the model of Law and Economics. Working rules are taken to be the rules which structure the decision making processes of legal institutions. That is, the working rules determine the framework in which legal institutions operate on a day to day basis. In our model, the term working rules is associated with institutions. Property rights are used in our model to describe the legal relations governing the allocation and distribution of resources in a society. They are the sanctioned behavioral relations among the members of a society that pertain to and delimit the permissible use of resources and goods and services which an individual must observe or incur the cost associated with nonobservance.[4]

In our model we will distinguish between three different types of property rights—private property rights, status rights, and communal rights. Private property rights give to the owner of an asset the exclusive rights to use it plus the right to transfer its exclusive use to another person. Private property rights will characterize the sanctioned legal-economic relationships in the market sector. Status rights are regarded as those property rights which are associated with the public sector. They are characterized as exclusive but nontransferable. Individual access to status rights depends upon meeting certain eligibility requirements set forth by the legal institutions operating within the framework established by their working rules. Finally, communal rights are defined as nonexclusive and hence nontransferable rights to certain resources or goods. That is, under communal rights everyone has the right to use the resources or goods and no one has the right to exclude anyone from the use of those resources or goods. Such rights will reside in the communal sector of our model.[5] (The market, public, and communal sectors will be fully developed in Section B of this chapter).[6]

Returning to our model of Law and Economics, its approach will be seen to be in marked contrast to neoclassical economics where (a) the working rules which govern the structure of the choice-making legal institutions of society are taken as given and (b) the prevailing structure of rights which emerges as a result of the decisions of the legal institutions is taken as given. As stated by Svetozar Pejovich:

> The second level of social interaction involves decision-making processes, individual choices, the content of contractual arrangements, and activities within the set of opportunity choices defined by the prevailing property rights. Traditionally, economic theory has been primarily concerned with the analysis of social interactions at this level of economic activity—that is, with the analysis of equilibrium solutions *within a given institutional framework.*[7] (emphasis added)

In Law and Economics, however, the legal institutions (their structure, conduct, and performance) are at center stage and are treated as endogenous decision-making units. They are no longer considered exogenous as is the "government" in welfare economics. The legal institutions are treated in much the same manner as consumers and producers have been treated in welfare economics. That is, the consuming units, the firms, and the prevailing legal institutions (e.g., courts, legislatures, the bureaucracies, etc.) are not given immutably by nature but are themselves a response to economic needs and flexible in response to changes in those needs.[8]

A. THE DESCRIPTIVE MODEL: INSTITUTIONS AND LEGAL RELATIONS

Our model is comprised of the following legal institutions each of which, through its respective complex process of decision making, makes choices which may ultimately determine the character of economic life.[9] (See Figure II.1.)

• The Legislature—including federal, state and local legislative bodies.

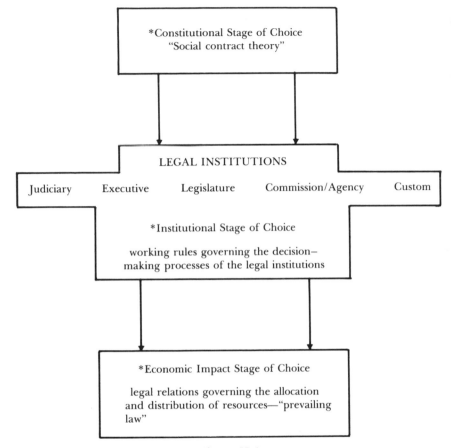

Figure II.1.

- The Judiciary—including federal, state and local judicial bodies as well as accompanying support or associated services.
- The Executive Offices—including the office of President, governors of the several states, and local executives.
- Government Commissions and Bureaucratic Agencies—including federal, state and local regulatory commissions (e.g., I.C.C., local zoning commissions, etc.) and government agencies (e.g., E.P.A., welfare agencies, natural resource departments in state governments, etc.).
- Custom—an eclectic assemblage of traditional or informal decision–making units (e.g., religious organizations, grassroot issue groups, etc.).

In focusing on these legal institutions, three concerns have come to dominate those contributing to the literature of Law and Economics. First, it becomes necessary to describe and understand the emergence of such institutions—the constitutional stage of choice. Second, it is necessary to describe and understand both the structuring and the revising or restructuring of the legal institutional decision-making processes—the institutional stage of choice. Finally, the consequent economic impacts of choices from prevailing or potentially revised institutions must be analyzed and understood—the economic impact stage of choice. In attempting to address these concerns, those contributing to the literature of Law and Economics have divided their labors to describe these three different levels of choice.

Before delving into a description and analysis of each of these stages of choice, it is important to understand the role of and the relationships among the individual participants in the legal-economic arena. These relationships can be illustrated by the use of a simple diagram which captures the faccts of the independence and the interdependence of individuals that comprise a society (see Figure II.2). Each individual has a spherc of interests or an opportunity set which can be thought of as an array of alternative lines of action with an opportunity cost attached to each line of action.[10] It is generally recognized that, in a society, the spheres of interests are not mutually exclusive but often overlap as illustrated in the diagram (shaded lens). That is, while some individual actions may not have any impact whatsoever on other individuals in the society (unshaded regions), oftentimes, one individual's sphere of interests is contrary to, or overlaps, another's sphere of interests, resulting in an area of mutual interdependence. How that mutual interdependence—the overlap of contrary interests—is channeled by a society and ultimately acted out contributes to shaping the character of economic life.

For instance, if a society were in a state of anarchy with no mutually agreed on property rights or working rules to channel instances of overlapping spheres of interests, then the area of interdependence can be viewed as an area of conflict rather negative in character. Each individual will have essentially two basic options to increase his welfare, or as it is often referred to, his utility (where utility is defined as a subjective measure of satisfaction derived from the acquisition of goods and services). One option is to devote his labor and other resources to producing those goods and services that advance his utility. The other option in an anarchistic society of unrestricted behavior entails plundering and acting in a predacious manner to acquire those goods and services that add to his utility. An individual will mix or combine these two options in a manner which best enhances his welfare. Further, each individual

Spheres of Interest

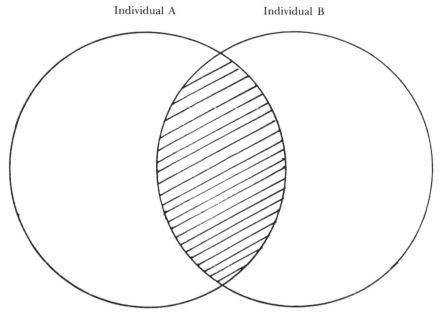

Individual A   Individual B

Figure II.2.

knows that since the second option is a viable line of action for other individuals, it will also be to his advantage to protect his self-proclaimed sphere of interests by devoting resources to defend those interests. Of course, with this protective-defensive resource diversion the individual sacrifices some utility that could have been acquired through the production of that which would have advanced his welfare. Thus, we can depict an anarchistic society as being at point A, where U_{A1} and U_{B1} show the respective utility levels of individuals A and B (see Figure II.3).

Contemplating the opportunity costs associated with the protective-defensive resource diversions, individuals will come to recognize the negative impact of these resource diversions upon the character of their economic life. As a consequence, they will seek to rechannel the nature of their conduct in instances of overlapping spheres of interests under anarchy. That is, because of the prospects of improvement in their individual utilities, there exists a potential for a social contract or constitution which spells out, among other things, the behavioral limits of what is or is not mutually acceptable conduct when spheres of interests overlap. Described in our model as the constitutional stage of choice (akin to social contract theory), it is at this level that the ultimate character of economic life is cast. The establishment of a constitutional mechanism for determining working rules and property rights channels the conduct of individuals comprising a society characterized by mutual interdependence.[11]

In the abstract, the individuals in such a society can be thought of as formulating constitutional mechanisms (i.e., "rules of the game") under the "veil of ignorance."[12] That is, each individual, if uncertain as to his actual position in a subsequent specific collective choice, will not work to adopt basic rules that directly promote any class or group interest but will work to adopt those rules which can be generally agreed upon. This concept has been most clearly articulated by James M. Buchanan and Gordon Tullock:

> We try only to analyze the calculus of the utility-maximizing individual who is confronted with the constitutional problem. Essential to the analysis is the presumption that the individual is *uncertain* as to what his own precise role will be in any one of the whole chain of later collective choices that will actually have to be made. For this reason he is considered not to have a particular and distinguishable interest separate and apart from his fellows. This is not to suggest that he will act contrary to his own interest; but the individual will not find it advantageous to vote for rules that may promote sectional, class, or group interests because, by presupposition, he is unable to predict the role that he will be playing in the actual collective decision-making process at any particular time in the future. He cannot predict with any

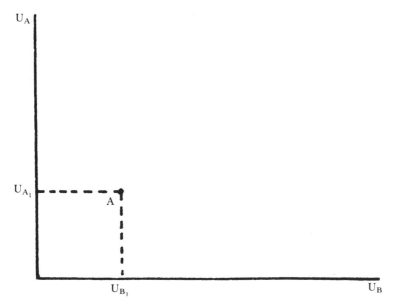

Figure II.3.

degree of certainty whether he is more likely to be in a winning or a losing coalition on any specific issue. Therefore, he will assume that occasionally he will be in one group and occasionally in the other. His own self-interest will lead him to choose rules that will maximize the utility of an individual in a series of collective decisions with his own preferences on the separate issues being more or less randomly distributed.[13]

It is important to note that, while in the abstract, the notion of working to adopt rules that do not promote any particular group interest has some appeal, in reality the assumption of absolute uncertainty is difficult to meet because participants in the legal–economic arena may be aware of their actual positions in subsequent collective choices. If in fact the constitution would be framed under the "veil of ignorance," then it will serve to limit conflict and channel behavior from protective-defensive actions to more productive endeavors, thereby enhancing each individual's welfare. By working out the social contract or constitution, society can be thought of as moving from point A to point S, with each individual now being better off—U_{A2} and U_{B2} (see Figure II.4).

Returning to our model, it must be emphasized that the social contract that emerges at this constitutional stage of choice will directly affect (perhaps subtly) the character of economic life. For example, constitu-

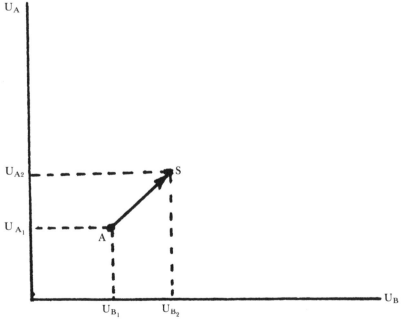

Figure II.4.

tional choices must be made as to whether a one or two house legislature will be established or whether a majority or perhaps two thirds vote will determine a legislative choice. In addition, since constitutions are not immutable, the methods by which constitutional rules can be revised are developed at this level of choice. Further, it should be noted that the relationships among emergent institutions is also partially resolved at the constitutional stage of choice. We are thinking specifically of the choices that govern which institutions will prevail over others in making choices—for example, a system of checks and balances. The essential point to be understood here, in light of our descriptive model, is that whatever legal institutions come to characterize a society, they owe their development, existence and legitimacy to the initial choices made at the constitutional stage of choice.[14] Once the constitution is framed, it will then provide the basis for the emergence of legal-economic institutions which alter the allocation and distribution of resources in society (see Figure II.1) and in turn, provide the foundation for subsequent movements away from point S in Figure II.4 (a matter which will be taken up in Section B of this chapter).

The second level of choice—the institutional stage of choice—attended to in Law and Economics focuses directly on the structure and choices of the legal institutions (commonly referred to as the "state"), as well as the revision of those institutional structures and the consequent changes in the choices of the institutions. As such, the decision-making processes of a legal institution may be partially established by the rights and rules worked out at the constitutional stage of choice, but also may be a partial function of the decisions of other institutions often under complex procedures. An example of this would be a court decision which imposes certain restrictions or obligations upon a legislative body or government agency. However, most of the decision-making processes of an institution are formally worked out by the institution itself in developing its own working rules. Examples of this might include: judiciary—rules of evidence; legislature—committee structures and procedures; agencies—determining the method by which standards are arrived at (E.P.A., O.S.H.A., F.D.A., etc.); regulatory commissions—rules governing intervenors at rate hearings for a regulated utility. These examples are intended only to serve as illustrations that working rules, that structure and are structured by an institution, determine the decision-making processes of the institution that ultimately structure the property rights governing the allocation and distribution of resources. In recognition of this Alan Randall suggests the following:

> An analytical approach to [the study of institutions] needs to be directed toward . . . the study of the outcomes in terms of output and distribution of income,

wealth, and human and civil rights of alternative structures of property rights. . . . Since institutional choice is a partial function of the distribution of power, publication of information about the process of choice may enable the people to confront the issues of both choice and power more effectively.[15]

As in the case of constitutions, legal institutions are not served up immutably by nature, but rather are themselves a response to economic needs and, as such, can and do undergo structural revisions. Any change in the working rules of a legal institution will revise the decision-making processes of that institution and, as a result, may alter the choices as to which structure of property rights will prevail. It is these choices as to the structure of property rights to which we now turn by exploring the economic impact stage of choice inasmuch as it is this stage of choice that comprises the most prominent interface between Law and Economics.

B. THE ECONOMIC IMPACT STAGE OF CHOICE: THE INTERFACE BETWEEN LAW AND ECONOMICS

By examining the economic impact stage of choice, the interface between Law and Economics becomes more apparent. In the context of our model, the purpose of this section is to demonstrate the fundamental manner in which the prevailing and emerging legal institutions affect the character of economic life. Conceptually, we begin with the notion of three distinct systems for organizing and controlling the allocation and distribution of resources: the market sector, the public sector, and the communal sector. While we will initially treat each sector as if it exists separate and apart from the other sectors, we are doing so to explore the nature of each sector. Once this is accomplished, we will integrate these sectors to better describe the manner in which, typically, all three systems operate interdependently to allocate and distribute resources.

1. The Market Sector

Once a social contract that establishes private property rights is framed, then the participants in the economic arena are able to specialize according to comparative advantage and engage in trade within the market sector in order to improve their individual utilities (see Figure II.5, Panel [a]). This is distinct from a state of anarchy previously described, where there are no private property rights. Under anarchy, individuals would have little incentive to engage in market exchange because they could not anticipate, with any certainty, that the trading partner would actually live up to the terms of the agreement.

As described earlier, the emergence of the social contract has brought

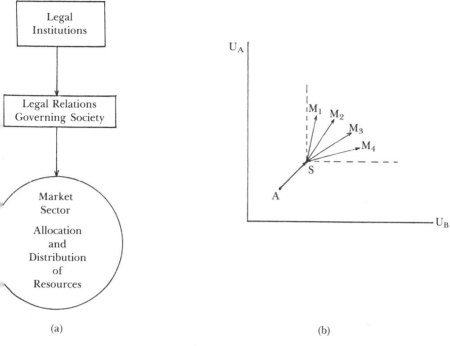

(a)   (b)

Figure II.5.

he participants from point A (anarchy) to point S (see Figure II.5, Panel b]). With the establishment of private property, and with the market as a system of social control, it is now possible for the individuals to further enhance their welfare by specializing and engaging in exchange through trade. This process of trade is conventionally viewed as a purely voluntary endeavor and characterizes what we are calling here the market sector. The voluntary nature of this market process is such that no individual will engage in a trade that leaves him worse off. Thus, trade will bring the participants from point S to some point to the northeast. In this polar case, where the only method of allocation and distribution is through the private market sector, society would come to rest at some point among the array of potential outcomes depicted by $M_1, M_2, M_3, \ldots$ (Figure II.5, Panel [b]). The final allocational and distributional outcome would be arrived at once all the gains from trade have been exhausted.

In order to gain more insight into the market sector, we will look more deeply into its treatment in Law and Economics, emphasizing the property rights approach. In the pure market sector, all property rights are held as bundles of fee simple absolute rights[16] or, as it is more often articulated in the literature, all rights are said to be fully nonattenuated.[17] These two notions, fee simple absolute rights and nonattenuated rights, seem to be treated synonomously in Law and Economics. As a result, our discussion can concentrate safely on nonattenuated property rights alone. According to the conventional definition of property rights, what are owned by individuals are not goods or resources but are the rights to use goods and resources. Armen A. Alchian and Harold Demsetz stated, "What are owned are socially recognized rights of action."[18]

In order for a set of property rights to be nonattenuated, there must be no restrictions on the owner's right to use or transfer resources or goods. Randall defines a set of nonattenuated property rights as:

1. Completely specified, so that it can serve as a perfect system of information about the rights that accompany ownership, the restrictions upon those rights, and the penalties for their violation.
2. Exclusive, so that all rewards and penalties resulting from an action accrue directly to the individual empowered to take action (i.e., the owner).
3. Transferable, so that rights may gravitate to their highest-value use.
4. Enforceable and completely enforced. An unenforced right is no right at all.[19]

As a consequence of the notion of nonattenuation described above, scholars writing in the field of Law and Economics have broadened the conventional definition of "output" and of "factors of production." In place of calling them output and factors of production, they are referred to as effective commodities and effective resources, respectively. An effective commodity is the physical commodity plus the associated property rights to use or transfer the commodity, while an effective resource is the physical resource plus the rights to use or transfer the resource.[20] Thus, the individual owner's right to use or transfer a commodity or resource may be limited by the prevailing restrictions stated by the legal institutions (this will be discussed later in this section). Focusing on the conception of a fully nonattenuated structure of property rights as set forth by Randall, it can be seen to provide the foundation or basis from which market exchange can take place in order to achieve a Pareto efficient outcome. Eirik G. Furubotn and Svetozar Pejovich state it the following way: "The logic of competition (i.e., the heeding of alternative uses) indicates that a more complete and definite specification [i.e. movements toward a nonattenuated structure of rights] of individua property rights diminishes uncertainty and tends to promote efficient allocation and use of resources."[21] Randall states it the following way.

> If actual distributions of income, wealth, legal rights, etc., coincide with the distributional preferences of society, if all rights are nonattenuated, and if all of the requirements of pure competition are satisfied, unfettered markets will result in socially optimal production and consumption patterns, given resource scarcity and the existing tastes and preferences of the participants in those markets.[22]

While the market, as described in our model, is just one of the three systems of social control, the fact that under certain circumstances it generates Pareto-efficient solutions has lead many to advocate the market as the preferred system of control. Inasmuch as the market sector activities of production and consumption are much of what neoclassical microeconomics is all about and has succeeded in describing with great analytical rigor, it seems appropriate that the market sector should be analyzed here in more detail than the public and communal sectors. The analysis will focus on the inevitable interrelationships between the legal institutions and the market sector—these are the "legal relations governing society" in Figure II.5, Panel [a]. There are three points that the reader should keep in mind that are implicit in advocacy of the market sector (often described as a laissez-faire system) as the preferred system of social control. In highlighting these points our purpose is not to denigrate the market but to make certain that the reader is aware of what may be subsumed in the rhetoric of market advocacy.

First, under a market sector allocation and distribution of resources, any initial private assignment of property rights will yield efficiency, as long as all rights are fully specified. It is sufficient to observe that if all existing property rights were randomly redistributed among all households in society, a new state of general equilibrium incorporating the new distribution of resources in the economy would also satisfy the necessary conditions for Pareto efficiency. Because there are an infinite number of random redistributions of property in any society, it follows that there is also, literally, an infinite number of Pareto optimal outcomes, each corresponding to a different initial distribution of property rights.[23] Thus, any assignment of property rights will yield an efficient solution. However, the distribution of goods and services will vary with alternative assignments of rights. The final welfare of society is a function of the allocation and distribution of resources in a society. From the perspective of Law and Economics, which concerns itself with both allocation and distribution, Pareto efficient market outcomes only speak to the former of these two concerns and are silent as to the latter. That is, Pareto efficiency either assumes the prevailing distribution of resources or ignores any mention of the distribution of resources in a society (which may amount to the same thing). Warren J. Samuels has gone further to suggest that other factors are also subsumed under the notion of Pareto optimality. He states:

> Not only is there a multiple number of Pareto-optima represented on the contract curve, which reflects alternative initial endowments, but there are an infinite number of Pareto-optima reflecting the many other assumptions and the multiplicity of substantive contents of each of them. Pareto-optimum varies, for example, with income and wealth distribution, with the power structure, and, most significantly for policy issues, with the law.[24]

The second point is that even though a final allocation of resources is efficient it may not be desirable, even if we ignore distributional questions. Some efficient allocations may so violate the moral and ethical norms of society that the achievement of efficiency may reduce societal welfare. Examples might include broad based wholesale and retail markets for nuclear weapons, or the street-cart or machine vending of heroin and other drugs or narcotics. While a completely nonattenuated structure of property rights would imply a free market for these goods, the "efficient" market outcomes for nuclear weapons and drugs may be totally undesirable from society's viewpoint.

As alluded to earlier, proponents of market allocation advocate movements toward a nonattenuated structure of rights. But, as these examples indicate, an inherent ambiguity arises which will now be explored. The following quote typifies the thrust of the literature which advocates the market as the preferred system of social control based on the concept of nonattenuated rights. As stated by Randall, the call is for

> ... policies aimed at promoting distributional justice, promoting competitive structures (or structures which perform in the manner of competitive structures) in resource markets, *eliminating, to the extent possible, market imperfections attributable to attenuated structures of property rights,* and assisting, or at least not impeding, the process of market adjustment to changing relative scarcity.[25] (emphasis added)

Elsewhere Randall stated: "While any specification of nonattenuated property rights may lead to efficiency, many possible specifications will be at variance with the moral and ethical value system of society."[26] Thus, what first appears as unqualified support of nonattenuated rights—". . . eliminating, *to the extent possible,* market imperfections attributable to attenuated structures of property rights,"—later becomes qualified—*to the extent ethical.*

That the right of ownership to a commodity or resource is not, and can hardly be expected to be, completely nonattenuated has been generally recognized in the literature.[27] In most cases we can expect that, to some extent, the use and transfer of all commodities and resources will be partially restricted in accordance with the determinations made by individuals in the legal-economic arena. While these restrictions may range from substantial to minor, the important point to be understood is that there will be some restrictions, i.e., some degree of attenuation worked out through the legal institutions. Consequently, advocacy of a market sector allocation and distribution of effective commodities and effective resources leaves at issue what degree of attenuation is appropriate to conform with the ethical mandates of society.

This question can be conceptually analyzed by use of a simple diagram which analyzes the notion of attenuation (see Figure II.6). Costs are measured on the verticle axis while the degree of nonattenuation of effective commodities is measured on the horizontal axis.[28] The notion conveyed by the Randall and Furubotn and Pejovich quotes (above) suggests that efficiency would dictate that society adopt the "fully nonattenuated" set of property rights. However, if there are demoralization costs associated with either adopting such a set of rights or moving towards fully nonattenuated rights structures, then the issue is somewhat more complex.

In a purely competitive market setting, movements toward a fully nonattenuated structure of rights will decrease costs of production due to unambiguous gains in exchange of the factors of production. That is, the more rights are nonattenuated, the greater the efficiency, thus the lower the costs of production. Conversely, the greater the degree of attenuation, the more inefficiencies arise due to a variety of market impediments, thus the higher the costs of production. Consequently,

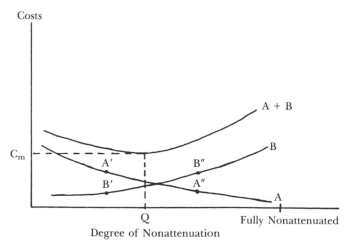

Figure II.6.

there will be an inverse relationship between the degree of nonattenuation of rights and the costs of production. This cost function can be depicted as curve A. For example, the passage of blue laws (such as those which require the closing of all retail stores on Sunday in order to provide for peace, quiet and tranquility) inherently provides some impediments to the market by introducing a constraint on the transfer of goods and services that was not there before passage of the law. The inefficiency (i.e., an increase in costs) associated with the passage of such a blue law can be depicted as a movement from A″ to A′.

In addition, there are costs that result from the establishment of a system of property rights which is at variance with the moral and ethical norms of society. Though this has not been fully developed in the literature, it seems that, given their existence, these costs would most likely increase as the structure of rights become more and more nonattenuated.[29] This cost function can be depicted as curve B. With respect to the example of blue laws, if the opening of retail stores on Sunday runs counter to the morals and ethics of the community, the individuals may incur costs such as B″. Passage of the blue laws which closes all retail stores or Sunday may reduce their demoralization costs down to B′.

Vertically summing these two societal costs yields cost function A + B, the total costs of moving towards a nonattenuated structure of property rights. A society wishing to minimize its costs would attenuate the rights to effective commodities (and resources) to a point such as Q where minimum cost C_m is realized. In this particular example, point Q might be attained by passing blue laws which focus on some retail stores but to the exclusion of others.

As should be evident from this analysis, isolated recommendations for adopting property rights structures which are more and more nonattenuated in order to establish "efficient" markets seem to be based on the narrow concern for cost function A. However, as demonstrated here, if these recommendations are followed, society may have the luxury of unfettered markets but at the expense of a demoralized society.

Thus, in the context of our model of Law and Economics, discussion of the market sector assumes that an antecedent determination of the degree of attenuation has been made. In practice, it is of course the role of the participants in the legal-economic arena to work through the legal institutions to specify the varying degrees of attenuation for specific effective commodities and effective resources in an attempt to enhance their welfare.

The final interdependence between the legal institutions and the market sector concerns the enforcement of both the social contract and private contracts that provide the basis of exchange and production. With respect to the social contract, the absence of enforcement may lead society back toward anarchy, from S to A in Figure II.5, Panel [b].

Enforcement of the social contract is the most basic of Adam Smith's four justifiable categories of government involvement in the market economy.[30] With respect to private contracts, the existence of violation detection and enforcement mechanisms (courts, police, etc.) provides incentives to adhere to the agreements that promote gains from trade (movements from S to $M_1, M_2, M_3, \ldots$). It must be noted that the process of detection and enforcement of the social contract and private contracts entails an opportunity cost equal to the amount of the diversion of resources into detection and enforcement and away from production. Again, the participants in the legal-economic arena will work through the legal institutions to provide that level of enforcement which comports with society's needs.

In summary, in establishing the legal relations governing society in the market sector, the legal institutions provide the guidelines for transactions between parties by assigning, detecting and enforcing, and specifying property rights (i.e., determining the degree of attenuation). The guidelines enable a society to advance its welfare from point S to some point like $M_1, M_2, M_3, \ldots$ (Figure II.5, Panel [b]).

Thus, the market sector allocation and distribution of resources depend upon the interrelationship between the legal institutions and the market. Changes in legal institutions or changes in the choices made by the legal institutions will affect market outcomes. Clarence Ayres suggests that the organizational structure of society, i.e., the institutions, is the predominant determinant of the allocation and distribution of resources.

> The object of dissent is the conception of the market as the guiding mechanism of the economy or, more broadly, the conception of the economy as organized and guided by the market. It simply is not true that scarce resources are allocated among alternative uses by the market. The real determinant of whatever allocation occurs in any society is the organizational structure of that society—in short, its institutions. At most, the market only gives effect to prevailing institutions. By focusing attention on the market mechanism, economists have ignored the real allocation mechanism.[31]

Contrary to his emphasis, we assume that both the market mechanism and the legal institutions influence market outcomes without placing emphasis on either. Our purpose in the remaining chapters is to provide a better understanding of this interrelationship between law and economics.

2. *Public Sector*

The public sector can be conceived of as yet another arena of organizing and controlling the allocation and distribution of resources in a society. In this polar case the allocation and distribution of all resources will be determined in the public sector. That is, the legal institutions will define and assign status rights which establish eligibility requirements for individuals to gain access to goods and resources. This situation may be referred to as "government regulation" in its broadest sense. Thus, legal institutions, in making an array of such complex choices as judge and jury verdicts, legislative statutes, agency pronouncements concerning specific standards and utility commissions' adoptions of new rate structures, affect the final public allocation and distribution of resources in society (see Figure II.7, Panel [a]). The impact of a public sector allocation and distribution of resources upon the individuals' utilities can be depicted in Figure II.7, Panel [b]. Starting from the social contract, point S, the outcomes ($P_1, P_2, P_3, P_4, \ldots$) represent a possible array of legal-institutional choices. It should be noted that within the context of a public sector determination, individuals can work or operate through the legal institutions to enhance their welfare jointly (e.g., P_2, P_3) or, unlike the market sector, one at the expense of another (e.g., P_1, P_4).

3. Communal Sector

In a similar manner, individuals of a society, acting through legal institutions, may decide that commodities or resources will be commu-

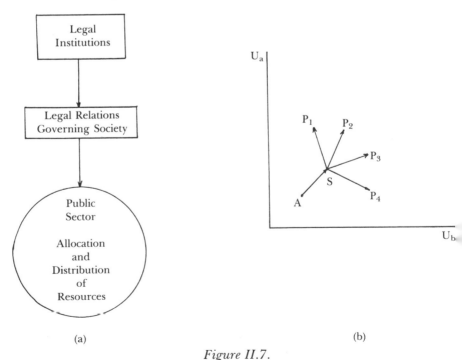

(a)   (b)

Figure II.7.

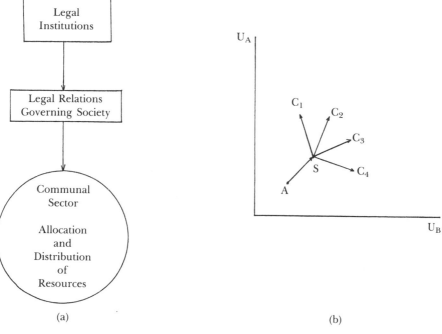

Figure II.8.

nally owned.[32] In this polar case, rights would be assigned equally to each individual, resulting in a communal allocation and distribution (see Figure II.8, Panel [a]). It is understood that once rights are communally assigned the commodity or resource is equally available to all (i.e., non-exclusive) and hence nontransferable. Their being "nontransferable" refers to the fact that the communally owned commodity or resource cannot be transferred from one individual to the next, indeed it is already available to all. Again, starting from the social contract, point S, the possible outcomes $(C_1, C_2, C_3, C_4, \ldots)$ are depicted in Figure II.8, Panel [b].

4. The Complex Legal-Economic Arena

While describing each of these sectors separate and apart from each other serves an heuristic function, a deeper appreciation of the complexity of the legal-economic decision making process emerges upon the recognition that the character of economic life is determined by all three systems of social control: the market sector, the public sector, and the communal sector (see Figure II.9). The relative scope and content of each of the systems of social control is the result of a collective determination of the individual participants in the legal-economic arena. Their

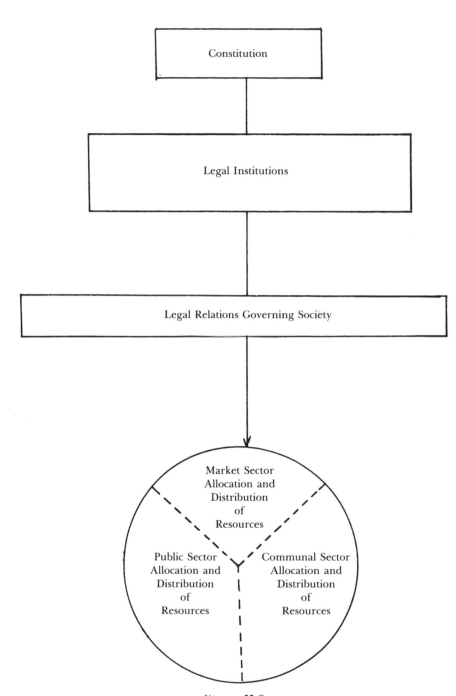

Figure II.9.

participation in the choice-making processes will establish the working rules of the legal institutions and the structure of property rights, both of which will serve to govern the combined allocation and distribution of resources.

The participants in the legal-economic arena will endeavor to revise the constitution, to structure and restructure the working rules and property rights, and through the market, public, and communal sectors will achieve an allocation and distribution of resources that enhance their individual welfare beyond that established in the initial social contract. This is accomplished under the recognition that neither (1) the constitution, (2) the decision-making processes of the legal institutions (i.e., the working rules), nor (3) the legal relations governing the size and scope of the market, public, and communal sectors are given immutably by nature but are themselves a response to economic needs and flexible in response to changes in those needs.

Specifically, working through the legal institutions, the individual participants restructure institutions, work to revise institutional choices within prevailing institutions, or engage in both activities concurrently.[33] In doing so, they alter the legal relations among members of society and thereby redetermine (perhaps only incrementally) the relative scopes of the market, public and communal sectors in the society. For example, at the institutional stage of choice, participants may work: (1) to revise rules for determining legislative committee structures; (2) to determine who may have standing in a court of law or raise or lower the maximum limits for litigation in a small claims court; (3) to expand or limit the role of the intervenor at rate hearings; (4) to alter the method or process by which pollution permits are obtained; and (5) to broaden or curtail that which comes under the notion of executive privilege.

At the economic impact stage of choice, legal-economic participants may work: (1) to determine which goods, services, and resources will be directly under the state's supervision (e.g., more or less public or private education); (2) to determine status rights by defining eligibility requirements for individuals to gain access to certain goods or resources, the rights to which are not transferable among individuals in society (e.g., welfare, foodstamps, etc.); (3) to enhance or diminish the degree of attenuation of effective commodities and resources (e.g., residential, commercial, and industrial zoning restrictions, blue laws, price supports and price ceilings); (4) to have specific rate structures adopted at public utility hearings; (5) to have a parcel of land made readily available for private development or have the same parcel declared communal property for conservation or wilderness purposes; (6) to either assign the right to an upstream chemical firm which allows it to dump its residuals into the stream or assign the right to the downstream farmer who uses the water for crop irrigation to have unpolluted water available; and (7) to have environmental commissions either closely monitor and strictly enforce standing environmental laws or rarely monitor and thus loosely enforce the same laws.

These examples are intended only to illustrate that individual participants in the legal-economic arena can and do restructure institutions and work to revise institutional choices within prevailing institutions. In doing so these individuals alter the legal relations among members of society and thereby redetermine the relative scopes of the market, public, and communal allocations and distributions of resources (see dashed boarders—Figure II.9) all of which goes toward shaping the character of economic life.

Figure II.10 shows clearly the nature of the process described above. Starting at point S, with the establishment of the social contract, the concurrent legal-economic choices as to the market, public and communal sectors (M_1, P_1, and C_1, respectively) result in a complex vector which depicts the combined impact of the legal-economic process. That is, participants in the legal-economic arena will endeavor to structure or revise working rules and property rights in order to achieve an allocation and distribution of resources that enhance their individual welfare beyond point S. As depicted here, society would end up at point L_1, one

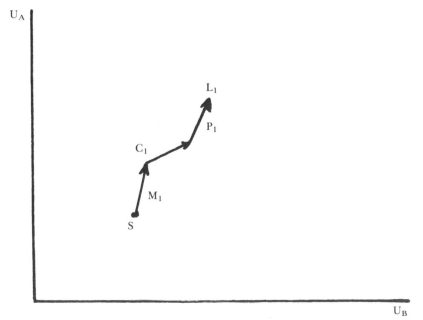

Figure II.10.

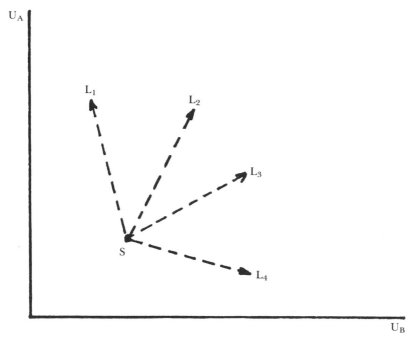

Figure II.11.

possible outcome. An array of possible outcomes is depicted in Figure II.11. In working through the legal-economic institutions to revise working rules or property rights, individuals may enhance their welfare jointly, L_2, L_3, or sometimes at the expense of others, L_1, L_4 (where each vector is a function of the combined and concurrent market, public and communal sector activities as described above).

In the context of our model, the final allocation and distribution of resourcers depends upon the choices made at the constitutional, institutional, and economic impact stages of choice. The consequent character of economic life that emerges in light of the institutional choices must be seen to be an expression of the values of those who participated in and prevailed at each stage of choice in the legal-economic arena. We now turn our attention to a discussion of the inevitable introduction of those values into institutional choice.

C. THE NECESSITY OF CHOICE

It must be recognized that there is a continuing necessity of choice (i.e., an introducing of values) at the constitutional stage of choice, the institutional stage of choice, and the economic impact stage of choice. Any final allocation and distribution of resources (reflected as L_1, L_2, L_3, L_4, . . .) that results from this overall process is an expression of the values of those who have participated at each stage of choice in the legal-economic arena. The necessity of choice has been recognized by many. In writing on the institutional level of choice Buchanan states:

> Man must look to *all* institutions as potentially improvable. Man must adopt the attitude that he can control his fate; he must accept the necessity of choosing. He must look on himself as a man, not another animal, and upon 'civilization' as if it is of his own making.[34]

Samuels, in writing on the interrelations between legal and economic processes and their economic impact, also states:

> There is, first of all, an existential necessity of choice over relative rights, relative capacity to visit injury or costs, and mutual coercive power (or claims to income). The economy, in which the legal process is so obviously involved, is a system of relative rights, of exposure to costs shifted by others, and of coercive impact of others. In choosing between conflicting rights' claimants, furthermore, the choice is between one interest or another. The choice is over capacities to participate in the economic decision-making process—over seats at Spencer's banquet table. These choices are a function of rights which are a function of law; so that, *inter alia*, income distribution—through relative claims to income—is a partial function of law. It is ineluctable, then, that government is involved in the fundamental character, structure, and results of the private sector. Policy issues thus become which or whose rights will government operate to effectively secure, which rights will government no longer operate to effectively secure and which new rights, that is, the use of government to change the effective pattern of rights or realization of interests. . . .
>
> If the issue is one as to which interest government will be used to support, part of the character of the legal process is clarified. The legal system (government, law) is not something given and external to the economic decision-making process. Rather, since government is a mode though which relative rights and therefore relative market (income securing) status is given effect, the critical question is *who* uses government for *what* ends. . . .
>
> Simply put, the question of whose interests the state will be used to effectuate reduces in part to the question of which specific interests or values will dominate in a particular case. This ultimate specificity of choice is the existential burden of man, which no reference to general or neutral principles or choices will avoid.[35]

Perhaps Kendall P. Cochran expresses it best. In writing on the necessity of moral assumptions in shaping the future character of economic life, he states:

> In sum, man, as a social being, has a degree of control over his future destiny. Today and yesterday are *irretrievably gone*. But the future *can* be of his own making. If one were to take a purposeful, a moral look at the future and ask himself, ask his generation, 'What do we want to do with it?' he would find that meaningful alternatives were available. But only if we make a clearly defined choice regarding the

moral assumption we choose to use. And *that* is the moral imperative for members of the economics profession. The only alternative is one of laissez-faire indifference. And the consequence of that moral position, for laissez-faire indifference is equally a moral position, will be that meaningful alternatives are not made available and known to society.[36]

This leaves us with the problem of choosing the "appropriate" institutional arrangements or rearrangements for shaping the character of economic life. That there exist competing theories (economic, as well as noneconomic) to prescribe the "appropriate" institutional arrangements is incontrovertible.[37] As stated earlier in this work, the formulation of alternative theories is to be encouraged in the marketplace of ideas. And, it is the very availability of such theories that once again brings to the forefront the necessity of choice, for society must choose among them to analyze and shape its legal-economic institutions.

Essentially, the practitioners of Law and Economics have taken two tracks in their attempt to choose "appropriate" institutional arrangements. One track analyzes and advocates the structuring of legal institutions on the basis of Pareto optimality. The second approach describes the economic impacts of comparative institutional arrangements. Both tracks recognize that in Law and Economics the legal institutions are no longer exogenous variables as perceived in welfare economics but are now methodologically endogenous to the system. Given their endogenous placement the revision of institutional structures becomes part of a circular process which can be characterized in the following manner. The legal-economic participants, driven by the desire to maximize utility, function not only in the market sector but also in the public and communal sectors, via the legal institutions.[38] As to the latter two sectors, the legal-economic participants, recognizing the incentives inherent in the public and communal sectors, will pursue their interests and opportunities for advantage by working through or modifying the legal institutions in order to revise status rights or communal rights in an attempt to enhance their welfare. Further, within the market sector, changes in demand, scarcity of resources, or technology will create incentives for the legal-economic participants to work through or modify the legal institutions in order to either maintain or revise private property rights or to create new rights in the market in an attempt to enhance their welfare. What is essential to understand is that in the context of this circular process, legal institutions undergo revisions in their structure.

In an attempt to provide some guidelines as to what constitutes "appropriate" institutional arrangements and rearrangements, contributors to the first track described above have set forth theories and methods of analysis that rely heavily on the Pareto efficiency concept borrowed from welfare economics, outlined in Chapter I. Utilizing this principle or one of its variants, these practitioners attempt to determine the "appropriate" structure and hence conduct of legal institutions from which would emerge the "proper" character of economic life. While such attempts are extremely useful in describing the allocation and distribution of resources generated through Pareto-structured institutions, there is no basis to claim they are "appropriate" in any positive sense.

As one reviews the contributions in this area of Law and Economics, it remains unclear whether the designing or evaluating of legal institutions is to be accomplished through recourse to *only* the Pareto optimality criterion. That is, whether what is being set forth is the view that one should make Pareto optimal institutional revisions or that one should *only* make Pareto optimal institutional revisions is not at all clear.

It is our assertion that all attempts to determine the "proper" or "appropriate" legal institutions and legal arrangements by use of the Pareto-efficiency criteria fall strictly within the domain of normative analysis, claims to the contrary notwithstanding. This is our judgment and rests on three suppositions. First, as explained in Chapter I, welfare economics and its underlying Pareto principle are generally considered normative. Second, there is a necessity of having to introduce one's own value judgments to use any one of the economic criteria available—the Pareto principle is just one—to prescribe legal institutional structures. That a "wide consensus" may exist among some practitioners of Law and Economics asserting that the Pareto principle is particularly well suited for this endeavor does not negate the antecedent ethical presupposition required for its adoption. And third, the quest for appropriate or optimal arrangements based on economic criteria is only one, albeit an important, consideration in determining the institutional and legal arrangements of a society. As stated by Milton Friedman:

> It has been long known that there are alternative institutional arrangements that would enable the formal conditions for an optimum to be attained. Furthermore, the institutional arrangements adopted are likely to have important noneconomic implications. So it is necessary both to make a choice and to introduce additional criteria in making the choice. . . . Economic institutions do not operate in a vacuum. They form part, and an extremely important part, of the social structure within which individuals live. They must also be judged by their noneconomic implications, of which the political implications—the implications for individual liberty—are probably of the most interest and the ethical implications the most fundamental.[39]

The second tract taken up by some contributors to Law and Economics views the discipline as one concerned more with the description of the economic impacts of comparative institutional arrangements. The attempt generally has been to avoid prescription and try to rigorously describe, in a more positive sense: (1) the systematic relationships between the structure of the legal institutions and the market, public and communal sectors as systems of social control and (2) the resulting allocation and distribution of resources. Conceptually, perhaps "ideally", the systems of control are given equal footing and subjected to a similar type of economic impact analysis (allocation and distribution). Unfortunately, this has not been the case. Our observation is that much of the Law and Economics literature focuses on questions of allocation rather than questions of distribution. In addition, it concentrates its efforts on critiquing "governmental regulation," reflecting a partiality toward private-market economic activity.[40] This is neither good nor bad, but it is incomplete. Our view is in line with what Ronald H. Coase suggests. Notwithstanding his predisposition toward the private-market sector, he states:

> The discussion of the problem of harmful effects . . . has made clear that the problem is one of choosing the appropriate social arrangement for dealing with the harmful effects. All solutions have costs and there is no reason to suppose that government regulation is called for simply because the problem is not well handled by the market or the firm. Satisfactory views on policy can only come from a patient study of how, in practice, the market, firms and governments handle the problem of harmful effects. . . . It is my belief that economists, and policy-makers generally, have tended to over-estimate the advantages which come from governmental regulation. But this belief, even if justified, does not do more than suggest that government regulation should be curtailed. It does not tell us where the boundary line should be drawn. This, it seems to me, has to come from a detailed investigation of the actual results of handling the problem in different ways.[41]

Pure descriptive analysis cannot advocate any system of social control nor can it advocate a particular legal-institutional arrangement. It should be content with describing the full array of economic impacts (including both the allocation and distribution of resources) of alternative institutions and legal arrangements. In doing so, a comparative institutional approach to Law and Economics can help unmask the options open to individuals in a society. There remains a continuing necessity of choice as to which institutions should prevail in society, the structure of those institutions, and the emergent character of economic life. Once the options are made known through a comparative institutional approach, the participants in the legal-economic arena may be able to make a more informed choice.

NOTES AND REFERENCES

1.   John Rawls, *A Theory of Justice* (Cambridge, Mass: The Bellnap Press, 1971), p. 4.
2.   As developed below, legal institutions include the judiciaries, executive branches of government, legislatures, government commissions and agencies, and custom.

3. Werner Z. Hirsh, *Law and Economics: An Introductory Analysis* (New York: Academic Press, 1979), pp. 4–5.

4. As stated by Taylor, "Private property is a public fact, or it is no fact at all . . . . My right of property in a thing depends not upon my claim to it, but precisely upon your readiness to admit my claim as privileged. . . . For we have property only because first we consent to have community. . . . Outside of the bond of community a man owns nothing." John F. A. Taylor, *Masks of Society* (New York: Appleton, Century, Crofts, 1966), pp. 108–109.

5. For a more thorough discussion of these terms, see John H. Dales, "Rights and Economics," in Gene Wunderlich and W. L. Gibson, Eds., *Perspectives of Property* (University Park: Institute for Research on Land and Water Resources, Pennsylvania State University, 1972), pp. 149–155; Hirsch, *Law and Economics*, pp. 17–21; Richard McKenzie and Gordon Tullock, *Modern Political Economy* (New York: McGraw Hill Book Co., 1978), pp. 75–91; A. Allan Schmid, "A General Paradigm of Institutions and Performance," in A. Allan Schmid, *Property, Power, and Public Choice: An Inquiry into Law and Economics* (New York: Praeger Publishers, 1978), pp. 3–7.

6. A similar sector breakdown is contained in McKenzie and Tullock, *Modern Political Economy*, p. 80.

7. Svetozar Pejovich, *Fundamentals of Economics* (Dallas: The Fisher Institute, 1979), pp. 21–22.

8. For an attenuated version of this notion see Harry G. Johnson, "Reflections on Current Trends in Economics," *Australian Economic Papers*, Vol. 10, No. 16 (June 1971), pp. 1–11 at 10. It should be noted that this perception is different from the Marxian theory of law as outlined by Isaac D. Balbus, "Commodity Form and Legal Form: An Essay on the 'Relative Autonomy' of the Law," *Law and Society Review*, Vol. 11, No. 3 (Winter 1977), pp. 571–588. For a discussion of alternative perspectives on this issue see Mark Tushnet, "Truth, Justice, and the American Way: An Interpretation of Public Law Scholarship in the Seventies," *Texas Law Review*, Vol. 57, No. 8 (November 1979), pp. 1307–1359.

9. If an institution makes choices that have no bearing on the allocation and distribution of resources we do not consider those choices within the domain of Law and Economics. It should be noted that throughout the remaining chapters our examples will usually focus on the legislature, judiciary, and government commissions and agencies though similar statements can be made with respect to the executive branch and custom. A similar descriptive model is provided in Carl A. Auerbach, "Law and Social Change in the United States," *UCLA Law Review*, Vol. 6, No. 4 (July 1959), pp. 516–532. A similar analytical model is provided by Schmid, *Property, Power, and Public Choice*, pp. 3–23.

10. Opportunity cost is defined as the highest valued alternative that must be sacrificed or foregone as a result of choosing a particular course of action. For a discussion of opportunity sets see Warren J. Samuels, "Welfare Economics, Power, and Property," in Wunderlich and Gibson, *Perspectives of Property*, pp. 61–148 at 63–67; McKenzie and Tullock, *Modern Political Economy*, pp. 79–80; Alan Randall, *Resource Economics* (Columbus, Ohio: Grid Publishing, Inc., 1981), p. 39.

11. A synoptic review of the constitutional literature would include: James M. Buchanan and Gordon Tullock, *The Calculus of Consent* (Ann Arbor: University of Michigan Press, 1965), pp. 63–84 and 303–340; Henry G. Manne, Ed., *The Economics of Legal Relationships* (St. Paul: West Publishing Co., 1975), pp. 67–120; Dennis C. Mueller, *Public Choice* (Cambridge: Cambridge University Press, 1979), pp. 11–18, 227–260; Richard A. Posner, *Economic Analysis of Law*, 2nd ed., (Boston: Little, Brown and Co., 1977), pp. 491–496; Charles K. Rowley and Alan T. Peacock, *Welfare Economics* (New York: John Wiley and Sons, 1975), pp. 103–159.

12. See Rawls, *A Theory of Justice*, pp. 136–142.

13. Buchanan and Tullock, *The Calculus of Consent,* p. 78.

14. The actions taken at the constitutional stage of choice are accomplished through the sovereign powers which originated in common law. These powers include the police power, eminent domain, taxing, proprietary, and spending powers. See Raleigh Barlowe, "Federal Programs for the Direction of Land Use," *Iowa Law Review,* Vol. 50, No. 2 (1965), pp. 337–366. In our model, the scope of these powers is endogenous and can be altered by the legal economic participants working through the constitutional processes.

15. Alan Randall, "On Appraising Environmental Institutions: Comment," *American Journal of Agricultural Economics,* Vol. 56, No. 4 (November 1974), pp. 823–825 at 824–825.

16. Raleigh Barlowe, *Land Resource Economics,* 3rd ed., (Englewood Cliffs: Prentice Hall, 1978), pp. 394–411.

17. Eirik Furubotn and Svetozar Pejovich, *The Economics of Property Rights* (Cambridge: Ballinger Publishing Co., 1974), pp. 1–9.

18. Armen A. Alchain and Harold Demsetz, "The Property Rights Paradigm," *Journal of Economic History,* Vol. 33, No. 1 (March 1973), pp. 16–27 at 17.

19. Randall, *Resource Economics,* p. 148.

20. See Furubotn and Pejovich, *The Economics of Property Rights,* p. 5. Furubotn and Pejovich speak only to effective commodities to which we have added the parallel notion of effective resources. It should be noted that output is broadly conceived to include "human rights," e.g., the right to vote, to publish, rights to one's body, etc. Ibid., p. 3.

21. Ibid., p. 6. This assertion remains an unsubstantiated proposition. See Armen Alchain, "Foreword" to Furubotn and Pejovich, *The Economics of Property Rights,* pp. xiii–xiv.

22. Alan Randall, "Growth, Resources and Environment: Some Conceptual Issues," *American Journal of Agricultural Economics,* Vol. 57, No. 5 (December 1975), pp. 803–809 at 805.

23. S. K. Nath, *A Reappraisal of Welfare Economics* (London: Routledge and Kegan Paul, 1969), pp. 28–31. Alan M. Feldman, *Welfare Economics and Social Choice Theory* (Boston: Martinus Nijhoff Publishing, 1980), pp. 51–58. A clear exposition of the nonuniqueness of Pareto efficient outcomes is contained in Randall, *Resource Economics,* pp. 143–154.

24. Samuels, "Welfare Economics, Power, and Property," pp. 74–75.

25. Randall, "Growth, Resources, and Environment," p. 806.

26. Randall, *Resource Economics,* p. 152.

27. Furubotn and Pejovich state the following:

Although our definition suggests that the right of ownership is an *exclusive* right, ownership is not, and can hardly be expected to be, an *unrestricted* right. The right of ownership is an exclusive right in the sense that it is limited *only* by those restrictions that are explicitly stated in the law. Such restrictions may range from the substantial to the minor. For example, on one hand, there is the serious case where an individual's right of ownership in an asset cannot be transferred for a price higher than the ceiling price established by the government; on the other, there is the situation where a land owner is constrained from building a fence within two feet of the property line.

Furubotn and Pejovich, *The Economics of Property Rights,* p. 4.

28. The same type of analysis could be applied to effective resources.

29. The actual behavior of this cost function is, of course, an empirical question. While we have shown it to be upward sloping over the entire range, it is possible that the curve may be U-shaped.

30. Adam Smith, *An Inquiry into the Nature and Causes of the Wealth of Nations* (New York: The Modern Library Edition, 1937), pp. 669–680.

31. Clarence E. Ayres, "Institutional Economics: Discussion," *American Economic Review*, Vol. 47, No. 2 (May 1957), pp. 13–27 at 26.

32. See Garrett Hardin, "The Tragedy of the Commons," *Science*, Vol. 162 (1968), pp. 1243–1248; see also Garrett Hardin and John Baden, *Managing the Commons* (San Francisco: W. H. Freeman and Co., 1977).

33. It must be noted that the participants in the legal-economic arena can also revise the position of point S by altering the constitution.

34. James M. Buchanan, "Law and the Invisible Hand," in Bernard H. Siegan, Ed., *The Interaction of Economics and the Law* (Lexington: Lexington Books, 1977), pp. 127–138 at 136.

35. Warren J. Samuels, "Interrelations Between Legal and Economic Processes," *Journal of Law and Economics*, Vol. 14, No. 2 (October 1971), pp. 435–450 at 442, 445.

36. Kendall P. Cochran, "Economics as a Moral Science," *Review of Social Economy*, Vol. 37, No. 2 (October 1974), pp. 186–195 at 194.

37. For a discussion of these competing theories, see Arthur A. Leff, "Economic Analysis of Law: Some Realism About Nominalism," *Virginia Law Review*, Vol. 60, No. 3 (March 1974), pp. 451–482 at 469–477.

38. Miliband states this process as follows:

> More than ever before men now live in the shadow of the state. What they want to achieve, individually or in groups, now mainly depends on the state's sanction and support. But since that sanction and support are not bestowed indiscriminately, they must, ever more directly, seek to influence and shape it altogether. It is for the state's attention, or for its control, that men compete.

Ralph Miliband, *The State in Capitalist Society* (London: Weidenfeld and Nicolson, 1969), p. 1. A review of the interrelationship between government and the economy in the context of the history of economic thought is provided by Warren J. Samuels, "The State, Law, and Economic Organization," *Research in Law and Sociology*, Vol. 2 (1979), pp. 65–99.

39. Milton Friedman, "Lerner on the Economics of Control," in Milton Friedman, *Essays in Positive Economics* (Chicago: University of Chicago Press, 1953), pp. 301–319 at 316, 317, 318.

40. H. H. Liebhafsky, "Price Theory as Jurisprudence: Law and Economics, Chicago Style," *Journal of Economic Issues*, Vol. 10, No. 1 (March 1976), pp. 23–43 at 40, and Richard L. Abel, "Redirecting Social Studies of Law," *Law and Society Review*, Vol. 14, No. 3 (Spring 1980), pp. 805–829 at 827.

41. Ronald Coase, "The Problem of Social Cost," *Journal of Law and Economics*, Vol. 3 (October 1960), pp. 1–44 at 18–19.

Chapter III

The Problem of Externalities

It is thus doubtful whether the term 'externality' has any meaningful interpretation, except as an indicator of the political beliefs and value judgments of the person who uses (or avoids using) the term.[1] (Dahlman, 1979)

In analyzing the manner in which law and economics interact, it is necessary to study the problem of externality. The vast literature on this topic is far too extensive for us to review here but we will attempt to briefly characterize its traditional treatment in neoclassical economics and property rights economics, as well as to direct attention to its formulation and treatment in the context of our model of Law and Economics.

There have been many definitions of externalities and many classifications of externalities within these definitions.[2] In introducing the concept of externalities we start with a definition from Bernard Herber which reflects the current and broadly accepted usage of the concept of externality in conventional neoclassical economics.

> An economic externality may be viewed as an economic gain or loss accruing to one or more recipient agents as the result of an economic action initiated by another agent—with the gain or loss not being reflected in a market price. The initiating or recipient economic agent may be either a producer or a consumer.[3]

Thus, an externality exists when the action of one consumer or producer enters the utility or production function of some other consumer or producer.

Defining an externality in this conventional sense focuses attention on economic activity in the private market sector and the functioning or disfunctioning of the purely competitive market. The purely competitive perfectly functioning market has the following characteristics: many buyers motivated by self-interests acting to maximize utility; many sellers also motivated by self-interests acting to maximize profits in atomistic industries; both buyers and sellers are unable to exert any control over market price and thus are price takers; prices serve as the guideposts for decision makers in the market to communicate scarcity; products are standardized (i.e., homogeneous); there are no barriers to entry or exit, thus buyers and sellers are free to enter or leave all product and factor markets; all buyers and sellers are fully informed as to the terms of all market transactions; and prevailing laws and property rights are enforced through the state.[4]

The conventional approach to externalities rests upon the recognition that this purely competitive market, by taking into account all costs and benefits, equates marginal social benefits (MBs) with marginal social costs (MCs) and thereby produces an efficient allocation of resources. However, it is also recognized that some activities of the economic actors in the economy, for a variety of reasons, can drive a wedge into the perfectly functioning markets which tends to result in some costs or benefits—those that are "external" to the market, hence the name "externalities"—going unaccounted for in market transactions. The existence of externalities will cause a divergence between the marginal social benefits and marginal social costs. The problem then is to find a mechanism to communicate any heretofore unaccounted external benefits or costs to the market participants. In doing so, externalities are said to be "internalized" thereby restoring an efficient allocation of resources to society (i.e., MBs = MCs).

A. A FORMAL PRESENTATION OF THE MARKET SECTOR

Given the preponderance of the literature that relates to market failure and the concept of externality, a more formal analysis of the market sector is in order. From society's standpoint, the significance of having MBs equal to MCs is best grasped by understanding what transpires when this equality does not hold. Consider Figure III.1 where the MBs and MCs for good X are depicted.[5] If the allocation of resources is such that quantity X_1 gets produced, then the MBs exceeds MCs for that quantity of good X. As additional resources are devoted to the production of good X, society would incrementally gain benefits in excess of costs as more and more X is produced and consumed. Once the quantity X_0 is produced where no further incremental gains are possible, i.e., where MBs = MCs, society is said to have achieved an efficient allocation of resources devoted to good X. If society had continued to devote even more additional resources to good X and had produced X_2, then the MCs would have exceeded the MBs. Clearly, each additional unit of X

Costs &
Benefits

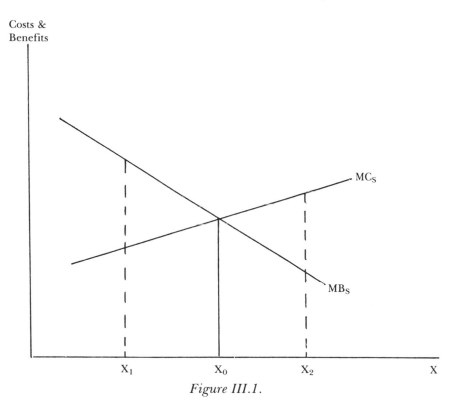

Figure III.1.

produced and consumed beyond X_0 would entail incremental costs in excess of benefits. By foregoing these additional units of good X and remaining at X_0, that quantity of good X which equates MBs to MCs, society achieves an efficient allocation of resources. By following this same process for all goods, society achieves a Pareto optimal allocation of resources throughout the economy. The important point to be understood is that when *all* benefits and costs are accounted for and when MBs = MCs for all goods, the outcome is said to be Pareto efficient.

Further, there is a body of literature that illustrates that a purely competitive, perfectly functioning market will achieve a Pareto efficient allocation of resources. This correspondence between the purely competitive market performance and Pareto efficiency is referred to as the duality theorem.[6] This literature has identified four necessary conditions that must be met in order for the market to achieve Pareto efficiency.[7] These conditions are summarized in Table III.1.[8] As indicated, the condition for a Pareto-efficient allocation of resources is that the MBs = MCs for every good. With the market sector as a means of social control, all decisions are made by individual producers and consumers attempt-

Table III-1.

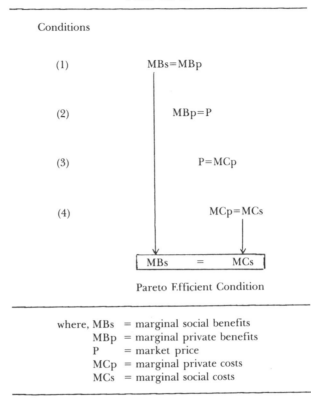

Conditions

(1) MBs=MBp

(2) MBp=P

(3) P=MCp

(4) MCp=MCs

| MBs | = | MCs |

Pareto Efficient Condition

where, MBs = marginal social benefits
MBp = marginal private benefits
P   = market price
MCp = marginal private costs
MCs = marginal social costs

ing to maximize profits and utility, respectively.[9] In order to achieve a Pareto optimal outcome through the market, it is necessary to fulfill the four conditions presented in Table III.1. In doing so, the market solutions generated will take into account all social benefits and social costs.

With respect to condition (1) shown in Table III.1, since Pareto efficiency requires that marginal social benefits be considered and utility maximization assumes the consumers consider only private benefits, then the condition that MBs = MBp means that all social benefits will be accounted for in the market sector by the activities of individual consumers. Condition (2), MBp = P, states that the price an individual consumer is willing to pay to acquire a good reflects perfectly his private marginal benefit derived from the good. In fulfilling this condition, each individual is maximizing his utility. Furthermore, these prices are the ones that will guide producers to allocate more or less resources to the production of various goods and thereby take into account the marginal private benefit assessments of the consumers. Condition (3), P = MCp, states that the price received by a producer perfectly reflects the marginal private cost of producing the good, i.e., the opportunity cost of using the resources needed to produce the good. In fulfilling this condition, each firm is maximizing its profits under perfect competition. Finally, since Pareto efficiency requires that all marginal social costs be considered and profit maximization assumes that the producers consider only private costs, then condition (4), MCp = MCs, means that all social costs will be accounted for in the market sector by the activities of individual producers. Given the fulfillment of these four conditions, purely competitive, perfectly functioning markets will generate Pareto efficient outcomes (as can be seen clearly from Table III.1).

B. MARKET FAILURE

The market sector, as a means for social control, will fail to generate a Pareto optimal outcome if any one of the four conditions is not met. That is, if there are deviations from the basic structural characteristics of the purely competitive market that drive a wedge into any one or more of the four basic equalities, then the condition for Pareto efficiency (MBs = MCs) will not be met. In reality, there are a variety of factors and forces at work in the economy that create such inequalities.[10] To these, we now turn.

The fulfillment of condition (1), MBs = MBp, can be intuitively grasped by considering what occurs when an individual consumes a steak. The benefit an individual acquires in eating the steak is probably not much different than the benefit society acquires by his action—he benefits by so much and society benefits by the same amount. However, there are many situations in which society's benefits differ from the benefits acquired by an individual when that individual takes a particular course of action. Instances where the benefits accruing to society exceed the benefits gained by an individual include an individual engaging in such activities as having his home landscaped and gardened, having the family inoculated for contagious diseases, or seeing that children acquire an education.[11] These examples can be depicted in Figure III.2 where MBs is the sum of private consumption benefits plus the external benefits accruing to society as a result of the private consumption decision, MBp plus XB. As outlined earlier, from society's standpoint, the efficient allocation of resources would be at X_0 units of good X where MCs = MBs. However, consumers in the market will make decisions with regard to private benefit assessments (i.e., along MBp) resulting in a solution where MBp = MCs. This corresponds to a nonoptimal, underallocation of resources at point X_1, where it is observed that MBs = MBp

Costs &
Benefits

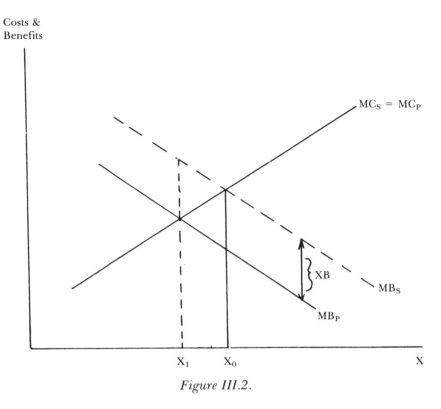

Figure III.2.

+ XB and therefore MBs > MBp, a violation of condition (1).

With respect to condition (2), MBp = P, it is difficult to imagine violations of this condition for consumers in the final goods and services market. However, monopsonists in resource markets (i.e., a single buyer or association of buyers with some control over the resource price) do violate this condition. An example of a monopsonistic firm in the labor market can be depicted in Figure III.3. This example requires some redefinitions as we shift to the labor market. In the labor market price (P) is now the price of labor (P_L) or simply the wage rate (W). MBs, which equals MBp, represents the marginal revenue product to the firm employing additional laborers (MRP_L). MCs equals MRCs, society's marginal resource cost, and represents the true opportunity cost incurred by society in supplying additional units of labor. MCp = MRCp represents the private marginal expense to the firm of acquiring additional units of labor. From society's standpoint, the efficient solution would dictate that the firm hire L_0 laborers and pay W_0 wage rate where $W_0 = MRP_L$ (rearticulated in terms of Table III.1, P = MBp). However, the firm in making its decision on how many laborers to hire will consider only the private cost of hiring additional laborers (i.e., move along MRCp) and hire L_1 laborers and pay W_1 wage rate. Thus, at L_1, $W_1 < MRP_L$ (i.e., P < MBp) a violation of condition (2).

With respect to condition (3), P = MCp, recall that in a perfectly competitive market each firm acts as a price taker—which means that each firm perceives that it has no control over the price of its output. As a result, each firm, within a limited range, can sell as much or as little of the good as it wants at the prevailing market price. If this is the case, then the marginal revenue (MR) of one additional unit sold is equal to the market price, (i.e., MR = P). Since, profit maximizing firms will always produce at the output where the marginal cost of the next unit is equal to the marginal revenue of that unit (MCp = MR), in a competitive industry, profit maximizing firms will produce at an output where marginal cost is equal, not only to marginal revenue, but also equal to price; that is, since P = MR and MR = MCp, then P = MCp.

Violations of condition (3) occur in cases of imperfect competition where firms, to some extent, exert control over the market price. Typ-

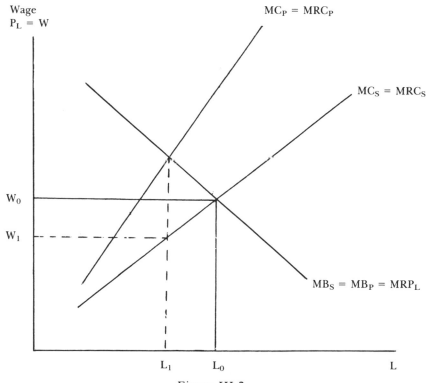

Figure III.3.

ically this is what transpires in various degrees in the market structures of pure monopoly, oligopoly and monopolistic competition. That is, firms in these market structures typically face a downward sloping demand curve, which implies that the marginal revenue of the next unit sold is less than the price for each quantity produced and sold (MR < P). As depicted in Figure III.4, efficiency would dictate that X_0 units be produced and sold for price P_0, where MBs = MCs. However, the firm will equate the marginal revenue (MR) to marginal private cost (MCp) and produce X_1 units and charge price P_1. As a result, the profit maximizing firm with some market power will produce at a level of output where price exceeds marginal private cost; that is, at X_1 since P > MR and MR = MCp, then P > MCp, a violation of condition (3).

The fulfillment of condition (4), MCp = MCs, can be illustrated by the example of an organic farm which avoids the use of any nonorganic fertilizers, pesticides or rodenticides. The implication is that all of the marginal private costs incurred to produce the farm products are equivalent to all the marginal social costs incurred by society. Violations of this condition are a result of the interdependence often brought on by the existence of common property resources and are probably the most

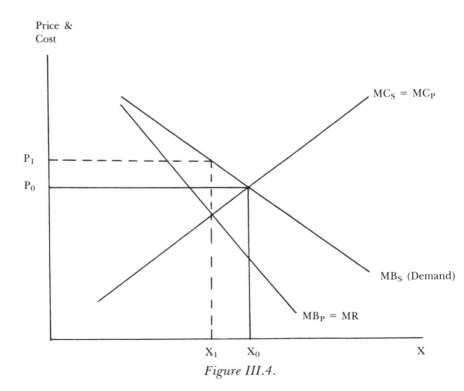

Figure III.4.

Costs & benefits

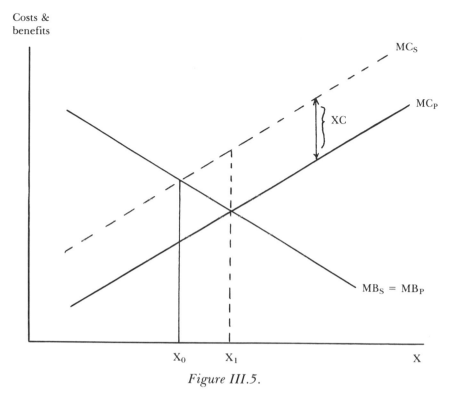

Figure III.5.

widely discussed case of externalities. Examples of this include air and water pollution, noise pollution, and the like. Exploring this a bit further, firms make their output decisions on the basis of the costs of production that result from the purchase of privately owned factors of production, i.e., the firm's marginal private costs (MCp). However, in cases where the firm utilizes a common property resource, the production of a good entails costs that are not borne by the firm but are borne by some other producers or consumers in the society, yielding external costs, XC, in Figure III.5.[12] The marginal social cost, MCs, equals the sum of MCp plus XC. From society's standpoint the efficient allocation of resources would coincide with the production and consumption of X_0 units of good X where MCs = MBs. However, the perfectly competitive firm will maximize profits by considering only private costs, MCp, resulting in a solution where MBs = MCp. This corresponds to a nonoptimal, overallocation of resources at point X_1, where it is observed that MCs = MCp + XC and therefore MCs > MBs, a violation of condition (4).

There are two other sources of market failure, one concerning information, the other enforcement, that we note. Both the lack of full information to market participants and the lack of complete enforcement of rights can drive a wedge into the equalities given by the four conditions specified in Table III.1.

Recall that one of the basic assumptions of a purely competitive, perfectly functioning market is that all consumers and producers have perfect information over all facets of all market transactions. However, if the requirement of perfect information is not met, then conditions arise that can serve to drive a wedge into the equalities given by conditions (2) and (3) and thereby prevent the market from attaining a Pareto optimal outcome.[13] For example, if a consumer is not fully informed as to the actual benefits to be derived from the acquisition of additional units of a good, then the price he is willing to pay for the good in an attempt to maximize his utility will likely be at variance with the actual benefits received. That is, the actual benefits received will not equal the price the consumer is willing to pay, i.e., $MBp \neq P$, since the price was based on an incorrect or incomplete assessment due to a lack of full information as to the benefits to be received. It should be noted that the impact upon the individual consumer brought on by the lack of full information can be to his benefit or detriment. If the impact on the consumer was to his benefit then $MB_p > P$, for example, the discovery of oil on the site of his vacation home. Whereas, if the impact was to his detriment then $MBp < P$. An example might be the unknown side-effects of medications. In either case $MBp \neq P$, which would preclude a Pareto efficient outcome.

In a similar manner, a producer who lacks perfect information, say with respect to market demand, scarcity of resources or technology, in an attempt to maximize profits, is likely to make output decisions that are at variance with the actual costs incurred, i.e., $P \neq MCp$. If the actual market demand for a producer's product, and therefore the market price, is not fully known due to a lack of perfect information, then the true market price may be greater or less than the producer's assessment of that price. An example might be a farmer who, in the short run, makes his output decision by equating his marginal private costs to the expected price of wheat, say $3.00 a bushel. If at harvest he finds that the actual price is greater than $3.00 then $P > MCp$. Likewise if it turns out that the market price is less than $3.00, then $P < MCp$. In either case, $P \neq MCp$, which prevents the attainment of a Pareto efficient solution.

The complete governmental enforcement of rights is another of the basic assumptions of purely competitive markets. The full enforcement of rights pertaining to contracts is one of the prerequisites for smoothly functioning, purely competitive markets.[14] The lack of protection of these rights underlying the market sector can drive a wedge into any one of the four conditions and thereby prevent the market from attaining a

Pareto optimal outcome. A simple example of a violation of each of the four conditions will make this apparent. The lack of enforcement of rights leading to a violation of condition (1) causing MBs $\neq$ MBp, can be illustrated by the case of an individual who, for his own fishing enjoyment, stocks his private lake with fish. If antipoaching or trespass laws are not enforced then MBs > MBp. Condition (2), MBp = P, will be violated if laws that allow for the establishment of unions to countervail monopsony power are not enforced; as a result, MRP_L > W (i.e., MBp > P). Condition (3), P = MCp, will be violated if antitrust laws go unenforced, i.e., P > MCp. And finally, condition (4), MCp = MCs, will be violated if nuisance laws that prohibit firms from discharging smoke into the air are not enforced, MCp < MCs.

C. TRADITIONAL SOLUTIONS TO THE PROBLEM OF EXTERNALITIES

It should now be evident that there are many underlying sources of externalities which manifest themselves by variously creating inequalities in any one or more of the four efficiency conditions thereby causing the market to fail to attain a Pareto-efficient outcome. We now turn to a brief review of some of the traditional solutions that have been proffered to remove or internalize externalities in the hope of restoring Pareto efficiency.

In approaching solutions to the problem of externalities there is one intuitive notion that the reader should be on guard against. One might think that if there were six or eight underlying causes of externalities resulting in inequalities of the four conditions, then by operating in a piecemeal fashion and eliminating the causes one by one, society will move sequentially towards a Pareto efficient solution. As demonstrated by Richard G. Lipsey and Kelvin Lancaster in their *General Theory of Second Best,* this is not the case. What they showed was that, provided at least one underlying cause remains unresolved or unrectified, it cannot be determined whether welfare will be improved by eliminating the other causes of externalities.[15] For example, in making the otherwise obviously efficient move of breaking up a monopoly, the allocation of resources may be made even more inefficient if the monopolist was a polluter. Fredrick M. Scherer, comments on the theory of second best:

> Because it states that maintaining competition whenever possible is not necessarily optimal but offers no guidance toward improved policies in the absence of information which cannot be obtained, the theory of second best is a counsel of despair. Still policy decisions must be taken, and if the data needed for second-best solutions are lacking, rough and ready ' third-best' approximations will at least be better, as E. J.

Mishan has advised, than 'standing by and sadly sucking our thumbs under the sign of second best.'[16]

Perhaps the best description of the present intellectual niche occupied by the theory of second best is provided by Charles K. Rowley and Alan T. Peacock:

> The less tortuous and more popular [avenue of escape] is that of paying lip service to the second-best theorem while proceeding (more or less brazenly, according to sensitivity) to an analysis based upon the 'piecemeal' principle.[17]

Notwithstanding the Lipsey and Lancaster contribution, there are several traditional solutions to the problem of externalities. These traditional approaches share the common characteristic that they tend to treat the government as an exogenous actor called on to rectify the underlying causes of inequalities in any of the four basic conditions necessary for an efficient allocation of resources.

We begin with the literature on public goods.[18] This body of work is largely devoted to describing the conditions under which the MBs ≠ MBp and, further, to analyzing various governmental approaches that attempt to restore equality in this condition. A public good is a good that is indivisible or non rival in consumption. That is, once a public good is provided additional consumption by one individual does not reduce the quantity available to other consumers. This is unlike the case of private goods where additional consumption by one individual does reduce the quantity available to other consumers. In addition, for public goods, exclusion of non-payers is too costly to be worth enforcing. Because of the characteristics inherent in public goods, the market cannot be relied upon to provide the efficient quantity. That is, since MBs > MBp, the market would persistently underallocate resources devoted to the production of public goods.

The traditional public goods literature has analyzed in great depth various methods by which the government might be able to ascertain the demand for public goods. Due to the difficulties associated with preference revelation in the context of the free rider problem, definitive solutions have proven elusive. Regardless of the actual method of demand revelation employed (e.g., sum of willingness to pay or sell), the government would obtain a biased estimate of consumer demand for public goods. As a result, many of the problems associated with public goods persisted, giving rise to various prescriptive approaches including real valued social welfare functions, axiomatic social welfare functions and conventional public choice theory (these will be explored in Chapter V).

Second, there is a body of literature that describes the manner in which the government can attempt to restore MBp = P in the case of monopsony (described earlier). This literature, among other things, focuses on the role of the government endorsing the establishment of unions in order to "countervail" the power exercised by the monopsonist and thus attempt to restore equality back into condition (2).[19]

With respect to condition (3), P = MCp, two sizable bodies of literature exist reflecting two different public policy approaches adopted in the U.S. in an attempt to restore or maintain equality with regard to condition (3). Antitrust comprises one track, where the role of government is seen to be that of outlawing and punishing abuses of monopoly power as well as prohibiting certain types of conduct that may lead to monopoly.[20] The second track of public policy does not secure equality in condition (3), P = MCp, but does attempt to minimize the amount by which price will exceed marginal private cost. This is the purported thrust of public utility regulation where a regulatory commission regulates a natural monopoly, for example electricity and telephone service.[21]

Finally, the existence of common property resources, such as air and water, results in an inequality in condition (4), MCp = MCs. Much of the literature devoted to analyzing problems relating to common property resources is in the area of environmental economics.[22] The thrust of this literature is to prescribe various governmental solutions including legislated standards, tax schemes, subsidy schemes, and others, all of which attempt to equate MCp with MCs.

Given the thrust of much of this traditional literature on externalities, we do not think it is too much a generalization to assert that the conventional solution to the externality problem has been based on the argument that the mere existence of externalities justifies the intervention of the "state" or "government" into the economy, in order to eliminate the underlying causes of market failure and attain Pareto efficient outcomes. In particular, a good deal of the literature focuses specifically on the role of government tax and subsidy schemes that attempt to ultimately equate MBs with MCs. This subset of literature owes its origin to the work of Arthur C. Pigou, who, in treating the government as an exogenous variable, proffered the use of tax and subsidy schemes to rectify a disfunctioning market.[23] In addition, implicit in this tradition, a distinction is drawn between emitors and recipients of externalities. We pay particular attention to the Pigovian tradition inasmuch as it provides a basis upon which to better understand the treatment of externalities in Law and Economics. Pigou stated:

But even in the most advanced States there are failures and imperfections. . . . There are many obstacles that prevent a community's resources being distributed . . . in the most effective way. The study of these constitutes our present problem . . . its purpose is essentially practical. It seeks to bring into clearer light some of the ways in which it now is, or eventually may become, feasible for governments to control the play of economic forces in such wise as to promote the economic welfare, and through that, the total welfare, of their citizens as a whole.[24]

He went on to say:

It is plain that divergences between private and social net product of the kinds we have so far been considering cannot . . . be mitigated by a modification of the contractual relations between any two contracting parties, because the divergence arises out of a service or disservice rendered to persons other than the contracting parties. It is, however, possible for the State, if it so chooses to remove the divergence in any field by 'extraordinary encouragements' or 'extraordinary restraints' upon investments in that field. The most obvious forms which these encouragements and restraints may assume are, of course, those of bounties and taxes.[25]

As will be seen, from the perspective of Law and Economics, the tax-subsidy scheme proffered by Pigou can be thought of as one solution with specific allocative and distributive economic consequences that must be compared to the economic consequences of alternative corrective legal-institutional arrangements.

D. LAW AND ECONOMICS AND THE PROBLEM OF EXTERNALITY

Notwithstanding the great influence of Pigou's contribution, the current treatment of externalities in Law and Economics has dispensed with the approach outlined above, in the sense that the government is no longer perceived as an exogenous actor. Further, from the perspective of Law and Economics, the domain of the problem of externality is not confined exclusively to a disfunctioning private-market sector. As a result, the problem is more complex and solutions somewhat more ambivalent, as will be seen. The appropriate place to start is with the work of Ronald H. Coase.

In his seminal article "The Problem of Social Cost," Coase analyzed the problem of esternalities and set forth bargaining as a solution to the externality problem.[26] Within this work, he dispensed with the emitor-recipient distinction by defining and focusing on the reciprocal nature of externalities. That is, if liability rules are fixed one way, then A imposes an externality on B. If, however, liability rules are reversed, then B imposes an externality on A. Thus, the question to be decided is: "Should A be allowed to harm B or B be allowed to harm A?" Coase's analysis of the bargaining solution to externalities and its impact on the allocation of resources was carried out in two different contexts—one in which market transactions costs are zero and another in which positive transactions costs exist.[27] Unfortunately, a great deal of the analysis of and attention to Coase's work has been of the case where market transactions costs are zero. The greater contribution of Coase, however, comes from the second case. Both are discussed here. In the first part of his article, Coase assumes zero market transactions costs and analyzes the effect of externalities on the allocation of resources.

The reader should note that at this point in his work, Coase views externalities as closely associated with, and external to, the market sector. Using the now famous example of the straying cattle who inflict crop damage on the farmers, Coase shows that the changes in the legal liability rules will not affect the final equilibrium output of cattle and crops. The market will insure that the highest valued commodity will be produced regardless of the initial assignment of liability rules. That is, if cattle are more highly valued in the market and the cattle owners do not possess the property rights to destroy crops, then the cattle owners will bribe the farmers to allow the cattle to graze and destroy some crops. The amount of cattle and crops that would result from this bargaining process is exactly the same as the amount of the two goods that would result if the cattle owners had owned the right to destroy some crops in the first place. Stated in a slightly different manner, the outcome of the bargaining process will be that which maximizes the value of output, as long as the rights are initially assigned to someone and then enforced. This is the Coase Theorem: under idealized conditions when market transactions costs are zero and where income effects are not relevant, the allocational results of voluntarily negotiated agreements will be invariant over differing assignments of property rights among the parties to the interaction.[28] The Theorem conceptually provides a market-like, bargaining solution to the problem of externalities where it is observed that: (1) the government has a more limited role to play than in the Pigovian approach—under the Coase Theorem, the government need only assign and enforce property rights—and, (2) the outcome is Pareto efficient.

The reader can decide for himself whether the Theorem stands on its merits by reading the onslaught of criticism and undying support which the Theorem has received.[29] We would note that from the perspective of our model of Law and Economics, the Coase Theorem is of little practical importance inasmuch as it relies so heavily on the assumption of zero market transaction costs. As Coase himself has stated:

> I would not wish to conclude without observing that, while consideration of what would happen in a world of zero transaction costs can give us valuable insights, these insights are, in my view, without value except as steps on the way to the analysis of the real world of positive transaction costs. We do not do well to devote ourselves to a detailed study of the world of zero transaction costs, like augurs divining the future by the minute inspection of the entrails of a goose.[30]

Presumably this statement can be directed at those who have critiqued the Theorem as well as at those who have tried to advance lassize-faire policies on its behalf. We would not wish to conclude without observing that one can only speculate on how an alternative theory of governmental regulation to resolve the externality problem would hold up on the assumption that the government transactions costs are zero. Furthermore, as we have established earlier in this work, most contributors to the discipline of Law and Economics are concerned with *both* the allocation and distribution of resources consequent to alternative legal arrangements. In this light, the Coase Theorem has one redeeming feature; that is, a direct corollary to the Coase Theorem would be: under conditions of zero transactions costs, society's concern should be with distributive questions because nothing can be said about allocation other than that allocation is not affected.[31]

Fortunately, in the second part of his article Coase analyzes externalities when market transactions costs are not zero.[32] Here his contribution is a major one. Coase acknowledges that when transactions costs are positive, allocative neutrality may break down. Specifically, he states:

> In these conditions the initial delimitation of legal rights does have an effect on the efficiency with which the economic system operates. One arrangement of rights may bring about a greater value of production than any other. But unless this is the arrangement of rights established by the legal system, the costs of reaching the same result by altering and combining rights through the market may be so great that this optimal arrangement of rights, and the greater value of production which it would bring, may never be achieved.[33]

Thus, Coase recognizes that the initial assignment of property rights makes a difference in the eventual allocation of resources in a world of positive transactions costs. In Law and Economics, the most important thrust of Coase's article then is not the claim that the initial assignments of property rights is not important but is the analysis of what happens to the production of output once we recognize that market transactions costs are positive and large enough to affect the production of goods and services.

Harold Demsetz and others have advanced considerably this line of reasoning by analyzing the concept of "externality" and examining the relationship between externalities, positive transactions costs, and the associated economic consequences of trying to internalize externalities.[34] The major thrust of this literature is to suggest that allowing "side effects" (alternately named in lieu of "externalities"[35]) to continue may be perceived as preferable once one recognizes that, due to positive transactions costs, the "optimal" allocation of resources is not attainable. That is, the message appears to be, since both (1) market solutions to externalities or "side effects" are costly and (2) governmental solutions to externalities or "side effects" are costly, then adopting either solution may force society to incur costs which exceed the value of realigning resources that are necessary to take the "side effects" into account.

For example, suppose a chemical firm is situated upstream from a farming community. The chemical firm dumps pollution into the water and the farmers use the water to irrigate their crops and some crop damage ensues. If the property rights structure is such that the chemical firm has the right to dump into the river then three possibilities must be considered. If the market transaction would cost $100 (e.g., $90 for farmers and $10 for the chemical firm); government regulation (including standard setting, monitoring and enforcing) would cost $150; and the side effects (i.e., crop damage) amount to $70, then allowing the side effects to persist is cheaper than adopting either the market or governmental mechanism. However, if the side effects are significant enough to exceed the costs associated with a market or governmental mechanism (i.e., collective fiat) then the issue is much more problematical. As Guido Calabresi and A. Douglas Melamed suggest:

> Since we are in an area where by hypothesis markets do not work perfectly—there are transaction costs—a decision will often have to be made on whether market transactions or collective fiat is most likely to bring us closer to the Pareto optimal result the 'perfect' market would reach. . . . The fact that both market and collective determinations face difficulties in achieving the Pareto optimal result which perfect knowledge and no transaction costs would permit does not mean that the same difficulties are always as great for the two approaches. Thus, there are many situations in which we can assume fairly confidently that the market will do better than a collective decider, and there are situations where we can assume the opposite to be true.[36]

Ryan C. Amacher puts it simply:

> In fact, the failure of government in many areas is every bit as important a social problem today as the failure of private market processes. The unromantic but real choice is between two mechanisms that are both imperfect.[37]

The essential point to be understood is that Law and Economics calls for a broader agenda of corrective measures than those set forth in the Pigovian tradition. It does not exclude Pigovian prescriptions but merely places them in competition with other solutions derived from legal-economic analysis. Registering his discontent with past reliance and over-emphasis on Pigovian solutions, Coase states:

> Analysis in terms of divergences between private and social products concentrates attention on particular deficiencies in the system and tends to nourish the belief that any measure which will remove the deficiency is necessarily desirable. It diverts attention from those other changes in the system which are inevitably associated with the corrective measure, changes which may well produce more harm than the original deficiency.[38]

However, this view must be moderated inasmuch as avoiding harmful effects may not have been Pigou's sole concern. As A. Allan Schmid reminds us, more is involved:

> The Pareto-criterion can be used against the Pigovian argument that the existence of externalities was a prima-facie case for direct government action via regulation or punitive taxation. But we must be careful of overkill. In putting Pigou down, some have tried to put down all regulatory action. Some new regulation was never intended to improve the efficiency of existing rights but only to change these rights. Since Pareto-optimality just carries out given rights, it cannot be used to select these rights. Pareto-efficiency is derived from given rights, not instructive of them. The Pareto-criterion carries out the implications of an original distribution of rights. There are as many Pareto-optimal solutions as there are ways to define and distribute rights, as shown above. One must not avoid the necessity of making a moral choice between A and B by adopting the Pareto-criterion, which only confirms the one already made by implying it should continue.[39]

Furthermore, it should be pointed out that the Coase/Demsetz approach, while comparative institutional in nature, utilizes the concept of efficiency in assigning rights. As Murry N. Rothbard observes, their use of efficiency to assign rights removes their work from the domain of positive analysis.

> Another serious problem with the Coase-Demsetz approach is that pretending to be value-free, they in reality import the ethical norm of 'efficiency,' and assert that property rights should be assigned on the basis of such efficiency. But even if the concept of social efficiency were meaningful, they don't answer the questions of why efficiency should be the overriding consideration in establishing legal principles or why externalities should be internalized above all other considerations. We are now out of *Wertfreiheit* and back to unexamined ethical questions.[40]

Bearing in mind the inherent distributional consequences of alternative solutions and the normative use of efficiency as a criteria (as described by Rothbard), the Coase/Demsetz approach seems to suggest the following calculus:

Compare SE to M and G where

   SE = "side effects"—those effects for which no account *seems* to be taken in the market place.
   M = the cost of providing a market arrangement to take the side effects into account; some market-like solutions include: (1) placing liability on the least cost avoider and allowing subsequent bargaining to rearrange rights, and (2) extending the firm, where such an extension allows the firm to rearrange production and thereby take the side effects into account.[41]

G = the cost of providing a government arrangement to take the side effects into account. The government, either by statute or more typically through administrative agency, can impose regulations to monitor, set standards, and enforce solutions.

Policy Options:

(i)   if SE < M and SE < G, the use of the market sector or the public sector to take the side effects into account is too costly, then allow side effects to persist;

(ii) if SE > M and SE > G and if M < G, then take the side effects into account through the market sector;

(iii) if SE > M and SE > G and if G < M, then take the side effects into account through the public sector.

Thus, the Coase/Demsetz approach can be interpreted as setting forth an analysis that looks to a broad array of solutions without closing the door on public sector solutions, including those often attributed to Pigou. In contrast, some "Coasians," who attach themselves to "the Theorem" and who prefer a preeminance of private market sector activity, would like to rely solely on market-like solutions to resolve externality problems. However, they can no longer unambiguously conclude that market-like solutions are preferable from the standpoint of efficiency except in a world of zero market transactions costs. Commenting on those who still contend that Coase advocated little or no governmental intervention, Calabresi states:

> Some may take Coase's analysis to suggest that little or no government intervention is usually the best rule. My own conclusions are quite different. His analysis, combined with common intuition or guesses as to the relative costs of transactions, taxation, structural rules and liability rules, can go far to explain various types of heretofore inadequately justified governmental actions. This is especially so if one considers the relevance of goals other than resource allocations to those situations where inadequate data makes resource allocations an unsatisfactory guide. Perhaps more precise data will some day prove some of these interventions to be improper from the standpoint of resource allocation. Then we shall have to choose, as we often do, between the bigger pie and other aims.[42]

Indeed, Coase perceived the issue as one of choosing the appropriate social arrangement.

> The discussion of the problem of harmful effects . . . has made clear that the problem is one of choosing the appropriate social arrangement for dealing with the harmful effects. . . . Satisfactory views on policy can only come from a patient study of how, in practice, the market, firms and governments handle the problem of harmful effects. . . . It is my belief that economists, and policy-makers generally, have tended to over-estimate the advantages which come from governmental reg-

ulation. But this belief, even if justified, does not do more than suggest that government regulation should be curtailed. It does not tell us where the boundary line should be drawn. This, it seems to me, has to come from a detailed investigation of the actual results of handling the problem in different ways.[43]

Finally, Carl J. Dahlman sums it up as follows:

> Transaction costs may prevent the establishment of a desirable allocation of resources, one that everyone would agree is better than the one attained when transactions are costly. In this case the Coase analysis implies one of two corrective measures: (i) find out if there is a feasible way to decrease the costs of transacting between market agents through government action, or (ii), *if* that is not possible, the analysis would suggest employing taxes, legislative action, standards, prohibitions, agencies, or whatever else can be thought of that will achieve the allocation of resources we have already decided is preferred. The implication of status quo is simply not there: the theory says to find practicable ways of diminishing transaction costs, by whatever kind of action is necessary, including governmental action.[44]

Thus, the Coase/Demsetz approach lays the foundation for a comparative institutional, legal-economic analysis which essentially lies at the heart of our model. Dahlman, in distinguishing between the traditional approach (see Section C above) and the comparative-institutional approach, advocates a method of analysis that underlies our model of Law and Economics. He states:

> The neatness of the Coase analysis lies in the fact that it dispenses completely with what Demsetz has called 'the Nirvana approach' and instead calls for what he labels 'the comparative systems approach' which explicitly attempts to ascertain the economic consequences of alternative ways of organizing the allocation of resources. The analysis thus directs attention to the point that institutions fulfill an economic function by reducing transaction costs and therefore ought to be treated as variables determined inside the economic scheme of things. The question then ultimately becomes: how can the economic organization be improved upon by endogenous institutional rearrangements? This is not the outlook of modern welfare theory where the government is seen as a force outside the economic system altogether, which will come to our aid and rectify the havoc wrought by endogenously working market forces, just like the classical *deus ex machina*. Coase opens the door for an economic theory of institutions, whereas modern welfare theory can only gaze into its crystal ball of mathematical abstraction and wisely state that heaven on earth is still far off—which is true, but of no particular consequence either for the correct conduct of economic policy or for the theory of externalities.[45]

Once one adopts a comparative institutional approach to study the interaction between law and economics, a fundamental difficulty arises with the very concept of "externality." That is, once you accept the notion inherent in our model of Law and Economics that the legal-economic actors of society treat the legal institutions as endogenous variables (i.e., in the context of a closed system) and alter the working rules and property rights in an attempt to maximize their gains, then the concept of "externality" itself begins to break down. The concept dissolves because in a closed choice-making system, comprised of constitutional, institutional, and economic impact stages of choice, there is no entity or sector from which to be external. All costs and benefits are internal, worked out in the legal-economic arena. The legal institutions are endogenous and there to be remade by the legal-economic actors.

Furthermore, from the perspective of Law and Economics, the so called "externalities," both positive and negative, can be created by the legal-economic participants acting in any one of the three sectors—market, public, or communal. These "externalities" are the interdependent costs and benefits of activities within the legal-economic arena; they are shifted about within this arena, coming to a temporary rest until the legal-economic actors once again engage in activities to rid themselves of costs and attempt to acquire benefits to advance their welfare.

The fact that "externalities" are internal to our model of Law and Economics may be disquieting to some and may go beyond the point that many practitioners of Law and Economics would prefer. That the concept of "externality" has a hold over those who contribute to the literature of Law and Economics is manifested in many ways. Once such way is that in the face of no concensus as to the nature or the definition of an externality, the practitioners of Law and Economics suggest one either formulates his own conception or adopts one of the many that exist.[46] Rarely do you hear, "dispense with it altogether." Yet another approach is to avoid referring to them as "externalities" and rename them. This is somewhat helpful because we believe it may logically result in dispensing with the concept altogether. For instance (as stated above) Demsetz prefers "side effects."[47] This does not help much because legal-economic actors, legal institutions, and all economic effects are by definition *inside*. In fact, Demsetz himself comes as close as anyone to dispensing with the concept of externality. After calling them "side effects" he goes even further to state:

> There exist no qualitative differences between side effects and what we may call 'primary' effects. . . . There is nothing special or qualitatively different about any of these effects . . . and any special treatment accorded to them cannot be justified merely by observing their presence.[48]

Coase called them "harmful" effects.[49] This does not help either since the legal-economic actors are at work in the ongoing process of formulating and reformulating what may be considered "harmful." This is done in many ways, for example, the process of defining effective resources and commodities through the attenuation process described earlier in Chapter II. Any antecedent determination of what constitutes a "harmful effect" will tend to predetermine the outcomes which are at issue. Further, consider the following definition of externality by Ezra J. Mishan:

> A consideration of this notation suggests that an external effect arises wherever the value of a production function, or a consumption function, depends directly upon the activity of others. What the notation alone does not succeed in conveying, however, is that the essential feature of the concept of an external effect is that the effect produced is not a deliberate creation but an *unintended* or *incidental* by-product of some otherwise legitimate activity.[50]

Mishan's definition seems designed to distinguish economic externalities (i.e., those linked to legitimate activities) from those external effects which are caused by "illegitimate" activities. The distinction is once again artificial in that it suffers from having to employ Coase's antecedent determination of what is "harmful"—this time—to what is "illegitimate." But, what is "illegitimate" is a function of the prevailing structure of rights. As should be evident, rights, and what is "illegitimate," are continually being revised (perhaps incrementally) by the legal-economic participants. Thus an antecedent determination of what is "illegitimate" takes as given what is often at issue.

Furthermore, the Mishan construction suffers from the additional problem of having to decide on "intentions." For example, smoke emitted from a factory is a by-product of the production of some market good, but in most situations, given the technology to reduce or eliminate the smoke, it is by no means unintended or necessarily incidental. It is not clear what the "intention" of the producer of the externality has to do with the definition of an externality; it is also not clear what Mishan would call the "intended" by-products of an activity.

Given that all economic impacts are internal and are to be worked by the legal-economic actors through the legal institutions, the concept of externality may be used to divert attention away from the choices confronting society. Its various formulations may mask or obscure options in order to reinforce certain ideological predilections. As Dahlman states:

> It is thus doubtful whether the term 'externality' has any meaningful interpretation, except as an indicator of the political beliefs and value judgments of the person who uses (or avoids using) the term.[51]

If Law and Economics were to dispense with the concept of externality, then the agenda for the practitioners is clarified. Coase simply states:

> A better approach would seem to be to start our analysis with a situation approximating that which actually exists, to examine the effects of a proposed policy change and to attempt to decide whether the new situation would be, in total, better or worse than the original one.[52]

NOTES AND REFERENCES

1. Carl J. Dahlman, "The Problem of Externality," *The Journal of Law and Economics*, Vol. 22, No. 1 (April 1979), pp. 141–162 at 156.

2. For a review of the neoclassical treatment of externalities see Jacob Viner, "Cost Curves and Supply Curves," in George J. Stigler and Kenneth E. Boulding, Eds., *Readings in Price Theory* (Chicago: Richard D. Irwin, Inc., 1952), pp. 198–232; Tibor Scitovsky, "Two Concepts of External Economies," *Journal of Political Economy*, Vol. 62, No. 2 (April 1954), pp. 143–151; James M. Buchanan and William C. Stubblebine, "Externality," *Economica*, Vol. 29, No. 116 (November 1962), pp. 371–384. See also E. J. Mishan, "The Postwar Literature on Externalities: An Interpretive Essay," *Journal of Economic Literature*, Vol. 9, No. 1 (March 1971), pp. 1–28.

3. Bernard Herber, *Modern Public Finance*, 4th ed., (Homewood: Richard D. Irwin, 1979), p. 36.

4. Campbell R. McConnell, *Economics*, 7th ed., (New York: McGraw-Hill Book Co., 1978), pp. 44–48, 531–532.

5. The MB_s curve is downward sloping reflecting the law of diminishing marginal utility, while the MC_s curve is upward sloping due to the law of diminishing returns.

6. Francis M. Bator, "The Anatomy of Market Failure," *Quarterly Journal of Economics*, Vol. 72, No. 3 (August 1958), pp. 351–379 at 353–356.

7. Inasmuch as most of the literature has focused on an analysis of how it is that the market as a means for social control can achieve Pareto optimal outcomes, it must be noted that any system of social control which satisfies these four conditions will also achieve Pareto optimal outcomes. For a discussion of how a decentralized socialist system can attain a Pareto optimal outcome see J. P. Gould and C. E. Ferguson, *Microeconomic Theory*, 5th ed., (Homewood: Richard D. Irwin, Inc., 1980), pp. 440–445.

8. The tabular approach for depicting these conditions is drawn from Paul Wonnacott and Ronald Wonnacott, *An Introduction to Microeconomics* (New York: McGraw-Hill Book Co., 1979), pp. 178–194.

9. The economics of property rights approach does not treat the individual in the firm as just a profit maximizer but instead he is regarded more broadly as a utility maximizer where profits may be one argument in the utility function. Eirik G. Furubotn and Svetozar Pejovich, *The Economics of Property Rights* (Cambridge: Ballinger Publishing Co., 1974), pp. 1–9.

10. Bator, "The Anatomy of Market Failure," pp. 351–379.

11. It is recognized that some consumption activities of one individual can serve to *decrease* the benefits to others. Some examples include an individual practicing on his trumpet late into the night and hand held radios blaring music on the street.

12. It is recognized that some production activities of one firm can serve to *reduce* costs of other firms. See James E. Meade, "External Economies and Diseconomies in a Competitive Situation," *Economic Journal*, Vol. 62, No. 245 (March 1952), pp. 54–67.

13. Alan Schwartz and Louis L. Wilde, "Intervening in Markets on the Basis of Imperfect Information: A Legal and Economic Analysis," *University of Pennsylvania Law Review*, Vol. 127, No. 3 (January 1979), pp. 630–682. For a review of the literature on the economics of information see Jack Hirschleifer and John G. Riley, "The Analytics of Uncertainty and Information - An Expository Survey," *The Journal of Economic Literature*, Vol. 17, No. 4 (December 1979), pp. 1375–1421.

14. Robert L. Birmingham, "Breach of Contract, Damage Measures, and Economic Efficiency," *Rutgers Law Review*, Vol. 24, No. 2 (Winter 1970), pp. 273–292. For a discussion of enforcement, in general, see George J. Stigler, "The Optimum Enforcement of Laws," *Journal of Political Economy*, Vol. 78, No. 3 (May/June 1970), pp. 526–536; and Harold Demsetz, "The Exchange and Enforcement of Property Rights," *Journal of Law and Economics*, Vol. 7 (October 1964), pp. 11–26.

15. R. G. Lipsey and Kelvin Lancaster, "The General Theory of Second Best," *Review of Economic Studies*, Vol. 24, No. 1 (1956–1957), pp. 11–32. Arthur Leff stated the theory of second best in this way, "One might assert a *general* theory of the second best as follows: 'If a state of affairs is the product of *n* variables, and you have knowledge of or control over less than *n* variables, if you think you know what's going to happen when you vary 'your' variables, you're a booby.' That is, in complex processes (which most social processes are) a move in the right direction is not necessarily the right move." Arthur A. Leff, "Economic Analysis of Law: Some Realism About Nominalism," *Virgina Law Review*, Vol. 60, No. 3 (March 1974), pp. 451–482 at 476.

16. Frederick M. Scherer. *Industrial Market Structure and Economic Performance*, 1st ed., (Chicago: Rand McNally and Co., 1970), pp. 25–26.

17. Charles K. Rowley and Alan T. Peacock, *Welfare Economics: A Liberal Restatement* (New York: John Wiley and Sons, 1975), p. 21.

18. For a discussion of public goods see Richard Musgrave, *The Theory of Public Finance* (New York: McGraw-Hill Book Co., 1959); Paul Samuelson, "The Pure Theory of Public Expenditure," *Review of Economics and Statistics*, Vol. 36, No. 4 (November 1954), pp. 387–389; and Paul Samuelson, "Diagrammatic Exposition of a Theory of Public Expenditures," *Review of Economics and Statistics*, Vol. 37, No. 4 (November 1955), pp. 350–356.

19. Some of the literature relevant to this area includes the economic models of trade union behavior, especially discussions of bilateral monopoly. See Allan M. Carter, *Theory of Wages and Employment* (Homewood: Richard D. Irwin, Inc., 1959), pp. 80–92; and John Kenneth Galbraith's discussion of "countervailing power" in John Kenneth Galbraith, *The New Industrial State*, 2nd ed., (Boston: Houghton-Mifflin, Co., 1971).

20. See Louis B. Schwartz, *Free Enterprise and Economic Organization, Volume I: Concentration and Restrictive Practices* (Brooklyn: The Foundation Press, Inc., 1966). See also Clair Wilcox and William G. Shepherd, *Public Policies Toward Business*, 5th ed., (Homewood: Richard D. Irwin, Inc., 1975), pp. 111–291.

21. Alfred E. Kahn, *The Economics of Regulation, Vols. I and II*, (New York: John Wiley and Sons, Inc., 1970). See also Wilcox and Shepherd, *Public Policies Toward Business*, pp. 331–511.

22. See, for instance, William J. Baumol and Wallace E. Oates, *The Theory of Environmental Policy* (Englewood Cliffs: Prentice-Hall, Inc., 1975); Edwin S. Mills, *The Economics of Environmental Quality* (New York: W. W. Norton and Co., Inc., 1978); and Joseph J. Seneca and Michael K. Taussig, *Environmental Economics*, 3rd ed., (Englewood Cliffs: Prentice-Hall, Inc., 1984).

23. For a clear and concise review of A. C. Pigou's work in this area see Herber, *Modern Public Finance*, pp. 36–43.

24. Arthur C. Pigou, *The Economics of Welfare* (London: Macmillan and Company, Limited, 1952), pp. 129–130.

25. Ibid., p. 192.

26. Ronald Coase, "The Problem of Social Cost," *Journal of Law and Economics*, Vol. 3 (October 1960), pp. 1–44 at 1–15.

27. In Law and Economics, transactions costs are defined to include search and information costs, bargaining and decision costs, and policing and enforcement costs. This definition can be seen to take into account a broader array of costs than those which typically concern neoclassical economics.

28. This is a paraphrase of James M. Buchanan, "The Coase Theorem and the Theory of the State," *Natural Resources Journal*, Vol. 13, No. 4 (October 1973), pp. 579–594 at 580.

29. See "Coase Theorem Symposium: Parts I and II," *Natural Resources Journal*, Vol. 13, No. 4 (October 1973) and Vol. 14, No. 1 (January 1974), respectively. See also Daniel T. Dick, "The Voluntary Approach to Externality Problems: A Survey of the Critics,"

*Journal of Environmental Economics and Management,*Vol. 2, No. 3 (February 1976), pp. 185–195; Donald H. Regan, "The Problem of Social Cost Revisited," *Journal of Law and Economics,* Vol. 15, No. 2 (October 1972), pp. 427–437; Cento G. Veljanovski, "The Coase Theorems and the Economic Theory of Markets and Law," *Kyklos,* Vol. 35, No. 1 (1982), pp. 53–74. Mark Kelman, "Consumption Theory, Production Theory, and Ideology in the Coase Theorem," *Southern California Law Review,* Vol. 25, No. 3 (March 1979), pp. 669–698.

30. Ronald H. Coase, "The Coase Theorem and the Empty Core: A Comment," *The Journal of Law and Economics,* Vol. 24, No. 1 (April 1981), pp. 183–187 at 187.

31. It should also be noted that in the zero transactions cost case the role of government can conceptually be further attenuated by ignoring the technological and spatial relationships between the parties. In commenting on the cattle and farmer example Joseph M. Steiner states that the mere observance:

> . . . that the cattle trampled the crops . . . tells us nothing about who should bear the loss . . . something is missing. That something is a normative or moral premise which must state: whenever two parties attempt to make inconsistent use of the same resource and harm results to one, liability is to fall on the other. But all that distinguishes the parties is that one, for essentially technological reasons, is able to appropriate the common resource to himself without the consent of the other. Why that is relevant to the location of liability is an engigma.

Joseph M. Steiner, "Economics, Morality, and the Law of Torts," *University of Toronto Law Journal,* Vol. 26, No. 3 (Summer 1976), pp. 227–252, at 246.

32. Coase, "The Problem of Social Cost," pp. 15–19 and pp. 19–44 *passim.*

33. Ibid., p. 16.

34. Demsetz, "The Exchange and Enforcement of Property Rights," pp. 11–26.

35. Ibid., p. 11.

36. Guido Calabresi and A. Douglas Melamed, "Property Rules, Liability Rules, and Inalienability: One View of the Cathedral," *Harvard Law Review,* Vol. 85, No. 6 (April 1972), pp. 1089–1128 at 1097.

37. Ryan C. Amacher, et al., *The Economic Approach to Public Policy* (Ithaca: Cornell University Press, 1976), p. 335. John M. Clark makes the same point in a slightly different manner:

> We must be on our guard . . . against the tendency of the reformer to compare the imperfections of existing conditions with the anticipated results of his reform measures, conceived as working perfectly. They will not work perfectly, and this had better be expected from the start. We should learn to compare existing imperfect conditions with the other imperfections which experience teaches us are sure to result from attempts to control.

John M. Clark, *Social Control of Business,* 2nd ed., (New York: McGraw-Hill Book Co., 1939), p. 493.

38. Coase, "The Problem of Social Cost," pp. 42–43.

39. A. Allan Schmid, *Property, Power, and Public Choice: An Inquiry into Law and Economics* (New York: Praeger Publishers, 1978), pp. 211–212. The Pigovian approach is contrasted to the Coase approach in Steven N. S. Cheung, *The Myth of Social Cost,* Cato Paper No. 16 (San Francisco: The Cato Institute, 1980), pp. 1–52, and Robert Cooter, "The Cost of Coase," *The Journal of Legal Studies,* Vol. 11, No. 1 (January 1982), pp. 1–33.

40. Murry Rothbard, "Law, Property Rights, and Air Pollution," *The Cato Journal*, Vol. 2, No. 1 (Spring 1982), pp. 55–99 at 59.

41. Ronald H. Coase, "The Nature of the Firm," *Economica*, Vol. 4, No. 16 (November 1937), pp. 386–405.

42. Guido Calabresi, "Transaction Costs, Resource Allocation, and Liability Rules—A Comment," *Journal of Law and Economics*, Vol. 11 (April 1968), pp. 67–73 at 73.

43. Coase, "The Problem of Social Cost," pp. 18–19.

44. Dahlman, "The Problem of Externality," p. 160.

45. Ibid., pp. 161–162.

46 Werner Z. Hirsch, *Law and Economics: An Introductory Analysis* (New York: Academic Press, 1979), pp. 8–11.

47. Demsetz, "The Exchange and Enforcement of Property Rights," p. 11.

48. Ibid., pp. 25–26.

49. See quote in text at footnote 43 (this chapter).

50. Mishan, "The Postwar Literature on Externalities," p. 2.

51. Dahlman, "The Problem of Externality," p. 156.

52. Coase, "The Problem of Social Cost," p. 43.

Chapter IV

The Economic Compensation Principle: Liability Rules And The Taking Issue

People become indignant when they observe violations of what they regard as property rights. They become aggressive when they perceive their own property rights to be violated. The substantial overlap between property as protected by the state and property as perceived morally, whether by accident, design or evolutionary necessity, helps preserve a society.[1] (Tideman, 1972)

This chapter attempts to bring together several topics in Law and Economics. The common thread that binds these topics together is the issue of compensation: the issue as to which rights in a society will be elevated to the status of protected rights—protected in the sense that if violated, holders of these rights should or could be compensated. The terrain here will be broad. It includes the principle of compensation in economics; tort law, including both intentional and unintentional torts together with the liability rules which protect persons and property from the actions of other parties; and the taking issue which arises in law when losses are sustained by individuals due to governmental actions accomplished under the power of eminent domain or police power. We recognize that, in law, liability rules of tort law and the taking issue are typically treated as separate topics. However, from the vantage point of Law and Economics, the questions surrounding the compensation issue in both of these areas of law exhibit sufficient commonalities as to be treated together.

This chapter begins with a brief elaboration of the economic compensation principle. The importance of this principle is not easily overstated. As will be seen in this and the following chapter, it lies at the heart of the theoretical economic approach to liability rules, much of the new law and economics, and conventional public choice theory as well.

A. THE COMPENSATION PRINCIPLE IN ECONOMICS

The economic compensation principle was born as a result of a search for value-free (i.e., positive) criterion to ground, scientifically, legal-economic policy prescriptions. Because a prospective policy or legal change often will result in some individuals being better off while others are worse off, economists have tried to set forth a scientific or value-neutral basis for evaluating such policies.

The body of literature which ultimately yielded what today is referred to as the economic compensation principle emerged as a response to the work of Lionel C. Robbins. In his classic work Robbins denied the scientific comparability of different individuals' preferences for a particular policy because of the impossibility of interpersonal comparisons of utility.[2] That is, utility is an ordinal, not a cardinal, measurement and the utility gained by one individual when consuming a certain quantity of good X is not comparable to the utility gained by some other individual when consuming the same quantity of good X.

The thrust of Robbins' assertion was that since there was no scientific way for aggregating individual preference orderings economists would have no basis for solving practical economic problems. Several years later he revised his methodological position to suggest that economists who are engaged in formulating policy should make their value judgments explicit and recognize that these came from outside economic science.[3]

In an effort to remove the stigma attached to the introduction of value judgments into the positive science of economic analysis, economists tried to find a way around the strictures set forth by Robbins. It was in this environment that the so-called compensation test emerged as a variant to the principle of Pareto optimality.[4] Thus, the compensation principle must be viewed as an attempt to provide economics with a criterion upon which to base policy without having to engage in interpersonal comparisons of utility and, at a minimum, to incorporate only those value judgments subsumed in the principle of Pareto optimality.

The compensation principle (sometimes referred to as "potential Pareto superiority" or the "Kaldor-Hicks criterion" or "Pareto-Wicksellian criteria") is used to determine which legal-economic improvements should be undertaken and, as such, is a logical extension of the more general notion of Pareto optimality.[5] Recall, a Pareto optimum is defined as a state from which it is impossible to improve anyone's welfare (i.e., a movement to a higher level of utility) by realigning the use of resources or consumption of commodities without impairing someone else's welfare. A change is recognized as a Pareto improvement (i.e.,

Pareto safe) only if at least one person believes himself better off after the change and no one believes himself worse off.

While the literature developing the compensation principle need not be fully explored here, what has emerged as the compensation principle is generally formulated as follows: A policy (a legal-economic action realigning resources) is said to be "potential Pareto superior" if those who would gain from the change *could,* from their gain, pay compensation to those who would lose and thereby restore the losers to their original position, with the gainers still remaining better off.[6] In its purest form, the compensation principle requires only a hypothetical willingness to pay and accept, i.e., it does not mandate actual payment of compensation. It is generally felt that the question as to whether actual compensation is to be paid to those who would lose from the adoption of the policy should be left to distributional considerations. Hal R. Varian has described this nuance of the compensation principle in the following statement which is typical of the literature:

> The usual argument in defense of the compensation principle is that the question of whether the compensation is carried out is really a question about income distribution, and the basic welfare theorems show that the question of income distribution can be separated from the question of allocative efficiency. The compensation criterion is concerned solely with allocative efficiency, and the question of proper income distribution can best be handled by alternative means such as redistributive taxation.[7]

Before providing several illustrative quotes which serve: (1) to describe the current conventional formulations of the compensation principle, and (2) to demonstrate the scope of its current usage, there are several points the reader should keep in mind. These points are raised to highlight the fact that a variety of questions and issues continue to surround the use of the compensation principle and it is best to be aware of them from the outset inasmuch as the principle occupies a rather important niche in the theory of Law and Economics.[8]

First, in order to apply the compensation principle the gains and losses must be measurable. In Law and Economics, the economic compensation principle can be applied to changes in property rights and working rules including liability rules, decision rules in taking issue cases, legal rules in common law, and political-bureaucratic rules related to government regulation. It is extremely difficult, if not impossible, to accurately identify the winners and losers and to measure the actual gains and losses brought on by legal changes in these areas. Consequently, actual employment of the economic compensation principle in Law and Economics is problematic.

Second, since the economic compensation principle analyzes changes in law, its use requires a well defined starting point. Typically, that starting point is the status quo structure of rights and rules. Thus, the use of the principle assumes that one can identify that structure. However, as will be seen, uncertainity, imperfect information, and the dynamic nature of the legal system makes it difficult to identify the status quo structure of rights and rules.

Finally, contributors to the literature in this area have reached no consensus on the "could" or "should" question (i.e., is it enough that compensation "could" be paid to proceed with the legal change or "should" it be paid). Since allocation and distribution are the paramount concerns of Law and Economics, the resolution of the question remains a fundamental issue.

The following illustrative quotes can give the reader an appreciation of the current conventional formulations of the compensation principle as it is presently employed in economics. These particular examples concern tariffs and environmental policies.

> For social policy, the fundamental issue reduces to this. At any moment in time, there is *a legally sanctioned structure of property rights in existence;* thus, if the prevailing structure is to be modified by social action designed to reduce or eliminate the effects of an externality, taxes *must be imposed* on those who will gain from the proposed legal change, and compensation paid to those who will suffer capital losses or loss of satisfaction as a result of the new law. . . . It is important to reemphasize that property rights are crucial to this new line of analysis; the justification for compensation to B rests, ultimately, on the idea that, at any given time, individuals can have 'rights' to create certain types of 'diseconomies.' Thus, an individual (B) who is undertaking a *lawful activity in good faith* (e.g., generating smoke) *must be compensated* if there is to be a change in the law that will redefine property rights and reduce his welfare position.[9] (emphasis added)

Donald T. Savage et al. stated it somewhat differently:

> Faced with this policy dilemma, economists have generally found recourse in an analysis known as the compensation principle. If a particular policy, such as tariff reduction or pollution abatement, redistributes income, that is, if the incidence of costs and benefits is unequal and if the benefits exceed the costs (as they presumably do in both tariff reduction and pollution abatement), then *it should be possible* for those who benefit to compensate fully those who bear the costs and still have a net gain.[10] (emphasis added)

Thus, the reader is left for himself to decide the could or should question. That is, while the latter quote remains ambiguous as to whether compensation would in fact be forthcoming, the former directly implies it will be.

As to what constitutes the "legally sanctioned structure of rights," (i.e., the prevailing law), which when altered should (or could) command compensation, the proponents of the compensation principle conventionally respond as follows:

> Compensation is required so long as the injured party previously was acting within the law. . . . The law is . . . 'a *set of expectations*, which include enforcement *standards as traditionally observed*, along with formal statute. A change in law, by my definition, involves an explicit modification of *normal expectations*.'[11] (emphasis added)

However, in contrast, Harold M. Hochman stated:

> In determining whether compensation must be considered an ethical requirement, the ability of individuals to anticipate change and adjust their behavior to curtail potential losses is crucial. . . . Not just existing rules of conduct, but changes in these rules, must be *justifiable*, and the process through which change is effected must itself be *fair*. Failing direct or indirect compensation, the fairness of a rule change is unambiguous only if the pre-existing rule was clearly *inconsistent with the social contract* or *'constitution'* that underlay it and if those whom the change has harmed have had an opportunity to anticipate and adjust to it. . . . Rules, even if *unfair or inefficient*, may as custom *underlie reasonable expectations*. Rule changes that disappoint such expectation may themselves be considered unjust. . . . In practice whether compensation (for past or for future losses) is appropriate, is a far more subtle issue. Although the Pareto criterion strictly interpreted requires compensation, it seems absurd to argue that individuals *unjustly deprived of rights* under an existing rule should compensate its beneficiaries if the rule is changed.[12] (emphasis added)

All this proceeds on the presumption that the law is comprised of doctrines that give unambiguous meaning to such notions as "lawful activity in good faith," "normal expectations," "standards as traditionally observed," "justifiable and fair process," "unfair or inefficient rules," "inconsistent with the social contract," "reasonable expectations," and "unjust deprivation of rights," so as to provide unalterable benchmarks to determine which changes in "law" will be subject to the requirement of compensation. In fact, legal doctrine does not give unambiguous meaning to these notions. In a dynamic society legal doctrine evolves and society's normal expectations change, thereby conveying new meaning to such concepts as "just," "reasonable," and "fair," etc. Thus, the compensation principle is seen to rest on evolving doctrines and expectations which alter the meaning of these terms over time.

Furthermore, aside from the problem brought on by evolving law, there exists a normative element in coming to terms with such notions as "just," "reasonable," and "fair." That is, given the inherent ambiguity of each of these terms, the practical use of the compensation principle would require an antecedent definition of what is "just," "reasonable," and "fair." There is a necessity of choice involved in normatively defining and thereby bringing practical meaning to these terms that serves to undermine the purported positive thrust of the compensation principle.

While some of the advocates of the compensation principle recognize it to be a normative construct, others suggest that its use eliminates (or at least minimizes) the need to invoke value judgments. That is, some believe that the compensation principle provides a positive basis to guide legal change. Part of their argument rests on the alleged ethical neutrality of using the status quo structure of rights to gauge whether or not there has been a change in the law that would require compensation. Robert D. Tollison and James M. Buchanan, respectively, have described the role of the status quo as follows:

> The modified Paretian-Wicksellian framework implies that the social scientist must be prepared to accept the status quo when analysis indicates that tractable 'solutions' to social problems are not possible. In the absence of possible agreement on change among broad segments of the citizenry, the social scientist has no means of saying that change is or is not desirable. He accepts what is for the simple reason that this is where he starts.[13]

> Full compensation is essential, not in order to maintain any initial distribution on ethical grounds, but in order to decide which one from among the many possible social policy changes does, in fact, satisfy the genuine Pareto rule.[14]

Building on the supposition that reliance on the status quo structure of rights is ethically neutral, they go beyond this to argue that use of the compensation principle, that incorporates the unanimous consent requirement, eliminates the need for value judgments. Tollison stated:

> The writers in this volume basically adopt a modified Pareto-Wicksell framework in their approach to social analysis. The reason is simple—we do not wish to make interpersonal utility comparisons; we are unwilling to play God. Given this constraint, we are forced to look at the revealed choice behavior of individuals as the basic informational input in determining 'goodness' or 'badness' of social policy. . . . Consensus is the only standard by which 'rightness' can be discerned under this approach.[15]

> The Paretian construction, because of the unanimity sanction, implies a truly participatory basis for social change. In this approach public policy is not something legislated by or for powerful lobbies or the wealthy capitalists; either everyone agrees or there is no change.[16]

Their overall approach is purported to be value-neutral and, as such, is recommended as the correct approach for legal-economic analysis.

> I can see no personal excuse for joining other economists in an attempt to hoodwink the public into thinking that we make more sense out of these issues [those which require value judments] than analysis allows, or that economists have a hot line to God. By opting out of discussions where explicitly normative statements lie at the very beginning of the analysis, economists might leave themselves more time for the positive theory of political economy.[17]

In marked contrast to those who believe that the use of the compensation principle is value-neutral there are those who disagree. As to the problem of determining the status quo structure of rights, Warren J. Samuels stated:

> This belief is reinforced by the legal pretense that rights have an abstract antecedent existence that government is obligated to protect. The economic reality is that rights which are protected are rights only because they are protected; they are not protected because they were preexisting. Rights are made and remade, through both the law and the market; they are not found.[18]

As to the dynamic nature of rights as opposed to some static and hence readily identifiable status quo structure of rights Joseph L. Sax stated:

> The essence of property, as we actually use the term, is not fixity at all, but fluidity. Property is the end result of a process of competition among inconsistent and contending economic values. Instead of some static and definable quantity, property really is a multitude of existing interests which are constantly interrelating with each other, sometimes in ways that are mutually exclusive. . . . It is more accurate to describe property as the value which each owner has left after the inconsistencies between the two competing owners have been resolved. And, of course, even then the situation is not static, because new conflicts are always arising as a result of a change in the neighborhood's character, or in technology, or in public values. These changes will revise once again the permitted and permissible uses which we call property. Property is thus the result of the process of competition.[19]

Finally, Samuels commenting on Buchanan's use of the Pareto-Wicksellian compensation scheme describes the normative elements involved. The dispute persists.

> What can I say about his specific normative approach? It is what he has frequently labelled the Pareto-Wicksell approach, advocating a conception of Pareto optimality specified in terms of a unanimity rule and a prejudice (his term) in favor of previously existing rights. He is therefore in favor of defending *some* status quo power structure. But *which* one? As a normative matter, unanimity is attractive (but limited in feasibility, as he recognizes) and maintenance of previously existing rights is not to be rejected out of hand. But one has to know just what the existing structure of rights is that can be changed only unanimously. A Pareto-optimal rule (unanimity) must presume the propriety of the status quo in order for it to have recommendatory force. But which status quo?[20]

Inasmuch as the compensation principle is used rather extensively in this and the subsequent chapter, perhaps it is best to understand it as follows. First, notwithstanding claims to the contrary, it is one normative construct which can be used as a basis for evaluating legal-economic policy prescriptions. Second, it states that a legal change from the status quo structure of rights (given all the difficulties in discerning that structure) should proceed upon the payment (or the possibility of payment) of compensation to those who are made worse off by those who are made better off, where the latter is greater than the former. Not to allow or require the change would be to refuse to generate a surplus of value sufficient to compensate those harmed by the change.

B. TORT LAW AND LIABILITY RULES

The field of torts embraces a group of civil, as opposed to criminal, wrongs, In law, a tort is said to arise when one party, intentionally or unintentionally, engages in an action which violates the rights (those associated with either effective commodities or resources) of another and thereby causes the latter party to sustain losses. An act upon one individual by another may sometimes be both a crime punishable by the state in a criminal prosecution and also a tort actionable by the victim in a suit for damages. Typically, the criminal prosecution, whose purpose is essentially punitive, is an entirely separate and unrelated proceeding from the tort action where the purpose is to compensate the damaged party for the losses sustained.

The past decade has produced a great deal of literature on the theoretical (typically, though not exclusively, economic) formulations of the law of torts. Our purpose in this part of this chapter is to place this literature in perspective so as to better understand the major thrust of the literature as well as to gain an appreciation of the complexity of the endeavor that has been undertaken. Before we proceed with a detailed examination of the literature there are several points to be made that may help to keep it in perspective.

First, it is a fact of life that as individuals proceed through an ordinary day they may occassionally fall victim to a "potentially" tortious act. That is, life is filled with a plethora of risks which may result in damages to individuals. As such, the character of economic life will be fashioned, in part, by the choices made by society as to which risks will be perceived, and thus treated, as what we might call "background" risks—risks which must be borne as part of group living. In addition, there are risks which are not background risks. These risks arise from acts that are defined as tortious, where the victim has recourse for damages. George P. Fletcher has recast John Rawls's first principle of justice in making this point:

> We all have the right to the maximum amount of security compatible with a like security for everyone else. This means that we are subject to harm, without compensation, from background risks, but that no one may suffer harm from additional risks without recourse for damages against the risk-creator. Compensation is a surrogate for the individual's right to the same security as enjoyed by others.[21]

Viewed from this perspective, tort law must be understood to be a dynamic area of law, malleable in its scope as the participants in the legal-economic decision making processes decide which actions create risks that fall within the domain of background risks and which actions fall within the domain of tortious conduct.

Second, in law, tort liability can be imposed on individuals for intentional wrongs (willful misconduct) or for unintentional wrongs. On the basis of policy considerations, in the latter case, liability may be imposed based on the standard of negligence (failure to use reasonable care) or on the standard of strict liability (where no fault exists). The point to keep in mind is that the character of economic life will be partly determined by the choices between, say, the use of negligence or strict liability. More typically, the choice is between which specific negligence standard or which specific strict liability standard will be used.

Third, there appears to be two dominant schools of thought that contribute to the theoretical foundations of the law of torts. These two schools of thought can be referred to loosely as "the economic approach" and "the justice-fairness approach," respectively. While contributors *within* each school of thought may engage in debates over ancillary issues, proponents of each school of thought appear united on their different respective premises from which to analyze tort law.

The first school of thought, the economic approach, operates from the premise that the discipline of economics can be used to help provide the theoretical foundations of tort law. That is, they believe that economics can provide a rational foundation of tort law and thereby produce a systematic body of rules to resolve disputes. It has been argued that this approach propogates a system of legal formalism which conceptionally reduces the dispute resolution process down to a self-contained, apolitical, and logical process of mere rule application.[22] The flavor of this approach can be best captured by the following series of descriptive quotes:

> Many of these theories draw heavily, if not exclusively, on economics. The appeal of economics to legal scholars engaged in this endeavor derives partly from the evident importance of economic considerations in appraising schemes for the allocation and compensation of accident losses and partly from the widespread belief that economics is value-free and furnishes firm conclusions and prescriptions when the law is evaluated against the benchmark of economic efficiency.[23]

> The economic approach to liability law is to use market-like processes to establish a price for tortious conduct that approximates as closely as possible the market price which would obtain if market transactions were possible.[24]

> Efficiency is a widely used criterion in discussion of public policy because most people still believe that maximization of value is an important goal of society.[25]

Proponents of the economic efficiency school of thought typically treat criteria other than economic efficiency as follows:

> [If one does not adopt economic efficiency] this leaves us with only two reasons on which to base our choice of entitlement. The first is the relative worthiness of silence lovers and noise lovers. The second is the consistency of the choice, or its apparent consistency, with other entitlements in the society. . . . The first sounds appealing, and it sounds like justice. But it is hard to deal with. Why, unless our choice affects other people, should we prefer one to another? . . . *The usual answer is religious or transcendental reasons.*[26] (emphasis added)

The school of thought that advocates the use of economics as its mode of analysis is in marked contrast to the other school of thought that advocates the use of such notions as justice or fairness or distribution. The justice-fairness school of thought essentially takes the position that a blameworth injurer should compensate the innocent victim. Why? "It's just and fair!" The essence of their approach is subsumed in their critique of the economic approach.

Joseph M. Steiner, commenting on the economic approach to tort law, states:

> One might say that it is a distributively neutral approach. . . . But distribution of wealth is what this branch of law is about. . . . We are dealing here with the distribution of individual rights and, therefore, with individual liberties. The issues we face, then, are essentially and inescapably political and we should be wary of any simple formulae which purport to provide even theoretical solutions. . . . The underlying principle of a law of interaction damage must still be a *distributive* principle.[27]

Richard A. Epstein makes a similar point:

> It is a mistake to dwell too long upon questions of cost, for they should not be decisive in the analysis of the individual cases. Instead it is better to see the law of torts in terms of what might be called its political function. . . . The first task of the law of torts is to define the boundries of individual liberty.[28]

Cento G. Veljanovski suggests the following:

> *If* the object of tort is to correct market inefficiencies then economic efficiency does not constitute an adequate theory of liability unless it is combined with a normative theory of rights or entitlements. Once this is recognized then . . . the answer to the question whether accident victims should be compensated by those who injure them and under what conditions depends fundamentally on the value judgment as to whose rights should be protected by law. Justice is thus seen not as a goal which necessarily competes with economic efficiency but an essential ingredient of an economic theory of tort liability.[29]

Fletcher, continuing this line of critique, states:

> The thrust of the academic literature is to convert the tort system into something other than a mechanism for determining the just distribution of accident losses. . . .

One can speak of formulae, like the Learned Hand formula, and argue in detail about questions of cost, benefits and trade-offs. This style of thinking is attractive to the legal mind. . . . Why should the rhetoric of reasonableness and foreseeability appeal to lawyers as a more scientific or precise way of thinking? The answer might lie in the scientific image associated with passing through several stages of argument before reaching a conclusion. The paradigm of reasonableness requires several stages of analysis: defining the risk, assessing its consequences, balancing costs and benefits. . . . If an argument requires several steps, it basks in the respectability of precision and rationality. Yet associating rationality with multi-staged argumentation may be but a spectacular lawyerly fallacy—akin to the social scientists' fallacy of misplaced concreteness (thinking that numbers make a claim more accurate). . . . With close examination one sees that these formulae are merely tautological constructs designed to support an aura of utilitarian precision.[30]

Fletcher believes the agenda confronting contributors to the field of tort law should include the following:

What is the relevance of risk-creating conduct to the just distribution of wealth? What is the rationale for an individual's 'right' to recover for his losses? What are the criteria for justly singling out some people and making them, and not their neighbors, bear the costs of accidents? These persistent normative questions are the stuff of tort theory, but they are now too often ignored for the sake of inquiries about insurance and the efficient allocation of resources.[31]

It should be noted that, perhaps because of: (1) the persistence of these critics or (2) the realization by the proponents of the economic approach to tort law that they are dealing with an area of law that is attempting to correct wrongs inflicted upon individuals in society, the proponents of the economic approach admit that criteria other than efficiency (for example, distribution) could be incorporated into the dispute resolution decision making process. Epstein makes the same observation:

A knowledge of the economic consequence of alternative legal arrangements can be of great importance, but even among those who analyze tort in economic terms there is acknowledgement of certain questions of 'justice' or 'fairness' rooted in common sense beliefs that cannot be explicated in terms of economic theory.[32]

Guido Calabresi and A. Douglas Melamed recognize the following:

Economy efficiency is not, however, the sole reason which induces a society to select a set of entitlements. Wealth distribution preferences are another. . . . We should also recognize that efficiency is not the sole ground for employing liability rules rather than property rules. Just as the initial entitlement is often decided upon for distributional reasons, so too the choice of a liability rule is often made because it facilitates a combination of efficiency and distributive results which would be difficult to achieve under a property rule. . . . The final reasons for a society's choice of initial entitlements we termed other justice reasons, and we may as well admit that it is hard to know what content can be poured into that term.[33]

Calabresi and Jon T. Hirschoff not only suggest the possible inclusion of distributional factors but also ask how best to incorporate them into the various components of the dispute resolution tort system.

> Sorting out the relevant effects lumped under the term distribution, therefore, is a necessary task for society in choosing among liability rules. But when that is done another series of questions remains: which, if any, of the distributional considerations are appropriate to judicial decisions among liability rules, which are appropriate to ad hoc jury determinations, and which can only be properly settled by legislatures?[34]

In a less open manner Richard A. Posner also recognizes that society may hold social values other than the efficient use of resources paramount:

> Since the efficient use of resources is an important although not always paramount social value, the burden, I suggest, is on the authors to present reasons why a standard that appears to impose avoidable costs on society should nonetheless be adopted.[35]

The recognition of the potential inclusion of justice or fairness by those who advocate an economic approach raises the following question which, as of this writing, seems unresolved.

> Once it is admitted that there are questions of fairness as between the parties that are not answerable in economic terms, the exact role of economic argument in the solution of legal question becomes impossible to determine. It may well be that an acceptable theory of fairness can be reconciled with dictates of economic theory in a manner that leaves ample room for the use of economic thought. But that judgment presupposes that some theory of fairness has been spelled out, which, once completed, may leave no room for economic considerations of any sort.[36]

Fourth, much of the literature in both schools of thought is dominated by a concern for what can be termed "corrective justice," where the concern is solely on the litigant parties and where the quest is to choose from among various liability rules that provide remedies for tortious acts.[37] Both schools of thought focus on an intricate and detailed discussion of a subset of liability rule remedies that direct attention away from other possible remedies that typically come under the heading of "government regulation." The formal inclusion (or at a minimum the recognition of the existence) of governmental regulation as a remedy does not negate the need for liability rules but may reduce the scope of their application. For example, in Figure IV.1 let the entire circle represent all costs associated with automobile accidents, (actual damages suffered by victims, litigation expenses, legal administrative costs, enforcement costs, etc.) before the government does three things: (1) installs traffic signals, (2) installs stop signs, and (3) erects median barriers. Now, it seems clear that if the government installs traffic signals at certain intersections the

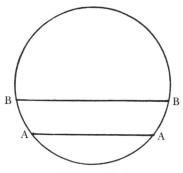

Figure IV.1.

net savings to society could be the area beneath AA.[38] Further, it may be that if the government installed stop signs at other intersections, the additional *net* savings may be the area circumscribed by ABBA. Finally, if the government decided to erect median barriers on all major streets and highways it might not result in any additional net savings, leaving society with the same net savings area below BB, which corresponds to the savings due to taking actions (1) and (2).[39] However, as can be seen, even with the government regulations, society is still in need of tort liability rules to resolve disputes over the incidence of the accident costs above BB—the domain of corrective justice remedies.

The essential point to be made is that in the midst of a detailed discussion of alternative liability rules (which follows in a subsequent section of this chapter), there always remains the potential remedy of government regulation. However, unless the government action would entirely eliminate all costs (unlikely), there remains a need for liability rules to resolve tort disputes. The literature that examines remedies for tortious acts focuses attention on liability rules with an uneven recognition of the governmental regulation remedy.

Before we turn to the formal discussion of liability rules there is one additional point the reader should keep in mind with respect to the literature discussed in this section. The contributors to the literature often bolster their arguments by the propitious choice of examples. This is evident throughout the literature but particularly recognizable in the ongoing debate over the preferred use of strict liability versus negligence standards to resolve tort disputes. The argument essentially centers on the legitimacy of the question: Did person A "cause" person B to incur damages? The proponents of the use of the negligence concept often rely on examples which give the appearance of reciprocal cause. That is, following Ronald H. Coase they argue that the disputed losses resulted because both parties wished to make inconsistant use of a common resource. Thus, it is not surprising to see such examples as: the cattle rancher and adjoining farmer,[40] the doctor and the confectioner,[41] built-in safety devices and careful driving for railway crossings,[42] defect-free radar and careful flying in the airplane case,[43] and shoveling snow and careful walking in the sidewalk case.[44] In marked contrast, those who advocate the use of strict liability often rely on examples where the "cause" is clear. For example: "A pummeled B;"[45] "a landlord lunges at the plaintiff and her husband with a pair of pliers;"[46] and "suppose a man (B) is minding his own business reading in a library. A comes up and punches him in the face."[47] One might think that in law these two types of examples conform to the distinction between intentional and unintentional torts. However, practioners of the new law and economics seem to believe this distinction is not relevant. As Posner states:

> The distinction between intentional and unintentional torts—thought by most tort lawyers to be fundamental—is both confusing and unnecessary.[48]

1. The Role of Liability Rules in Law and Economics

In order to understand the role of liability rules in Law and Economics, one should start with Coase's analysis of the zero transactions costs case (see Chapter III). Consider Figure IV.2.[49]

In this figure we assume that individual X is the victim of the pollution and Y is the originator of the pollution. The line labeled MBx is the marginal benefit of individual X when additional units of pollution abatement are added; the line labeled MCy is the marginal costs for the polluter of increased pollution abatement. If transactions costs are zero, then, as Coase points out, the assignment of liability to X or to Y will result in the same amount of pollution abatement, X*; that is, the amount of pollution abatement is invariant over different assignments of liability. In Figure IV.2, if liability is initial assigned to party X, then bargaining would begin at point A (no abatement and 100% pollution). At A, the marginal benefit to party X of one unit of pollution abatement is clearly greater than the marginal cost of the abatement by party Y; therefore X would bribe Y to produce some abatement. This process would continue until point X* is reached, beyond which the bribe is insufficient to cause Y to engage in any further abatement. Alternatively, if the liability is placed on party Y, bargaining would begin at point B (100% abatement and no pollution) and proceed to X* as party X accepts bribes from party Y to allow additional pollution. Thus, while the bargaining process will bring about the X* solution regardless to whom liability is assigned, it should be noted the placement of liability will affect the distribution of income.

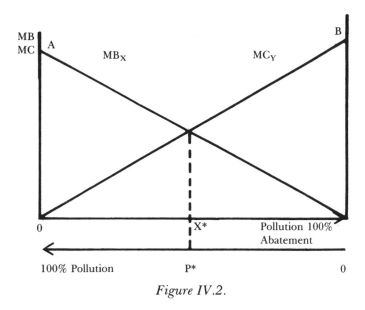

Figure IV.2.

As already discussed in Chapter III, if transactions costs are not zero, the ultimate solution will vary depending upon the assignment of liability. There are two cases that will be considered. The first case occurs when transactions costs are positive but not so high as to preclude subsequent bargaining solutions (see Figure IV.3). The second case occurs when transactions costs are so high as to preclude bargaining (see Figure IV.4).[50]

Case (1): Transactions Costs are Positive—With Bargaining. In Figure IV.3, MB′x depicts the marginal benefits of additional units of pollution abatement to party X adjusted for transactions costs, when X is liable. MC′y is party Y's marginal savings in costs associated with reductions in pollution abatement adjusted for transactions costs, when Y is liable. It is assumed that only the party that is liable bears the transactions costs and, in this example, the transactions costs for party X are assumed to be greater than the transactions costs for party Y.

If liability is assigned to party X, the bargaining process will begin at point A and proceed to point C along curve MB′x (where MB′x=MCy), yielding X′ pollution abatement. Alternatively, if party Y is assigned liability, bargaining commences at point B and proceeds to point D along curve MC′y (where MC′y=MBx), yielding X″ pollution abatement. Inasmuch as X″ is preferred to X′ (closer to X*), then what emerges is that the party that has the smaller transactions costs, in this example party Y, should bear the liability. This reasoning is inherent in Coase's approach where he states:

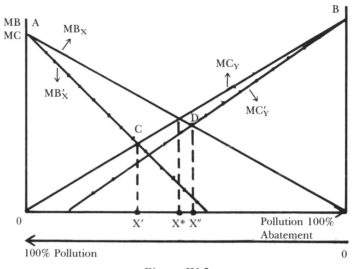

Figure IV.3.

Of course, if market transactions were costless, all that matters (questions of equity apart) is that the rights of the various parties should be well-defined and the results of legal actions easy to forecast. But as we have seen, the situation is quite different when market transactions are so costly as to make it difficult to change the arrangement of rights established by the law. In such cases, the courts directly influence economic activity. It would therefore seem desirable that the courts should understand the economic consequences of their decisions and should, insofar as this is possible without creating too much uncertainty about the legal position itself, take these consequences into account when making their decisions. Even when it is possible to change the legal delimitation of rights through market transactions, it is obviously desirable to reduce the need for such transactions and thus reduce the employment of resources in carrying them out.[51]

Case (2): Transactions Costs are Positive—No Bargaining Possible. When transactions costs are so high as to preclude any bargaining, the analysis can be depicted in Figure IV.4. As can be seen, once transaction costs are incorporated into the figure, MB′x and MC′y are now coincident with the vertical axes. The assignment of liability to party X would result in zero pollution abatement, point E, due to the prohibitively high costs of bargaining any move from point E. Likewise, the assignment of liability to party Y would result in 100% pollution abatement, point F.

Since neither of these two polar solutions is efficient, it appears that Coase's suggestion in such an instance would be to rely on common law solutions to determine liability.[52] Coase argues that use of the standard of reasonableness inherent in the common law would approximate an efficient solution. He states:

The problem which we face in dealing with actions which have harmful effects is not simply one of restraining those responsible for them. What has to be decided is whether the gain from preventing the harm is greater than the loss which would be suffered elsewhere as a result of stopping the action which produces the harm. In a world in which there are costs of rearranging the rights established by the legal system, the courts, in cases relating to nuisance, are, in effect, making a decision on the economic problem and determining how resources are to be employed. It was argued that the courts are conscious of this and that they often make, although not always in a very explicit fashion, a comparison between what would be gained and what lost by preventing actions which have harmful effects.[53]

What this suggests, with reference to Figure IV.4, is that the courts should consider (through implicit approximation) MBx and MCy in an attempt to arrive at point X*. It should be apparent that the courts may not be perfect evaluators of all the relevant costs and benefits and, as a result, the court determined solution (X'c or X"c) may differ from X*. It is in this sense that this approach is characterized as approximating a market solution.

Building on the work of Coase, Calabresi and Melamed have extended the analysis of rights and their protection.[54] They analyzed both liability rules and property rules as means of protecting the rights of an individual to take an action as well as the rights of an individual to be protected from the action of another. That is, they developed a framework of analysis that intergrates various legal relationships which, in law, are typically treated in the separate areas of property and tort law.

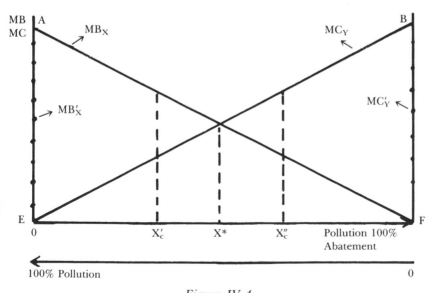

Figure IV.4.

Following their lead we will use the term entitlements to refer to these rights.

Calabresi and Melamed describe the choices that confront society in the following manner. "First order" decisions must be made as to the initial assignment of entitlement; that is, society, through the legal-economic institutions, must first decide to whom to assign the initial entitlement. Using our pollution example, does party Y have the right to pollute or does party X have the right to be free from pollution. They suggest that the criteria for setting entitlements can be based on economic efficiency, distributional preferences, or other justice considerations. Once initial entitlements are set, a series of "second order" decisions must be made. These decisions involve the manner in which entitlements are to be protected. They identify three methods of protecting entitlements: property rules, liability rules, and inalienability rules.[55] The choices confronting society can be dipicted in Figure IV.5.

The first order decision requires a choice as to whether the victim has the entitlement to be free from pollution (Cases I and II) or the injurer has the entitlement to pollute (Cases III and IV). The second order decision requires a choice as to whether the entitlement (whichever way assigned) should be protected by a property rule (Cases I and III) or a liability rule (Cases II and IV).[56] The property rule grants the holder of an entitlement an injunction to protect his entitlement whereas the liability rule awards him damages when his entitlement is violated.

In Case I, the victim is granted the entitlement to be free of pollution and protected by a property rule which allows the use of an injunction to enforce his entitlement. In this case, it may be possible for the victim to accept a bribe in lieu of exercising his right of injunction and thereby allow some pollution to occur. In Case II, the victim is again granted the entitlement to be free from pollution, but the entitlement is protected by

	(1st Order Decision)	
	Possessor of Entitlement	
(2nd Order Decision)		
Protection Rules	Victim (X)	Injurer (Y)
Property Rules	Case I	Case III
Liability Rules	Case II	Case IV

Figure IV.5.

a liability rule with the injurer liable for any damages suffered by the victim. However, unlike Case I, the victim does not have the option of enjoining the polluting activity. In Case III, the injurer (the polluter) is granted the entitlement to pollute and that entitlement is protected by a property rule. Thus, the victim is enjoined from taking any action. In this case, it is also possible that the polluter may prefer to abate some of the pollution in exchange for the payment of a bribe by the victim. In Case IV, the polluter is granted the entitlement to pollute and that entitlement is protected by a liability rule. This case differs from the other three inasmuch as the victim, if somehow successful in getting the government to prohibit the pollution, would be liable and required to pay, to the polluter, compensation based on the benefits received from the pollution abatement undertaken by the polluter.

In conjuction with the Calabresi and Melamed approach, a body of literature has emerged that tries to assess the allocative and distributive effects of the use of injunctions versus the awarding of damages in the nuisance area of tort law. While many contributors to this literature advocate the use of damages rather than injunctions, A. Mitchell Polinsky, in analyzing this question under a wide variety of assumptions, concludes that damage remedies cannot be unambiguously favored over injunctions.[57] Beyond this literature that assesses the allocative and distributive effects of injuctive versus damage remedies there is an even larger body of literature that analyzes the allocative and distributive effects of various liability rules (Case II), for example, the negligence standard, strict liability, and a host of variations. It is to this literature that we turn our attention.

2. *Liability Rules*

Historically, the development of the common law of tort has been influenced by the tension between two dominant theories: strict liability and negligence. Under the doctrine of strict liability, an individual who causes harm (the injurer) to another individual (the victim) is liable for damages regardless of whether or not the injurer was at fault, unless his actions were excused or justified.[58] Under the doctrine of negligence, the injurer is liable for damages if his actions were intentional or if he failed to take reasonable care to avoid inflicting the harm, i.e., if he is at fault.[59] In the early U.S. common law, prior to 1900, the courts predominantly employed various versions of strict liability. That is, the courts ruled, for the most part, that potential injurers must act at their own peril.[60] During the early twentieth century, a system of negligence began to replace the heretofore dominant system of strict liability. Even in the period in which the negligence system flourished, it should be noted that there remained pockets of strict liability in areas such as ultra hazardous activities.[61] Currently it appears that strict liability is once again becoming the dominant rule.[62]

In general, the economic approach to analyze liability rules can be viewed as one method of determining which risks in society will be considered background risks resulting in costs borne by the victim and which risks will be considered risks arising from tortious acts resulting in costs borne by the injurer. From this perspective, the objective of the economic approach is to develop a standard of liability (e.g., a specific strict liability or negligence rule) that determines the scope of background risks in such a manner as to minimize total interaction damage costs. This can be depicted in Figure IV.6, where the area of the circle is equal to the sum of all costs due to interaction damage situations, hereafter referred to as to total accident costs (inasmuch as we will use accidents for illustrative purposes). Let Cx represent all costs borne by victims: those costs, Cx, are borne by the victims because the liability rule chosen considered the risks associated with those costs part of background risks and thus noncompensable. Let Cy represent all costs borne by the injurers and compensable to the victims because they are not part of background risks in accordance with the chosen liability rule. In this diagrammatic context, the economic approach to tort law will be seen as an attempt to determine which specific liability rules result in the circle with the smallest area (i.e., least cost).

Utilizing this type of diagram, one can gain a better understanding of the differences between various types of liability rules. For instance, in Figure IV.7, we compare three types of liability rules—no liability (Panel a), strict liability (Panel b), and negligence (Panel c).

The no liability rule establishes a system under which injurers typically are not liable for damages (victims bear most of the costs) inasmuch as

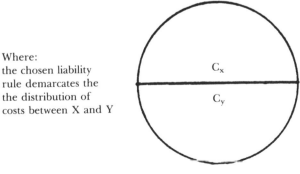

Where:
the chosen liability
rule demarcates the
the distribution of
costs between X and Y

C_x

C_y

Figure IV.6.

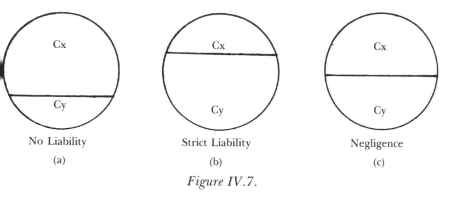

Figure IV.7.

this liability rule treats most risks as background risks. The strict liability establishes a system under which injurers typically are liable for damages (and thus bear most of the costs) inasmuch as such a liability rule typically treats few risks as background risks. Negligence establishes a system under which injurers are liable for damages only if they are negligent, i.e., only if they are at fault. Thus, it is evident that the choice of a liability rule will result in a different distribution of costs. It should be noted that although the three circles in Figure IV.7 have been drawn with the same area for expositional purposes, we do not mean to imply that total costs are invariant with respect to the specific liability rule employed. In fact, much of the economic approach operates on the premise that total accident costs do vary with the liability rule chosen.

Some of the liability rules are based on the negligence standard that will be discussed in some detail. Thus, it is important to understand the concept of negligence as used in common law. In order to gain an intuitive understanding of this concept consider the following quote by Chief Justice Rosenberry, in *Osborne v. Montgomery*.

> Every person is negligent when, without intending to do any wrong, he does such an act or omits to take such precaution that under the circumstances present he, as an ordinarily prudent person, ought reasonably to foresee that he will thereby expose the interest of another to an unreasonable risk of harm. In determining whether his conduct will subject the interests of another to an unreasonable risk of harm, a person is required to take into account such of the surrounding circumstances as would be taken into account by a reasonably prudent person and possess such knowledge as is possessed by an ordinarily reasonable person and to use such judgement and discretion as is exercised by persons of reasonable intelligence and judgement under the same or similar circumstances.[63]

The choice from among the various specific negligence liability rules will determine "reasonableness" and thereby serve to delimit the distribution of costs between victims and injurers.

Viewed from this perspective, the economic approach to the analysis of liability rules in tort law attempts to determine which of the specific negligence standards (of which there are several) and specific strict liability standards (likewise) are costminimizing, resulting in the circle with the smallest area. In this manner, the approach serves to inform society of the efficiency consequences of its choices.

Why this approach has proven attractive to legal scholars has already been mentioned. By focusing on costs, it provides a scheme to furnish firm prescriptions as to the choice of a specific liability rule thereby determining which losses are compensable—a scheme based on "value-free" economics.[64] Our position is different. First, there is a necessary introduction of value judgments in choosing from among the various liability rules. Second, we disagree with the notion that either negligence or strict liability is an objective standard, in contrast to Posner who states:

> Characterization of the negligence standard as moral or moralistic does not advance analysis. . . . Negligence is an objective standard. . . . To characterize the negligence concept as a moral one is only to push inquiry back a step.[65]

This ignores the essential point that "negligence" in and of itself is a meaningless concept unless the analyst has a particular construct of negligence in mind. It is not only not an objective standard, it is not a standard at all. Discussions of negligence or strict liability rules require an antecedent, value-laden choice as to which specific negligence liability rule or specific strict liability rule is being used. The illumination of the normative choices underlying characterizations of specific negligence and strict liability rules does not push inquiry back a step, but may serve to unmask the choices that are available to society.

Furthermore, it should be apparent from Figure IV.8 that the choice of a liability rule has simultaneously both efficiency and distributive consequences with respect to the pattern of costs. As can be seen clearly in the example, the total sum of accident costs is minimized by choosing a negligence liability rule that produces total costs equal to $600 as opposed to a strict liability rule that produces total costs equal to $1000. However, the distribution of costs differs depending on the liability rule chosen. The logic of the purported value-free economic approach dictates that the liability rule which minimizes the total costs should be chosen. Sole reliance on the economic approach serves to legitimize the specific distribution of risk associated with the chosen liability rule and thus forgoes a detailed analysis of the distributive incidence of costs, an important part of Law and Economics.

If one adopts Posner's position that efficiency should be the predominant value employed in choosing a standard of liability and if one be-

A Strict Liability Rule   A Negligence Liability Rule
(a)   (b)

Figure IV.8.

lieves that distribution is best handled by alternative means (a political determination), then one could suggest that the dispute resolution system in tort law should be converted to a two-staged process.[66] The first step would be to employ that liability rule which is cost minimizing thereby delimiting the distribution of costs between injurers and victims in a certain manner. For example, again using Figure IV.8, the negligence rule is more efficient than the strict liability and thus will be chosen. Then, following their belief that distributive questions can be separated from questions of efficiency and that the answer to distributive questions is a political choice, a second stage in the tort legal process would entail, what might be called, a "distributive hearing."

The entire purpose of this hearing is to alter the distribution of costs based on such political notions as "justice," "fairness" or "equity." The incidence derived from the first stage, where $C_x = \$300$ and $C_y = \$300$ could be politically altered to, say, $C_x = \$200$ and $C_y = \$400$. This scheme appears to follow the precepts of the economic compensation principle, in the sense that in the first stage, the efficient choice of the negligence liability rule produces a gain in costs savings for the injurer, party Y, equal to $500. At the same time the choice imposes a loss in the form of increased costs on the victim, party X, equal to $100. Consequently, Y's gain of $500 is sufficient to potentially compensate party X for his loss of $100. Thus, if the distributive hearing establishes the final incidence of costs at $C_x = \$200$ and $C_y = \$400$, this can be seen to be consistent with the compensation principle in that it restores party X to his initial position and leaves party Y better off by $400. We are not advocating such a system, but it is suggested as one system which seems to conform to the economic compensation principle. It should be noted that as the outcomes of the distributive hearings became known and if they were consistent, the very incentive system which was incorporated into the structuring of the liability rule to gain cost minimization in the first place would be altered.

Though it may be an unworkable scheme, it is raised here as a vehicle by which the justice or fairness approach outlined earlier can be compared to the economic approach. The former camp believes that liability should be placed on one party or another based on what is just or fair while the latter must live with whatever liability rule minimizes costs. It seems to explain why, as one commentator has stated, "The debate between these two camps has been unsatisfactory, neither party venturing to meet the other on its own territory."[67] For example, compare the following two statements by leading practitioners of the economic approach and the justice-fairness approach, respectively:

> Since the efficient use of resources is an important although not always paramount social value, the burden, I suggest, is on the authors to present reasons why a standard that appears to impose avoidable costs on society should nonetheless be adopted. They have not carried this burden.[68]

> Once it is admitted that there are questions of fairness as between the parties that are not answerable in economic terms, the exact role of economic argument in the solution of legal question becomes impossible to determine. It may well be that an acceptable theory of fairness can be reconciled with the dictates of economic theory in a manner that leaves ample room for the use of economic thought. But that judgment presupposes that some theory of fairness has been spelled out, which, once completed, may leave no room for economic considerations of any sort.[69]

3. Specific Liability Rules

As stated previously, there are several specific formulations of both the negligence standard and the strict liability standard. While the literature in this area is too vast to treat exhaustively, we will present several of the most commonly discussed liability rules to acquaint the reader with the nature of the work being done in this area.

The typical place to start is with the Learned Hand rule of negligence. It is commonly thought that Hand merely gave explicit formulation to the standard that the courts had applied throughout the period that the negligence standard flourished.[70] In *United States vs. Carrol Towing Co.,* Hand stated:

> Possibly it serves to bring this notion into relief to state it in algebraic terms: if the probability be called P; the injury, L; and the burden, B; liability depends upon whether B is less than L multiplied by P: i.e., whether $B < PL$.[71]

The specific liability rules we will investigate can be best understood by employing a simple numerical example. Let C^X_A be the costs of accidents borne by the victims (X) of accidents. Let C^Y_{AV} be the costs of avoiding accidents by the injurers (Y). Let P_A be the probability that the accident will occur if no avoidance is taken. Let P'_A be the probability that the accident will occur if some avoidance activities are undertaken. We will assume, for the sake of simplicity, that the probability of an accident occurring is .8 if no avoidance measures are taken and is .2 if avoidance measures are taken.

Case [i] Simple Learned Hand. Under this liability rule, the injurer is liable for accident damages if the expected accident costs (the probability of an accident occuring times the victim's accident costs) are greater than the costs that the injurer must bear to avoid the accident. Otherwise, the injurer is not negligent and the victim bears the damages. In symbols: if $P_A \cdot C^X_A > C^Y_{AV}$ then Y is negligent and thus liable. It is argued by some that this liability rule minimizes the sum of accident plus avoidance costs. To understand this, consider the following numerical example. Let $C^X_A = \$1000$, $C^Y_{AV} = \$500$, $P_A = .8$ if no avoidance measures are taken, and $P'_A = .2$ if avoidance action is taken. In this case, the simple Hand formula asserts that the injurer should be liable because (.8 × $1000) is greater than $500. Since he is liable, the injurer will engage in accident avoidance measures thereby reducing the probability of accidents to .2, resulting in expected accident costs equal to $200 and avoidance costs equal to $500 for a sum of $700. If the simple Hand formula was not followed in this situation and the injurer was not ruled liable, then he would not engage in avoidance activities and expected accident costs would be $800 and avoidance costs would be zero for a sum of $800. Inasmuch as the $700 is less than the $800, adherence to the simple Hand formula minimizes the sum of costs.

Consider an alternative case where the simple Hand formula would indicate that the injurer should not be liable. Let $C^X_A = \$1000$, $C^Y_{AV} = \$1500$, $P_A = .8$ and $P'_A = .2$. Since (.8 × $1000) is less than $1500, the injurer is not liable and the victim bears the costs. To show the efficiency of this solution consider the following. Since the injurer is not liable he will refrain from any accident avoidance activities, yielding expected accident costs equal to $800 (.8 × $1000) and avoidance costs equal to zero for a sum of $800. Note that if the courts had not followed the simple Hand formula and the injurer was ruled liable, he still would not engage in avoidance activities which would have resulted in expected accident costs of $200 (.2 × $1000) and avoidance costs of $1500, for a sum of $1700. The reason is that, if liable, it would be cheaper for the injurer to pay the accident damages of $800 to the victim for a sum of costs equal to $800. Thus, in this case, the use of the simple Hand formula, which places liability on the victim, results in the same total sum of costs as placing liability on injurers. The only difference is in who bears the costs.

Case [ii]   Hand   Formula   with   Contributory   Negligence—Version 1.   Under this liability rule, the injurer is liable for accident damages if the expected accident costs are greater than his avoidance costs *and* the expected accident costs are less than the victim's costs of avoidance. (Use of the simple Hand formula implicitly assumes that the victim can not avoid the accident. This liability rule relaxes that assumption.) In symbols: If $P_A \cdot C^X_A > C^Y_{AV}$ and if $P_A \cdot C^X_A < C^X_{AV}$ then Y is negligent and therefore liable. Otherwise, Y is not negligent and the damages are borne by the victim. This version of the Hand rule assumes that contributory negligence is an absolute defense for the injurer; that is, if the victim could have avoided the accident at a cost less than the expected accident costs, the victim is negligent even if the injurer's avoidance cost might be lower. Thus, this rule, in some instances, is not cost minimizing.

Consider the following example. Let $C^X_A = \$1000$, $C^Y_{AV} = \$500$, $C^X_{AV} = \$600$, $P_A = .8$ if no avoidance activities are taken, and $P'_A = .2$ if either the injurer or the victim takes avoidance activities. In this situation, since $P_A \cdot C^X_A$ is not less than C^X_{AV}, i.e., (.8 × \$1000) is not less than \$600, the Hand formula with contributory negligence—version 1 asserts that the victim is liable. Since he is liable, the victim will engage in accident avoidance measures costing \$600 and thereby reduce the probability of an accident to .2 resulting in expected costs of \$200. The total costs here are \$600 plus \$200, or \$800. If the courts had not followed the rule and liability had been reversed, that is, the injurer held liable, then the total costs would have been smaller. If the injurer had been held liable, he would have engaged in avoidance activities costing \$500 and would also have reduced the probability of an accident to .2, resulting in expected accident costs of \$200. In this example, a decision holding the injurer liable would have produced total costs equal to \$500 plus \$200, or \$700, clearly lower than the total costs if the victim were made liable. Thus, the Hand formula with contributory negligence—version 1 is not cost minimizing.

Case [iii]   Hand   Formula   with   Contributory   Negligence—Version 2.   Under this liability rule, the injurer is liable for accident damages if the expected accident costs are greater than his avoidance costs *and* the expected accident costs are greater than the victim's avoidance costs *and* the victim's avoidance costs are greater than the injurer's avoidance costs; otherwise, the victim is liable for damages. In symbols,

$$\text{If } P_A \cdot C^X_A > C^Y_{AV}$$
$$\text{and if } P_A \cdot C^X_A > C^X_{AV}$$
$$\text{and if } C^X_{AV} > C^Y_{AV}$$

then the injurer is negligent and therefore liable; otherwise the victim is liable. This rule is similar to version 1 analyzed above. The only difference is the comparison of injurer's and victim's avoidance costs. Using the same numerical example as in version 1, liability will be reversed. Again, let C^X_A = \$1000, C^Y_{AV} = \$500, C^X_{AV} = \$600, P_A = .8 if no avoidance activities are taken, and P'_A = .2 if either party takes avoidance measures. In this situation, the Hand formula with contributory negligence—version 2 asserts that the injurer is liable because (.8 × \$1000) > \$500 and (.8 × \$1000) > \$600 and \$600 > \$500. Since he is liable, the injurer will engage in avoidance activities costing \$500 and thereby reduce the probability of an accident to .2 resulting in expected accident costs of \$200, for a sum of \$700. Alternatively, had the victim been held liable by the court, he would have engaged in avoidance activities costing \$600, and expected accident costs of \$200 (.2 × \$1000) resulting in total costs of \$800. Thus, adherence to this version of the Hand rule does minimize the sum of accident costs.

Case [iv] **Strict Liability with Contributory Negligence—Version 1.** Under this rule, the injurer is liable for all accidents unless the victim is negligent, i.e., unless the expected accident costs are greater than the victim's avoidance costs. In symbols, the injurer is liable *unless*

$$P_A \cdot C^X_A > C^X_{AV}$$

It should be noted that this rule is similar to rule [ii] above; the only difference is that under this rule the cost of accidents that are not worth avoiding by either party (i.e., when $P_A \cdot C^X_A < C^X_{AV}$ and $P_A \cdot C^X_A < C^Y_{AV}$) are borne by the injurer rather than the victim as rule [ii] would have it. Further, since this rule (like rule [ii]) does not compare avoidance costs, it is not cost minimizing just as rule [ii] is not necessarily cost minimizing. To see this point, consider the same example used to analyze rule [ii]. Let C^X_A = \$1000, C^Y_{AV} = \$500, C^X_{AV} = \$600, P_A = .8, and P'_A = .2. In this situation, using rule [iv], the strict liability rule with contributory negligence—version 1, the victim is liable since (.8 × \$1000) is greater than \$600. Since the victim is liable, he will spend \$600 on avoidance and reduce expected accident costs to \$200, for a total of \$800. If the injurer had been held liable, he would have taken \$500 worth of avoidance activities and would have reduced expected accident costs to \$200, for a total of \$700. Thus, this rule, which makes the victim liable in this situation, is not cost minimizing.

Case [v] **Strict Liability with Contributory Negligence—Version 2.** Under this liability rule, the injurer is liable unless the victim can avoid the accident at a cost lower than the expected accident costs *and* lower than the injurer's avoidance costs. In symbols, the injurer is liable *unless*

$$P_A \cdot C^X_A > C^X_{AV}$$
$$\text{and } C^X_{AV} < C^Y_{AV}$$

This rule is comparable to rule [iii]; the only difference is that the injurer is liable for all accidents that are not worth avoiding, whereas under rule [iii], the victim would be liable. Using the same example used to analyze rule [iii], again, let $C^X_A = \$1000$, $C^Y_{AV} = \$500$, $C^X_{AV} = \$600$, $P_A = .8$ if no avoidance activities are taken, and $P'_A = .2$ if either party takes avoidance measurers. In this situation using rule [v], strict liability with contributory negligence—version 2, the injurer is liable because $800 (.8 × $1000) is greater than $600 but $600 is not less than $500. Since he is liable, the injurer will engage in avoidance activities costing $500 and thereby reduce expected accident costs to $200 for a sum of $700. Alternatively had the victim been held liable, he would have engaged in avoidance activities costing $600, reducing expected accident costs to $200, resulting in a sum total of cost equal to $800. Thus adherence to this version of the strict liability rule also minimizes the sum of accident costs as did rule [iii].

Case [vi] Least Cost Avoider Liability Rule. This is Calabresi, Melamed, and Hirschoff's version of strict liability. They suggest the following:

(1) That economic efficiency standing alone would dictate that set of entitlements which favors knowledgeable choices between social benefits and the social costs of obtaining them, and between social costs and the social costs of avoiding them; (2) that this implies in the absence of certainty as to whether a benefit is worth its costs to society, that *the cost should be put on the party or activity best located to make such a cost-benefit analysis;* (3) that in particular contexts like accidents or pollution *this suggests putting costs on the party or activity which can most cheaply avoid them;* (4) that in the absence of certainty as to who that party or activity is, the costs should be put on the party or activity which can with the lowest transaction costs act in the market to correct an error in entitlements by inducing the party who can avoid social costs most cheaply to do so; and (5) that since we are in an area where by hypothesis markets do not work perfectly—there are transaction costs—a decision will often have to be made on whether market transactions or collective fiat is most likely to bring us closer to the Pareto optimal result the 'perfect' market would reach.[72] (emphasis added)

We do not mean to suggest that the party in the best position to make the cost-benefit analysis is always in the best position to act upon it; where that is not the case, the decision requires weighing comparative advantages.[73] (emphasis added)

Although subject to a variety of interpretations, we believe they are arguing the following. Their strict liability rule introduces additional costs into the analysis. Specifically it adds the cost of actually calculating, by both parties, the relevant cost benefit ratios for avoiding accidents. Under this rule the injurer is liable for any accident unless the victim can avoid the accident at a total cost lower than the expected accident costs *and* lower than the injurer's total avoidance costs, where total avoidance costs (C_{TAV}) equal the usual avoidance costs (C_{AV}) plus the cost of calculating the relevant costs and benefits ($C_{C/B}$) for both parties. In symbols the injurer is liable *unless*

$$P_A \cdot C^X{}_A > C^X{}_{TAV}$$
$$\text{and } C^X{}_{TAV} < C^Y{}_{TAV}$$
$$\text{where } C^X{}_{TAV} = C^X{}_{AV} + C^X{}_{C/B}$$
$$\text{and } C^Y{}_{TAV} = C^Y{}_{AV} + C^Y{}_{C/B}$$

This rule is perfectly comparable to rule [v] and yields exactly the same results except that the costs of calculating the relevant costs and benefits of avoiding the accident are explicitly included in the avoidance costs.

Calabresi seems to narrow the approach by suggesting that the cheapest cost avoider can be determined by identifying the party with the lower cost of calculating the cost benefit ratio. This is true when the injurer's usual avoidance costs ($C^Y{}_{AV}$) are greater than the victim's usual avoidance costs ($C^X{}_{AV}$) *and* the injurer's costs of calculating the cost benefit ratio ($C^Y{}_{C/B}$) are greater than the victim's costs of calculating the cost benefit ratio ($C^X{}_{C/B}$). That is, ($C^Y{}_{AV}$) is greater than ($C^X{}_{AV}$) *and* ($C^Y{}_{C/B}$) is greater than ($C^X{}_{C/B}$). Conversely, it is also true when ($C^Y{}_{AV}$) is less than ($C^X{}_{AV}$) *and* ($C^Y{}_{C/B}$) is less than ($C^X{}_{C/B}$).

As Calabresi and Hirschoff point out, this need not be the case.[74] In a case where the party that has the lowest costs of calculating the cost benefit ratio is not the party in the best position to act upon the calculation, the rule remains efficient as can be seen in the following example. Let $C^X{}_A = \$1000$, $C^Y{}_{AV} = \$200$, $C^X{}_{AV} = \$150$, $C^Y{}_{C/B} = \$100$, $C^X{}_{C/B} = \$250$, $P_A = .8$, and $P'_A = .2$. Under the least cost avoider rule, the injurer is liable since his total avoidance costs ($\$200 + \$100 = \$300$) are less than the victim's total avoidance costs ($\$150 + \$250 = \$400$). Under this rule, the injurer would engage in avoidance at a cost of $300 which would result in expected accident costs of $200 for a sum total of costs equal to $500. Alternatively had the victim been held liable, he would have engaged in $400 ($150 + $250) of avoidance costs which would result in expected accident costs of $200, for a total of $600. This illustrates the rule is cost minimizing.

The difference between Calabresi's approach and two previous approaches (rules [iii] and [v]) is now clear. By his incorporation of the cost benefit calculation costs, liability is reversed in our example. That is, using Calabresi's approach the injurer is liable in this example; whereas under rule [iii] or rule [v], the victim would be liable because his avoidance costs (C^X_{AV}) are less than the avoidance costs of the injurer (C^Y_{AV}).

Implicit in the analysis of this liability rule, as well as the other liability rules discussed here, is the assumption that the courts have perfect information about all of the costs associated with accidents. This assumption is clearly invalid. As a consequence Calabresi, Hirschoff, and Melamed in extending rule [vi] explicitly introduce uncertainty into their analysis. In situations where there is uncertainty about which party is the least cost avoider, they propose that the courts should place liability ". . . on the party or activity which can with the lowest transaction costs act in the market to correct an error in entitlements by inducing the party who can avoid social costs most cheaply to do so."[75] This is referred to as the "best-briber" criterion and is perfectly analogous to the Coasian case where transactions costs are positive but not so high as to preclude subsequent bargaining solutions (see text circa Figure IV.3).

As indicated earlier, it should be clear that the preceeding list is not an exhaustive list of all possible liability rules. John P. Brown and Steven Shavell explore the efficiency implications of a variety of liability rules in addition to the ones analyzed here.[76] It should be noted that all those who seek efficient liability rules implicitly base their analysis on the economic compensation principle in the sense that efficient liability rules minimize total interaction damage costs and thereby produce a surplus in value (a net gain in cost savings) when compared to inefficient rules. The existence of the surplus in value indicates that the winners' gain is sufficiently large to enable them to potentially compensate the losers. Thus, the economic compensation principle lies at the heart of the economic approach for choosing appropriate liability rules.

In summary, what emerges from this kind of analysis is the conclusion that many of these rules, given different assumptions, produce efficient results. If the minimization of total interaction damage costs is the goal of tort law, efficiency can be used to choose among competing liability rules. However, since many rules are efficient, the efficiency criteria is not decisive. To understand this point, we need only to compare rule [iii], the Hand formula with contributory negligence—version 2, with rule [v], strict liability with contributory negligence—version 2. These two rules always place liability on the same party when the avoidance costs of each party are less than the expected accident costs. Both rules place liability on the party that can avoid the accident at the lowest costs. However, if the expected accident costs are lower than the two parties' respective costs of avoidance, then the two rules will assign liability differently. That is, rule [iii] would place liability on the victim and rule [v] would place liability on the injurer. Neither party will engage in any avoidance activities because avoidance is too costly. Therefore, both liability rules will produce identical total accident costs which are equal to the expected costs of accidents. The only difference is whether the injurer bears the costs as is the case under rule [v] or the victim bears the cost as is the case under rule [iii]. This is purely a distributive question.

Further, if as some suggest, "justice or fairness are the stuff of tort law"[77] and "it is a mistake to dwell too long upon questions of cost,"[78] then inefficient liability rules cannot be ruled out as working rules to guide a judiciary concerned with justice or fairness. Referring back to Figure IV.8, if justice dictates the choice of a strict liability rule because of a preference for that particular distribution of costs that results from the rule, then the fact that a negligence liability rule produces a lower total cost is irrelevant because that distribution of costs may be deemed unjust. The economic approach and the justice–fairness approach have yet to be reconciled.

C. THE TAKING ISSUE

The taking issue arises as a result of governmental actions that are accomplished under the power of eminent domain and the police power and that inflict losses on some members of society. The purpose of this section is to describe the manner in which the taking issue arises in law, to examine the issues involved in resolving such cases, and to explore the nature of the choices confronting society in this area of law. This matter remains a complex issue of public policy and continues to command the attention of legal–economic scholars and the courts due to the expansive character of modern land use regulations.[79]

Typically, disputes involving the taking issue have been resolved in the courts where the resolution of these cases is based upon a choice from among a host of decision criteria, rules, and doctrines developed in case law as well as by legal scholars who have undertaken much of the development, inquiry, and analysis of legal tests. The necessity for legal resolutions to the questions surrounding the taking issue requires the courts to choose one decision rule over another, the consequences of which affect the pattern of land use in a rather uncertain manner.[80]

As in the case of tort law, in taking issue cases, society is again faced with a choice—this time a choice as to which working rules or, more specifically, which decision rules to employ to resolve taking issue disputes. Broadly, the issue is whether the rights of individuals which are expropriated, diminished, or damaged consequent to a governmental action should or should not be elevated to the status of protected rights. However, unlike the discussion in the previous section concerning liability rules, where typically the two litigants were private parties, here the usual litigation is between the government (or public authority granted the power of eminent domain and the police power) and a private interest.

1. The Taking Issue: The Legal Setting

Inherent in sovereignty are the powers through which the government can exert control over the use of land. Within the limits set by the constitution (state and federal), the government can exercise its powers, which include eminent domain, the police power, taxing, proprietary, and the spending power.[81] Generally the control by government of land, air, and water resources is accomplished by regulating their use either by acquiring the rights to them through eminent domain or regulating them through the use of the police power. Viewed from the perspective of the individual landowner, these two powers have emerged as the most important governmental means for compelling or restricting individual landowners to use or not use certain natural resources in specific ways. They represent the two major exceptions to the right of absolute use of private property: the first is that the use of property is subject to the right of eminent domain, while the second is that private property is always held subject to reasonable regulation under the police power.

a. Eminent Domain and the Taking Issue. Eminent domain is the right held to be inherent in sovereignty whereby the right of private property is inferior to the right of the sovereign to take private property for public purposes. The power of eminent domain needed no constitutional recognition (although it is understood to be an implied power of the U.S. Constitution), because it is a power inherent in and one of the highest attributes of sovereignty. It antedates and exists independently of constitutions, legislation, and other provisions which are only declaratory of preexisting law. Eminent domain is understood to mean the power of the sovereign to take property for public use without the owner's consent and without compensation. Imposed upon the sovereign government by constitutional and statutory enactments is the right of the property owner to be compensated for his loss. The requirement of compensation has become so universal, it is usually included in the working definition of eminent domain.[82]

The Fifth Amendment of the Constitution of the United States provides "nor shall private property be taken for public use without just compensation."[83] So expressed, the provision for just compensation is a constitutional limitation on the exercise of the eminent domain power. Therefore, constitutionally, the government (or a subordinate agency which has been granted this authority) can exercise the unqualified right to condemn property for public purposes without the owner's consent, subject to the requirement of the payment of just compensation.

In eminent domain cases, the legal concern is focused on: (1) the issues surrounding the allowance or disallowance of the taking and the amount of compensation necessary, and (2) whether the consequential impact of an eminent domain action constitutes a compensable taking. As to the former concern, the issue is not whether the reduction of an individual's fee simple rights constitutes a taking—taking is directly implied under the concept of eminent domain—but whether the "admitted" taking by the government will be allowed in accordance with certain legal criteria. Thus, the (dis)allowance of taking under eminent domain centers on questions other than taking, for example, questions concerning public purpose, public use, condemnation procedure, and the valuation of just compensation.

It is with respect to concern (2) that the taking issue is raised; i.e., the question is whether a consequential impact of an eminent domain action constitutes a compensable taking.[84] In this case, an individual landowner can allege that, consequent to the government's use of the eminent domain power, he has suffered a loss which should be compensable under the applicable federal or state constitutional provision. For example, a city, using its power of eminent domain, may take a tract of property containing high density housing for urban renewal purposes. The owner of a food market located adjacent to the taken tract may suffer damages occasioned by the loss of his customers. The owner of the food market could claim that he has had his rights (rights to customers) taken without just compensation.[85] Generally, if the court holds that the government's action was not a taking of the market owner's rights but merely a damaging of rights which are not accorded a protected status, then the landowner can continue to utilize his market but under the burden of whatever restrictions or damages that took place. Alternatively, the court may rule that the consequential damages are in fact part of the eminent domain taking (or damaging) of the individual's rights and, as proscribed by the constitution, direct the government to pay just compensation to the market owner. Thus, the first limitation on the private use of property, the exercise of the power of eminent domain, does raise the taking issue over the question of consequential damages.

b. Police Power and the Taking Issue. As described earlier, the second major limitation on the private use of property is that it is held subject to the reasonable exercise of the police power. The police power, like that of eminent domain, is an inherent attribute of sovereignty. Police power is the duty of the sovereign to protect its citizens and to provide for the health, safety, welfare, morals, and good order of society. As long as the police power is exercised in such a way that it appears calculated to achieve a reasonable end within the concept of the welfare of the community, and as long as the means are reasonable and not arbitrary, courts have not interfered with its exercise.

Traditionally, however, where land use regulations have been promulgated under the police power, the common response has been one of landowners charging that their property is being taken without compensation. For example, the management of natural resources through land use regulation continues to be challenged in the courts, under the Fifth and Fourteenth Amendments, as an unconstitutional taking of property without compensation. The increasing frequency with which regulatory actions accomplished under the police power tend to collide with property interests safeguarded by constitutional prohibitions has been noted by Sax. He stated: "Nearly every attempt to regulate the private use of land, water, and air resources may be claimed to violate the taking clause."[86]

As related to the police power, the taking issue has been raised, procedurally, in either of two ways.[87] First, the taking issue can be raised through an inverse condemnation proceeding. That is, the private landowner can claim that the proposed police power regulation is an unconstitutional taking of property without just compensation and attempt to recover damages. The courts have typically reserved this remedy to be pursued for those cases where the government activity has involved the physical invasion of a property interest. It should be noted that recently a number of litigants have begun to pursue inverse condemnation damages for governmental activities that have impacts well beyond physical invasion. That is, they have attempted to win inverse condemnation awards for a broad array of "excessive" governmental regulations which they allege deprives them of their property.[88]

Under this procedure, the court may rule that the regulation is a valid exercise of the police power. The land use would then be guided in accordance with the regulation with no compensation paid. Alternatively, the court may rule that a taking has occured and award the individual landowner just compensation for those rights the government has affected through the imposition of the police power regulation. The private landowner would retain title to the "residual" rights and could engage in land uses within the governmentally proscribed regulations.

The second procedural method for raising the taking issue in response to a police power regulation is for the private land owner to seek a declaratory judgment for injunctive relief from the proposed governmental regulation, alleging that the regulation constitutes an unconstitutional taking of property without just compensation. Here, the landowner seeks to have the court rule that the government regulation is unconstitutional (or unconstitutional as applied) and therefore set aside the statute or ordinance. Where courts find that the ordinance falls within the valid scope of police power regulatory activity, the government's regulations regarding land use policy are upheld, and land use is guided accordingly. Alternatively, if the courts find that the regulation reaches so far as to constitute a taking, it is invalidated thereby removing the alleged burden of the regulation from the individual landowner. As such, the individual can then exercise control over the use of the land, always within other constitutionally valid police power regulations.

2. *Justice Holmes, the Taking Issue and Legal Rules*

In May of 1921, the Pennsylvania legislature passed and the Governor signed into law the Kohler Act. The Act prohibited the mining of coal where such mining would cause subsidence (i.e., sinking) of buildings (public buildings, churches, schools, hospitals, theaters, etc.), roadway bridges, railroad tracks, factories, homes, and stores.[89] In September, the Pennsylvania Coal Company, who owned the mineral rights below the home of the Mahons, informed them that mining operations beneath their property would soon commence and shortly thereafter cause subsidence. The Mahon's attempt to have the coal company's action enjoined was met with the charge by Pennsylvania Coal Co. that the Kohler Act amounted to a public taking of private property without just compensation. While the Supreme Court of Pennsylvania declared the Kohler Act constitutional, the U.S. Supreme Court found it to be unconstitutional in that it was thought that the Act tried to accomplish through the police power what should have been accomplished by eminent domain. In deciding the landmark case, Justice Oliver W. Holmes articulated the test which then became the basis for future decisions.

> Government hardly could go on if to some extent values incident to property could not be diminished without paying for every such change in the general law. As long recognized, some values are enjoyed under an implied limitation and must yield to the police power. But obviously the implied limitation must have its limits or the contract and due process clauses are gone. One fact for consideration in determining such limits is the extent of diminution. When it reaches a certain magnitude, in most if not in all cases there must be an excercise of eminent domain and compensation to sustain that act. So the question depends upon the particular facts. The greatest weight is given to the judgment of the legislature, but it is always open to interested parties to contend that the legislature had gone beyond its constitutional

power. . . . The general rule at least is, that while property may be regulated to a
certain extent, if regulation goes too far it will be recognized as a taking.[90]

Thereafter, each state court was left to decide which governmental
actions reached so far as to constitute a taking. As suggested earlier,
courts have a plethora of decision rules to resolve these cases, including
the harm-benefit rule, the fair compensation test, and the critical natural
features tests.[91] The harm-benefit rule provides for the positive enrich-
ment of the public through the extraction of the public good from
private property. It states that the government takes property by eminent domain because the government action is useful to the public and
under police power because the private action is harmful. In other
words, if the result of governmental regulation is to achieve a benefit for
the community, compensation must be paid, but if it is to terminate a
harmful activity, no compensation is necessary. The rationale of the
payment of compensation is to distribute more equitably the costs of
making a benefit generally available to the public. The fair compensation test suggests the introduction of a power between the police power
and eminent domain termed the accommodation power. This power,
together with the concept of fair compensation (less demanding than
just compensation), serves as an intermediary between the police power's
absence of compensation and the eminent domain power's requirement
of just compensation. The alleged need for the additional power together with fair compensation is based upon the premise that there is a
class of regulatory measures that fits neither into the scope of the traditional police power nor eminent domain power. The accommodation
power would escape the confiscation objection by affording burdened
landowners fair compensation in the form of appropriate economic
trade-offs. The critical natural features test focuses on the critical natural features of the land, the alteration of which will drastically affect
ecological integrity. The test essentially elevates the natural features of
land to special protective status. A paramount public interest in the
significant ecological ongoing functions limits the individual landowner's right to alter the land's features. Thus, regulations preserving
certain critical features of land can be upheld without compensation
despite great loss in economic development potential. A survey of the
literature suggests at least fifteen rules are available.

a. A Categorization of Taking Issue Cases.   These decision rules have
been applied in taking issue litigation in a rather uneven manner so as to
produce an area of law that has been described as "a welter of confusing
and apparently incompatible results," "a crazy quilt-work pattern of Supreme Court doctrine," and "artificial distinctions without basis other

than in semantics."[92] In an attempt to provide a more orderly treatment to this area of law the following categorization of taking issue cases is presented.

Recall that: (1) the taking issue in land use control is raised consequent to a government action founded upon the sovereign based powers of either the eminent domain or police power; (2) the landowners, alleging that a taking has transpired, can pursue remedies of either a damage award or invalidation of the government regulation; and (3) the court may rule on behalf of either the landowner or the government. Consequently, six categories or types of cases emerge.

Type 1   A claim for compensation arising from consequential damages due to a government action performed under the power of eminent domain, and the court rules on behalf of the government, whereby the landowner can continue to use his property, but under the burden of those damages that were consequent to the government action.[93]

Type 2   A claim for compensation arising from consequential damages due to a government action performed under the power of eminent domain, and the court rules on behalf of the landowner who would then receive compensation.[94]

Alternatively, as described earlier, the government may proceed to take an action based on the police power. As a result, an individual landowner may pursue either the remedy of inverse condemnation or declaratory relief.

Type 3   An inverse condemnation claim for monetary compensation arising from a government action based on the police power and the court rules on behalf of the government, thereby eliminating any requirement for compensation to the individual landowner.[95]

Type 4   An inverse condemnation claim arising from a government action based on the police power and the court rules on behalf of the landowner, who would then receive compensation for damages sustained in the taking.[96]

Type 5   A claim for declaratory relief asking that the government action, accomplished through the exercise of the police power, be delcared unconstitutional and the court rules on behalf of the government thereby ruling that the government regulation is a valid exercise of the police power.[97]

Type 6   A claim for declaratory relief asking that the government action, accomplished through the police power, be declared unconstitutional and the court rules on behalf of the landowner thereby finding the government action reaches beyond police power regulation and constitutes a taking of the individual's rights.[98]

It should be evident that, in both consequential damage eminent domain cases and inverse condemnation police power cases, regardless of who "wins" the particular case, the government determines the pattern of land use. "Winning" or "losing" the case from the individual landowner's point of view means being awarded or denied compensation, respectively, not maintaining control of the desired land use. However, the court's decision in a declaratory relief police power case does affect land use directly. If the individual landowner's claim is upheld in court then the landowner continues to control the use of the land. Alternatively, if the government prevails in the court, the land must then be utilized in accordance with the government regulation.

b. Legal-Economic Analysis of the Taking Issue.   Government regulations accomplished under the police power can be analyzed in a manner similar to our earlier analysis of liability rules where it was seen that the distribution of costs as well as the magnitude of these costs is contingent upon the choice of a specific liability rule to resolve tort disputes. In Figure IV.9 (which is similar to Figure IV.1), the area of the circle represents the total sum of interaction damage costs before any governmental regulation is passed. As Coase and Calabresi have observed, an alternative to the corrective justice approach of tort litigation to reduce interaction damage costs is government regulation, for example, police power zoning ordinances.[99] In Figure IV.9, a zoning regulation may have the effect of reducing total interaction damage costs to the area above line AA resulting in total net savings to society equal to the area below AA. In fact, several scholars have argued that zoning originated as a reform of nuisance law as a way of solving these disputes.[100]

More recently the focus of much government regulation, in particular zoning, appears to have shifted emphasis from the reduction of costs associated with nuisances to the creation of positive benefits that enhance the community environment.[101] Economic efficiency analysis indicates that a police power regulation that produces a benefit cost ratio greater than one, and thereby creates a surplus in value, should be undertaken. The logic of this approach has, at its base, the economic compensation principle.[102] In such a case, a decision not to go forward with the proposed regulation would be to refuse to generate a surplus of

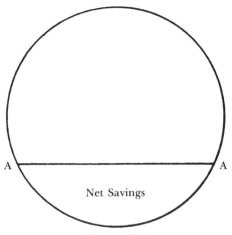

Figure IV.9.

value sufficient to enable the gainers to potentially compensate those harmed by the regulation and still remain better off.

Given a police power government regulation with a positive benefit cost ratio, there has been a debate in the literature as to the manner in which the losers, i.e., those who bear the costs of the regulation, should be treated. The issue can be analyzed using the concept of the attenuation of rights. The losers have had their rights attenuated; that is, they have suffered a diminution in the value of their effective commodities and effective resources (where effective commodities and effective resources are, as defined earlier, the commodities and resources plus all associated rights). There is a question as to whether the losers should be compensated for the losses they have sustained. In law, the judiciary will apply one of the various decision rules to determine if a compensable taking has occurred and compensate accordingly. In the economic approach to law, if the economic compensation principle is employed, the question of compensation remains unanswered; i.e., the "could" or "should" question remains unresolved.

Some of those who engage in the debate have suggested that, generally, compensation should be required for damages sustained as a result of police power regulations.[103] Those who argue this position adhere to the notion that the existing degree of attenuation of property rights is reflected in the prevailing law. They perceive the laws as a set of traditionally observed expectations. Thus, if a government regulation substantially alters any of these expectations, then a loss associated with a change in property rights (i.e., a "taking") has occurred and compensation is mandated.[104] Implicitly, this can be interpreted as an argument for the use of the power of eminent domain instead of the police power. But there are two problems associated with this approach. As discussed earlier, the notion of attenuation of rights presumes that a status quo structure of rights can be identified. However, in a dynamic society, evolving law constantly alters the structure of rights and thus makes identification difficult. Further, government regulation often involves situations where interdependencies among individuals in society exist. As a consequence, the question is not the degree of attenuation of rights, but whose rights will be attenuated.[105]

The alternative view to the debate suggests that as long as the gainers could compensate the losers, the government regulation should go forward without compensation and be treated as a legitimate police power action.[106] Implicit in this view is the notion that those who bear the costs of government regulation are also part of the group that benefits from these regulations. In this sense, the potential damage caused by government regulation can be viewed as part of the background risks borne by all members of society. Thus, losses sustained consequent to a government regulation are not compensable.

Finally, as to the remedy of declaratory relief (i.e., having the government regulation set aside if it constitutes a taking), a void exists in the legal-economic literature. The existence of this void can be partially explained by the argument that invalidation of the government regulation when the benefit cost ratio is greater than one would prevent the generation of a surplus of value. Clearly, from an efficiency standpoint, if the benefit cost ratio is less than one, few would disagree with setting the regulation aside.

In summary, in law, the courts must make a choice as to which decision rule should be employed to determine whether the damages associated with a police power regulation or consequential damages to an eminent domain action constitute a taking. As in the case of liability rules, this choice has a profound impact on the allocation and distribution of resources and, ultimately, the character of economic life.

NOTES AND REFERENCES

1. T. Nicolaus Tideman, "Property As a Moral Concept," in G. Wunderlich and W. L. Gibson, Jr., Eds., *Perspectives in Property* (University Park: Institute for Research on Land and Water Resources, Pennsylvania State University, 1972), pp. 202–205 at 202.

2. Lionel C. Robbins, *An Essay on the Nature and Significance of Economic Science* (London: Macmillan and Co., Limited, 1932).

3. Lionel C. Robbins, "Interpersonal Comparisons of Utility: A Comment," *Economic Journal*, Vol. 48, No. 192 (December 1938), pp. 635–641. For a review of these developments see John S. Chipman and James C. Moore, "The New Welfare Economics 1939–1974," *International Economic Review*, Vol. 19, No. 3 (October 1978), pp. 547–584 at 547–548.

4. Those credited with the development of the compensation principle include: E. Barone, "The Ministry of Production in the Collectivist State," in F. A. Hayek, Ed., *Collectivist Economic Planning* (London: G. Routledge Ltd., 1935); Nicholas Kaldor, "Welfare Propositions in Economics," *Economic Journal*, Vol. 49, No. 195 (September 1939), pp. 549–552; J. R. Hicks, "The Foundations of Welfare Economics," *Economic Journal*, Vol. 49, No. 196 (December 1939), pp. 696–712; Tibor Scitovsky, "A Note on Welfare Propositions in Economics," *Review of Economic Studies*, Vol. 9, No. 1 (November 1941–42), pp. 77–88. For a review of this literature see I. M. D. Little, "The Foundations of Welfare Economics," *Oxford Economic Papers*, Vol. 1, N.S. 227 (1949) and J. de V. Graaff, *Theoretical Welfare Economics* (London: Cambridge University Press, 1967).

5. The name of Wicksell is added to the name of Pareto since collective decision-making under a rule of unanimity is associated with the name of Knute Wicksell in modern public-finance theory analysis. He proposed institutional reforms that embodied unanimity in the reaching of tax and expenditure decisions. See Knute Wicksell, *Finanztheoretische untersuchungen* (Jena: Gustav Fischer, 1896). The central portion of this work appears in English translation as, "A New Principle of Just Taxation," in Richard Musgrave and Alan T. Peacock, Eds., *Classics in the Theory of Public Finance* (London: Macmillan and Company, Limited, 1958), pp. 72–118. J. S. Coleman reviewed the Wicksell criteria in "Individual Interests and Collective Action," *Papers in Non-Market Decision Making*, Vol. 1 (1966), pp. 49–62 at 51. He stated:

> Wicksell suggested that in this case the process of political adjustment was comparable to the process of voluntary exchange in the private sector of the economy, if the appropriate decision rule were used. The decision rule for Wicksell was one in which the first condition was that each expenditure should be associated with a particular tax, so that in the process of decision-making, individuals would know exactly what service they were buying. The second condition was that the tax should only be assessed upon a unanimous vote, based on the following consideration: both the level of taxes and the distribution of taxes should be adjusted until each individual was willing to pay his proportion at the given level. The result would be that the level would be adjusted upward by persons willing to assume a larger share in order to increase the level, up to the point that the marginal return of the additional service just equalled the marginal costs of the additional burden.

6. This is the Kaldor-Hicks version. Its main defect is that it gives contradictory (i.e., circular) results when comparing two efficient allocations. Though not readily evident from the test as articulated in the chapter, it has been demonstrated that in using the Kaldor-Hicks test, State 2 can be shown to be preferred to State 1. However, upon realigning resources to establish State 2, State 1 can then be shown to be preferred to State 2. To avoid this circularity Scitovsky added the refinement that in addition to conforming to the Kaldor-Hicks criteria, it is also essential that the losers not be able to bribe the potential gainers to forego the change. See J. de V. Graaff, *Theoretical Welfare Economics*, pp. 89–90 and S. K. Nath, *A Reappraisal of Welfare Economics* (London: Routledge and Kegan Paul 1969), pp. 94–101.

7. Varian also articulates a widely recognized, persistent problem with the compensation principle:

> Now it is clear that if the winners *do in fact* compensate the losers, the proposed change in the allocation will certainly be acceptable to all. But is not clear why one should think x′ is better than x merely because it is *possible* for the winners to compensate the losers.

Hal R. Varian, *Microeconomic Analysis* (New York: W. W. Norton and Co. 1978), p. 216.

8. The positive versus normative thrust of the compensation principle as well as other questions remain at issue. For example see: Harold M. Hochman and James D. Rodgers, "Pareto Optimal Redistribution," *American Economic Review*, Vol. 59, No. 4 (September 1969), pp. 542–557; Richard A. Musgrave, "Pareto Optimal Redistributions: Comment," *American Economic Review*, Vol. 60, No. 5 (December 1970), pp. 991–993; Harold M. Hochman and James D. Rodgers, "Pareto Optimal Redistributions: Reply," *American Economic Review*, Vol. 60, No. 5 (December 1970), pp. 997–1002; Harold M. Hochman, "Rule Change and Transitional Equity," in Harold M. Hochman and George E. Peterson, Eds., *Redistribution Through Public Choice* (New York: Columbia University Press, 1974), pp. 320–341; Warren J. Samuels, "Interrelations Between Legal and Economic Processes," *Journal of Law and Economics*, Vol. 14, No. 2 (October 1971), pp. 435–450; James M. Buchanan, "Politics, Property and the Law: An Alternative Interpretation of Miller et al. v. Schoene," *Journal of Law and Economics*, Vol. 15, No. 2 (October 1972), pp. 439–452; Warren J. Samuels, "In Defense of a Positive Approach to Government as an Economic Variable," *Journal of Law and Economics*, Vol. 15, No. 2 (October 1972), pp. 453–459; Warren J. Samuels, "Commentary: An Economic Perspective on the Compensation Problem," *Wayne Law Review*, Vol. 21, No. 1 (November 1974), pp. 113–134; Warren J. Samuels and Nicholas Mercuro, "The Role and Resolution of the Compensation Principle in Society," *Research in Law and Economics*, Vol. 1 (1979), pp. 157–194; and Nicholas Mercuro and Timothy P. Ryan, "Property Rights and Welfare Economics: Miller et al. v. Schoene Revisited," *Land Economics*, Vol. 56, No. 2 (May 1980), pp. 203–212.

9. Erik G. Furubotn and Svetozar Pejovich, "Property Rights and Economic Theory," *Journal of Economic Literature*, Vol. 10, No. 4 (December 1972), pp. 1137–1162 at 1142, 1143.

10. Donald T. Savage, et al., *The Economics of Environmental Improvement* (Boston: Houghton Mifflin Co., 1974), p. 73.

11. This is a quote from James M. Buchanan recounted in Victor Goldberg, "Public Choice-Property Rights," *Journal of Economic Issues*, Vol. 8, No. 3 (September 1974), pp. 555–579 at 562–563. (Goldberg's account of Buchanan's position is a synthesis of Buchanan's writings and personal correspondence between them.)

12. Hochman, "Rule Change and Transitional Equity," pp. 323, 324, 326, 327.

13. Robert D. Tollison, "Involved Social Analysis," in James M. Buchanan and Robert D. Tollison, Eds., *Theory of Public Choice* (Ann Arbor: The University of Michigan Press, 1972), pp. 3–7 at 4, 5.

14. James M. Buchanan, "Positive Economics, Welfare Economics, and Political Economy," *Journal of Law and Economics*, Vol. 2 (October 1959), pp. 124–138 at 129.

15. Tollison, "Involved Social Analysis," p. 4.

16. Ibid., p. 5.

17. James M. Buchanan, "What Kind of Redistribution Do We Want," *Economica*, Vol. 35, No. 138 (May 1968), pp. 185–190 at 189.

18. Samuels, "Commentary: An Economic Perspective on the Compensation Problem," pp. 118–119.

19. Joseph L. Sax, "Takings and the Police Power," *Yale Law Journal*, Vol. 74, No. 1 (November 1964), pp. 36–76 at 61.

20. Samuels, "In Defense of a Positive Approach to Government as an Economic Variable," p. 457.

21. George P. Fletcher, "Fairness and Utility in Tort Theory," *Harvard Law Review*, Vol. 85, No. 3 (January 1972), pp. 537–573 at 550.

22. See Izhak Englard, "The System Builders: A Critical Appraisal of Modern Tort Theory," *Journal of Legal Studies*, Vol. 9, No. 1 (January 1980), pp. 27–70 at 30–33.

23. Cento G. Veljanovski, "The Economic Theory of Tort Liability-Toward a Correc-

tive Justice Approach," in Paul Burrows and Cento G. Veljanovski, Eds., *The Economic Approach to Law* (London: Butterworths, 1981), pp. 125–150 at 125.

24. Paul H. Rubin, "Predictability and the Economic Approach to Law: A Comment on Rizzo," *Journal of Legal Studies,* Vol. 9, No. 2 (March 1980), pp. 319–334, at 320.

25. Richard A. Posner "Economic Justice and the Economist," *The Public Interest,* Number 33 (Fall 1973), pp. 109–119 at 113.

26. Guido Calabresi and A. Douglas Melamed, "Property Rules, Liability Rules, and Inalienability: One View of the Cathedral," *Harvard Law Review,* Vol. 85, No. 6 (April 1972), pp. 1089–1128 at 1102.

27. Joseph M. Steiner, "Economics, Morality, and the Law of Torts," *University of Toronto Law Journal,* Vol. 26, No. 3 (Summer 1976), pp. 227–252 at 228, 238, and 239.

28. Richard A. Epstein, "A Theory of Strict Liability," *Journal of Legal Studies,* Vol. 2, No. 1 (January 1973), pp. 151–204 at 203.

29. Veljanovski, "The Economic Theory of Tort Liability-Toward a Corrective Justice Approach," pp. 125–126.

30. Fletcher, "Fairness and Utility in Tort Theory," pp. 537, 571, and 573. Paul Burrows suggests the following:

> The important point in the current context is that the expected failure of bargaining solutions has serious consequences for the results of the efficiency analysis that has been used as a basis for judging alternative legal rules. Yet the study of the law and pollution control has been haunted for twenty years by the ghost of market solutions, and most lawyer-economists engaged in this activity have persisted in searching for the elusive ghost.

Paul Burrows, "Nuisance, Legal Rules and Decentralized Decisions: A Different View of the Cathedral Crypt," in Burrows and Veljanovski, Eds., *The Economic Approach To Law,* pp. 151–166, at 153.

31. Fletcher, "Fairness and Utility in Tort Theory," p. 538.

32. Epstein, "A Theory of Strict Liability," pp. 151–152.

33. Calabresi and Melamed, "Property Rules, Liability Rules, and Inalienability," pp. 1097, 1098, 1102, and 1110.

34. Guido Calabresi and Jon T. Hirschoff, "Toward a Test for Strict Liability in Torts," *The Yale Law Journal,* Vol. 81, No. 6 (May 1972), pp. 1055–1085 at 1077.

35. Richard A. Posner, "Strict Liability: A Comment," *Journal of Legal Studies,* Vol. 2, No. 1 (January 1973), pp. 205–221 at 221.

36. Epstein, "A Theory of Strict Liability," p. 152. The reader should note that the words "that judgement" do not refer to the previous sentence. Through a conversation with Professor Epstein we learned that at the time he wrote it, his essential point was that once a theory of fairness had been completed and spelled out, it might not leave any room for economic considerations.

37. See England, "The System Builders: A Critical Appraisal of Modern Tort Theory," p. 27.

38. We are aware that this is ultimately an empirical question.

39. In fact governmental action (3) could result in a net cost to society, thus, shifting the BB line back down.

40. Ronald Coase, "The Problem of Social Cost," *Journal of Law and Economics,* Vol. 3 (October 1969), pp. 1–44 at 3.

41. Ibid., pp. 8–10.

42. John P. Brown, "Toward an Economic Theory of Liability," *Journal of Legal Studies,* Vol. 2, No. 2 (June 1973), pp. 323–349 at 324.

43. Ibid., p. 324

44. Ibid.

45. Epstein, "A Theory of Strict Liability," p. 167.

46. Fletcher, "Fairness and Utility in Tort Theory," p. 550.

47. Mario Rizzo, "Law Amid Flux: The Economics of Negligence and Strict Liability," *Journal of Legal Studies*, Vol. 9, No. 2 (March 1980), pp. 291–318 at 311.

48. Richard A. Posner, *Economic Analysis of Law*, 2nd ed., (Boston: Little, Brown and Company, 1977), p. 119.

49. A similar diagrammatic exposition is presented in John A. C. Conybeare, "International Organization and the Theory of Property Rights," *International Organization*, Vol. 34, No. 3 (Summer 1980), pp. 307–334 at 309–312.

50. These two cases are eluded to in Wener Z. Hirsch, *Law and Economics: An Introductory Analysis* (New York: Academic Press, 1979), p. 20 and Posner, *Economic Analysis of Law*, 2nd ed., p. 36.

51. Coase, "The Problem of Social Cost," p. 19.

52. As expressed by Richard A. Posner:

> A very important, although for a time neglected, feature of Coase's article was its implications for the positive analysis of legal doctrine. Coase suggested that the English law of nuisance had an implicit economic logic. Later writers have generalized this insight and argued that many of the doctrines and institutions of the legal system are best understood and explained as efforts to promote the efficient allocation of resources.

Posner, *Economic Analysis of Law*, 2nd ed., pp. 16–17.

53. Coase, "The Problem of Social Cost," pp. 27–28. Coase's reliance on the "reasonableness" standard inherent in the common law is implicit in his discussion of cases. Ibid., pp. 19–28. Posner characterized Coase's work in this area as follows:

> The article makes three other important points, which are sometimes overlooked relating to the case in which the costs of transferring the property right are so high that a voluntary transfer is not feasible. (a) Placing liability on the party who causes the damages (the railroad in our example) may not produce the efficient solution to the conflict. (The reader can verify this by referring to our first example and assuming that the farmer has the property right and, because of heavy transaction costs, cannot transfer it to the railroad.) (b) The common law of nuisance can be understood as an attempt to increase the value of resource use by assigning property rights to those parties to conflicting land uses in whose hands the rights are most valuable. (c) In deciding whether governmental intervention in the economic system is appropriate, it is never sufficient to demonstrate that the market would operate imperfectly without intervention; government also operates imperfectly, so what is essential is a comparison between the actual workings of the market and of government in the particular setting.

Posner, *Economic Analysis of Law*, 2nd ed., pp. 35–36.

54. Calabresi and Melamed, "Property Rules, Liability Rules and Inalienability," pp. 1089–1128.

55. They define inalienability rules as rules that protect *and* regulate the original granting of an inalienable entitlement, one that cannot be transferred. Inasmuch as the literature on protecting entitlements concentrates on property and liability rules we will not explore the inalienability rules any further.

56. For this breakdown of rules and entitlements, see Ibid., pp. 1115–1116 and also A. Mitchell Polinsky, "Resolving Nuisance Disputes: The Simple Economics of Injunctive and Damage Remedies," *Stanford Law Review,* Vol. 33, No. 6 (July 1980), pp. 1075–1112 at 1095–1112; Burrows, "Nuisance, Legal Rules, and Decentralized Decisions," pp. 154–155.

57. See Polinsky, "Resolving Nuisance Disputes," pp. 1076–1077 at footnote 7 and pp. 1111–1112.

58. The doctrine of excuses and the doctrine of justification are explored in Epstein, "A Theory of Strict Liability," pp. 151–204.

59. Ibid., p. 152.

60. Ibid., p. 153.

61. For example, blasting, crop dusting, fumigating, ownership of wild animals . . . etc. remained as pockets of strict liability. These are explored in Fletcher, "Fairness and Utility in Tort Theory," pp. 547–549 and Steven Shavell, "Strict Liability versus Negligence," *Journal of Legal Studies,* Vol. 9, No. 1 (January 1980), pp. 1–26 at 24.

62. Charles O. Gregory, "Trespass to Negligence to Absolute Liability," *Virginia Law Review,* Vol. 37, No. 3 (April 1951), pp. 359–397.

63. *Osborne v. Montgomery,* 234 N.W. 372 (1931) at 379–380.

64. See text at footnote 23 (this chapter).

65. Richard A. Posner, "A Theory of Negligence," *Journal of Legal Studies,* Vol. 1, No. 1 (January 1972), pp. 29–96 at 31 and 32.

66. See Posner, as quoted in text at footnote 35 (this chapter). See also text at footnote 7 (this chapter). For a general critique of the efficiency approach see Duncan Kennedy, "Cost-Reduction Theory as Legitimation," *The Yale Law Journal,* Vol. 90, No. 5 (April 1981), pp. 1275–1283.

67. Steiner, "Economics, Morality and the Law of Torts," p. 228.

68. Posner, "Strict Liability: A Comment," p. 221.

69. Epstein, "A Theory of Strict Liability," p. 152. (See clarification at footnote 36 above).

70. Posner, "A Theory of Negligence," p. 32.

71. *United States v. Carroll Towing Co., Inc.,* 159 F. 2d 169 (1947) at 173.

72. Calabresi and Melamed, "Property Rules, Liability Rules, and Inalienability," pp. 1096–1097.

73. Calabresi and Hirschoff, "Toward a Test for Strict Liability in Torts," p. 1060.

74. Ibid.

75. Calabresi and Melamed, "Property Rules, Liability Rules, and Inalienability," p. 1097.

76. Brown, "Toward an Economic Theory of Liability," pp. 323–349 and Shavell, "Strict Liability versus Negligence," pp. 1–25.

77. Fletcher, "Fairness and Utility in Tort Theory," p. 539.

78. Epstein, "A Theory of Strict Liability," p. 203.

79. During the time this book was being drafted, the U.S. Supreme Court reviewed two important taking issue cases. See literature cited at footnote 88 of this chapter.

80. The term land use is used here, in the very broad sense, to include all uses or opportunities related to assertions of rights with regard to air, water, and land. As to the reason for this uncertainty, Arvo Van Alstyne has stated: "The existing uncertainties can be traced to the propensity of courts to avoid the difficult task of articulating a substantive decision between the competing claims of private right and community order by relying on procedural rules." Arvo Van Alstyne, "Taking or Damaging by Police Power: The Search for Inverse Condemnation Criteria," *Southern California Law Review,* Vol. 44, No. 1 (1971), pp. 1–73 at 13.

81. Raleigh Barlowe, "Federal Programs for the Direction of Land Use," *Iowa Law*

Review, Vol. 50, No. 2 (Winter 1965), pp. 337–366. He reviews police power, eminent domain, taxing, proprietary, and spending powers as related to land use.

82. See Ross D. Netherton, "Implementation of Land Use Policy: Police Power vs. Eminent Domain," *Land and Water Law Review*, Vol. 3, No. 1 (1968), pp. 33–57 at 38–39. For references regarding eminent domain see J. A. C. Grant, "The 'Higher Law' Background of the Law of Eminent Domain," *Wisconsin Law Review*, Vol. 6, No. 2 (1931), pp. 67–85.

83. The requirement has been incorporated into the Fourteenth Amendment (the constitutional injunction against deprivation by the government without due process of law) and controls the states. Joseph L. Sax, "Takings, Private Property and Public Rights," *The Yale Law Journal*, Vol. 81, No. 2 (December 1971), pp. 149–186 at 149. Allison Dunham, "Griggs vs. Allegheny County in Perspective: Thirty Years of Supreme Court Expropriation Law," *The Supreme Court Review* (1962), pp. 63–106 at 85. John D. Johnston, Jr., and George W. Johnson, *Land Use Control*, Volume IIB, (New York: New York University School of Law, 1974), p. 1414. Note that some states added "or damaged" after the word "taken"; otherwise the wording of state constitutions is virtually identical to the quoted clause of the Fifth Amendment to the U.S. Constitution. North Carolina is the only state which has no such clause; the duty to pay just compensation has been inferred from the state's due process clause. For a listing of the taking provision of each state constitution see John F. Fulham and Stephen Scharf, "Inverse Condemnation: Its Availability in Challenging the Validity of a Zoning Ordinance," *Stanford Law Review*, Vol. 26, No. 6 (June 1974), pp. 1439–1453 at 1444 footnote 3.

84. It must be underscored at this point that the possibility arises that a government action that gives rise to consequential damages and thus raises the taking issue can be founded upon Constitutional powers other than eminent domain. However, to simplify matters and to focus the scope of this chapter, we will concentrate on consequential damages that arise due to eminent domain actions, and the police power, fully cognizant that other constitutional powers besides these two may result in claims for consequential damages.

85. These are essentially the facts in *Woodland Market Reality Co. v. City of Cleveland*, 426 F. 2d 955 (1970).

86. Sax, "Takings, Private Property and Public Rights," pp. 149–150. For a comprehensive review of cases concerning land use regulation and the taking issue see Fred Bosselman, David Calles, and John Banta, *The Taking Issue: An Analysis of the Constitutional Limits of Land Use Control*, prepared for the Council of Environmental Quality, (Washington, D.C.: U.S. Government Printing Office, 1973), pp. 1–329.

87. These two procedures are described in John J. Costonis, "'Fair' Compensation and the Accommodation Power: Antidotes for the Taking Impasse in Land Use Controversies," *Columbia Law Review*, Vol. 75, No. 6 (October 1975), pp. 1021–1082 at 1034–1037.

88. As to whether to allow litigants to seek inverse condemnation as a remedy for cases beyond those of physical invasion is presently the paramount concern of taking issue litigation. For synoptic reviews on this matter see Wendy U. Larsen and Charles L. Siemon, "A Not So Quiet Revolution," *Environmental Comment*, (August 1980), pp. 8–11, and Ross Sandler, "Overview-Law: Inverse Condemnation," *Environment*, Vol. 22, No. 4 (May 1980), pp. 2–3. See also J. H. Beuscher, "Some Tentative Notes on the Integration of Police Power and the Eminent Domain by the Courts: So-Called Inverse or Reverse Condemnation," *Urban Law Annual*, (1968), pp. 1–14. Fulham and Scharf, "Inverse Condemnation: Its Availability in Challenging the Validity of a Zoning Ordinance," pp. 1439–1453. See also Donald G. Hagman, "Temporary or Interim Damages Awards in Land Use Control

Cases," (Parts I and II), *Zoning and Planning Law Report*, Vol. 4, Nos. 6 and 7 (June and July-August 1981), pp. 129–136, 137–144.

89. For a review of this case see Bosselman, Calles, and Banta, *The Taking Issue*, pp. 124–138.

90. *Pennsylvania Coal Co. v. Mahon*, 260 U.S. 393 (1922) at 413, 415.

91. These and other decision rules are described in Lawrence Berger, "A Policy Analysis of the Taking Problem," *New York University Law Review*, Vol. 49, Nos. 2 and 3 (May–June 1974), pp. 165–226 at 166–195; Frank Michelman, "Property, Utility, and Fairness: Comments on the Ethical Foundations of 'Just Compensation' Law," *Harvard Law Review*, Vol. 80, No. 6 (April 1967), pp. 1165–1258 at 1183–1201; Sax, "Takings and the Police Power," pp. 46–60; Arvo Van Alstyne, "Modernizing Inverse Condemnation: A Legislative Prospectus," *Santa Clara Lawyer*, Vol. 8, No. 1 (Fall 1967), pp. 1–36 at 13–25; Council on Environmental Quality, *Environmental Quality, 4th Annual Report*, (Washington, D.C.: U.S. Government Printing Office, 1973), pp. 121–153.

92. For citations to these and many other similar characterizations see Samuels and Mercuro, "The Role and Resolution to the Compensation Principle in Society," pp. 181–182 at footnotes 4 and 5.

93. See *Woodland Market Realty Company v. City of Cleveland*, 426 F.2d 955 (1970), U.S. Court of Appeals, Sixth Circuit.

94. See *Wilson v. City of Fargo*, 141 NW.2d 727 (1966), Supreme Court of North Dakota.

95. See *Moton v. City of Phoenix*, 410 P.2d 93 (1966), Supreme Court of Arizona.

96. See *Peacock v. County of Sacramento*, 77 Cal. Rptr. 391 (1969), California Court of Appeals.

97. See *Just v. Marinette County*, 201 NW.2d 761 (1972), Supreme Court of Wisconsin.

98. See *Morris County Land Improvement Co. v. Township of Parsippany-Troy Hills, N.J.* 193 A.2d 232 (1963), Supreme Court of New Jersey.

99. See text *circa* footnotes 37, 38, and 39. In addition, see Coase, "The Problem of Social Cost," pp. 18–19, 28 and Calabresi and Melamed, "Property Rules, Liability Rules, and Inalienability," p. 1097 where "collective fiat" is considered.

100. Robert H. Nelson, *Zoning and Property Rights* (Cambridge, Mass.: The MIT Press, 1977), pp. 7–21.

101. Netherton, "Implementation of Land Use Policy: Police Power vs. Eminent Domain," pp. 36–37.

102. It should be noted the compensation principle has survived in economics through its embodiment in conventional cost-benefit analysis. For an excellent critique see Duncan Kennedy, "Cost-Benefit Analysis of Entitlement Problems: A Critique," *Stanford Law Review*, Vol. 33, No. 3 (February 1981), pp. 387–445. From an efficiency point of view, few would argue that if the benefit cost ratio were less than one the regulation should go forward.

103. Robert C. Ellickson, "Alternatives to Zoning Covenants, Nuisance Rules, and Fines, as Land Use Control," *University of Chicago Law Review*, Vol. 40, No. 4 (Summer 1973), pp. 681–781 at 690 and 699. Bernard Siegan, *Land Use Without Zoning* (Lexington, Massachusetts: Lexington Books, 1972). For a similar interpretation of this literature see Costonis, "Fair Compensation and the Accommodation Power: Antidotes for the Taking Impasse in Land Use Controversies," pp. 1024–1033; and Nelson, *Zoning and Property Rights*, pp. 211–212.

104. This perception of law and the treatment of legal change runs parallel to the perception of some of those who advocate the use of the compensation principle with compensation as outlined in Section A of this chapter.

105. Nicholas Mercuro and Timothy Ryan, "The Role of Nonattenuated Rights in Positive Economics: A Critical Appraisal," *Journal of Economic Issues,* Vol. 13, No. 4 (December 1979), pp. 1007–1018.

106. The strongest endorsement of this position is presented by Bosselman, Calles, and Banta, *The Taking Issue.*

Chapter V

Economics and the Law

Ever since humanity recognized the need for social order, it has struggled with how to regulate the interaction of individuals. Central to that search has been the question, What is law? For it is law—whether written or unwritten, enforceable in a court or through less formal means—that regulates the interaction of those living in organized society. The laws each society create reflect the values that bind it together and represent that society's own compromise between ideals and the realities of human nature. Thus, the answer a society gives to that question provides a revealing portrait of itself. Our times are no different, and the variety of answers we have as yet proposed present incomplete and contradictory pictures of our self-image.[1]

The purpose of this chapter is to review the main components of the economic analysis of law, regulation, and non-market behavior as embodied in the new law and economics and public choice theory. By "Law" we are referring to the laws pertaining to the areas of property, contract, and tort law as well as the legal and political processes themselves. Our intent is not only to describe this literature but also to set forth its underlying ideological content.

A. THE NEW LAW AND ECONOMICS

The new law and economics (or as it is sometimes referred to, "the economic analysis of law") uses the standard theoretical tools of economic theory and empirical analysis to investigate the efficiency of the legal system in general and the common law in particular.[2] The scope of the law now covered in the new law and economics is vast. Much attention and emphasis has gone into analyzing the common law, specifically: (1) property law—the rules governing the acquisition of unowned things which determine the original property holdings of individuals, including rights over one's own body; (2) contract law—the rules governing the cooperative efforts among producers and consumers in the exchange of things that are already owned; and (3) the law of torts—the liability rules which protect persons and property from the aggression of third parties.[3] In addition, it focuses on criminal law and procedure and administrative law and procedure as well as other areas. This section will explore the literature pertaining to the efficiency analysis of the common law inasmuch as it is an important component of the new law and economics.

In the last few years, different definitions of efficiency have been employed in the efficiency of the common law literature. Jules L. Coleman has identified several notions of efficiency as follows:

> Economists as well as proponents of the economic analysis of law employ at least four efficiency-related notions, including: (1) productive efficiency, (2) Pareto optimality, (3) Pareto superiority, and (4) Kaldor-Hicks efficiency. If it constitutes a suitable efficiency criterion, Posner's wealth maximization would increase the total to at least five.[4]

Lewis A. Kornhauser not only recognizes the existence of multiple definitions but also points out that the analysis of the efficiency of the common law often shifts between these various definitions.

> The precise nature of the claim of either class depends on the definition given efficiency, on the particular list of rules considered feasible, and on those aspects of the world considered fixed or invariable in the model. A descriptive claim of efficiency may, therefore, rest upon any of at least six different definitions of efficiency and untold number of lists of possible rules. Arguments over the efficiency of a doctrine may shift between the various descriptive claims.[5]

Much of the new law and economics portends to be objective, neutral, and apolitical. That is, it views itself as drawing upon the prestige of the science of economics in an effort to create a system of legal thought based on a positive, efficiency analysis of the common law. Richard A. Posner has described the importance of utilizing this positive economic approach that purports to provide a deeper understanding of the common law. He states:

> Even in a quite extreme form—a prediction that *all* common law doctrines will eventually be shown to be based on efficiency considerations—the positive economic theory has the cardinal virtue of being the only positive theory of the common law that is in contention at this time.... That is not to say that any version of the efficiency theory must be accepted merely because there are no competing theories. If the theory had very little empirical support, one could take the position that there is no positive theory of the common law worth paying attention to. But despite our

inability to explain in an entirely convincing way why the common law should be efficient, and the incomplete and equivocal character of the data that support the theory, at least one can say that the theory deserves to be taken seriously, especially in its more moderate form of a claim that efficiency has been the predominant, not sole, factor in shaping the common-law system.[6]

1. Efficiency and the Common Law

Within the economic analysis of common law, two distinct but related trends are evident. One trend takes the structure of the legal institutions as given and studies the manner in which the conflicting parties in a legal dispute respond to the constraints that the system places on their behavior. Given the decision criteria established by the common law, prior to formal adjudication, the individuals are placed in a bargaining situation akin to the "gains-from-trade" paradigm of economics. The literature within this trend analyzes the behavior and decisions of the disputants as whether to voluntarily settle the dispute out of court or to have the matter litigated in court.

A second trend of the economic analysis of law explores the hypothesis that the procedural rules and practices that give the legal system its distinctive structure produce a system of common or judge-made law that tends toward efficiency. One aspect of this trend of analysis is the claim that the institutions of the common law have been designed to promote efficiency by fostering market transactions through contract. A second aspect of this trend concerns situations where transactions costs are so high as to preclude a private contract solution. Here the belief is that the common or judge-made law—in contrast to legislative or constitutional law—will result in outcomes that will bring about an allocation of resources that simulates that which the free market would have brought about had it been operable.[7] Both trends will be briefly explored.

The literature in the first trend uses expected utility maximization to provide theoretical insight to the issue of settlement prior to trial versus formal adjudication. This problem has been studied from the points of view of the plaintiff and the defendant in a civil case, or the defendant and the prosecutor where the prosecutor is litigating a criminal, labor, or antitrust case, or perhaps, representing an administrative agency. Typically, an economic model is employed to analyze the decision that must be made by the two parties in a potential litigation as to whether a case should be settled out of court or adjudicated. Given the resource constraints of both parties and their individual views on the probability of a conviction, both plaintiff (prosecutor) and defendant choose to settle or go to trial on the basis of which action gives them the higher expected utility.

To understand this process, for example in a civil case, let the expected judgment be $100,000 and assume that both parties agree on its size; let the probability that the plaintiff will be awarded the judgment be .40; let the defendant's trial cost be $10,000; and let the plaintiff's trial costs be $20,000. If this is the case, then the plaintiff's expected net gain from going to trial is $20,000 ($40,000 in expected gains minus $20,000 in trial costs) and the defendant's expected costs are $50,000 ($40,000 in payment plus $10,000 in trial costs). Since the plaintiff's expected net gain is $20,000 and the defendent's expected net cost is $50,000, then there is $30,000 range within which settlement can occur. That is, the plaintiff will settle for some amount over $20,000 while the defendent will settle for some amount less than $50,000.[8]

Alternatively, in a criminal case, utility of the prosecutor is defined as the expected number of convictions, weighted positively by the severity of the sentence. In a criminal case, the defendant would choose to settle, rather than go to trial, if the expected utility from settlement is higher than his expected utility from trial. The prosecutor would do the same if settlement, as opposed to going to trial, maximizes his expected utility. Thus, as in a civil case, if there is an expected gain for both parties from settlement, then a range exists within which a settlement may be secured.[9]

Additional considerations have been incorporated into the trial settlement models. Each subsequent extension of the model attempts to better describe the trial settlement patterns observed in law. Some of the factors that have been introduced into the model include: differential bargaining costs confronting the respective disputants, differences in the litigants' attitudes toward risk associated with the legal outcome, and the differential estimates by the litigants of the probabilities of winning a case. In addition, some of the models have attempted to describe the trial settlement pattern by analyzing the types of cases (large vs. small as measured by the monetary stakes involved) an administrative enforcement agency pursues. Finally, the various methods by which the legal costs of going to trial are allocated between the litigants has been analyzed in an attempt to explain the trial settlement pattern under each method.[10]

As to the second and related trend of the economic analysis of law which argues that the common law tends toward efficiency, three underlying explanations have been offered. These include: (1) inefficient rules are litigated more often than efficient rules and, as a consequence, the former will be overturned thereby increasing the stock of efficient rules over time; (2) litigants who benefit from an efficient rule invest more in the litigation, in an attempt to persuade the court, than those who favor an inefficient rule; and (3) judges actively seek or apply criteria which promote efficient outcomes. (A discussion of the judges purported pursuit of efficiency will be taken up in Section 2 of this chapter).

The first two explanations taken together with the logic of trial-settlement models underlie what has come to be known as "the economic theory of the evolution of common law." The evolutionary theory of common law has been articulated by Paul H. Rubin and George L. Priest. Rubin has described it as follows:

> The presumed efficiency of the common law and the decision to use the courts to settle a dispute are related. In particular, this relationship will occur because resorting to court settlement is more likely in cases where the legal rules relevant to the dispute are inefficient, and less likely where the rules are efficient. Thus, efficient rules may evolve from in-court settlement, thereby reducing the incentive for future litigation and increasing the probability that efficient rules will persist. In short, the efficient rule situation noted by Posner is due to an evolutionary mechanism whose direction proceeds from the utility maximizing decisions of disputants rather than from the wisdom of judges.[11]

He continues:

> If rules are inefficient, parties will use the courts until the rules are changed; conversely, if rules are efficient, the courts will not be used and the efficient rule will remain in force. An outside observer coming upon this legal rule would observe that the rule is efficient; but this efficiency occurs because of an evolutionary process, not because of any particular wisdom on the part of judges. If judges decide independently of efficiency we would still find efficient rules. Intelligent judges may speed up the process of attaining efficiency; they do not drive the process.[12]

Unlike Rubin and Priest, John C. Goodman attempts to make specific the reason why inefficient rules will be overturned.[13] Goodman assumes: (1) judges are amenable to persuasion by the litigants appearing before the court, (2) judges are completely unbiased with respect to efficiency, and (3) any increase in legal expense by either party will increase the degree of persuasion and thereby increase the probability of that party winning a favorable decision. Since the economic stakes are higher under inefficient rules, the party that initially has the liability has a greater incentive to spend a larger amount for litigation expenses than under efficient rules. The additional expenditurers in such litigation will increase the probability that the inefficient rule will be replaced by an efficient one. Goodman has described the system as follows:

> The explanation [for the development of common law] requires no particular assumption about litigation rates (litigation may occur randomly) and no particular assumption about the motivation of judges (judges may be initially neutral with regard to the issue of economic efficiency). We do assume, however, that judges are amenable to persuasion by the efforts of the litigants appearing before the court. A model of an adversary proceeding is proposed in which the probability that a particular litigant will win a favorable decision depends upon the efforts of both

litigants to influence the court and upon the weight of judicial bias. Since parties before the court have an obvious interest in the decision, they have incentives, not necessarily equal, to affect that decision through efforts that incur legal costs—expenses for legal research, factual investigation, forensic talent, and so forth. The fundamental assumption made throughout is that any increment in legal expenses c will induce an increment, however small, in the probability π of winning a favorable decision. . . . Even if the weight of past precedent favors inefficient solutions, the side with the greater economic stake in the issue will still have a higher probability of winning any succeeding case so long as the ratio of his economic stake to his opponent's exceeds the value of λ. . . . λ indicates the ratio of legal expenses by the two litigants that must be maintained in order to insure that they both have the same probability of winning. If $\lambda = 1$, the court will be said to be unbiased.[14]

In addition to these two prominent lines of thought on the evolutionary theory of common law, others have extended the analysis in several directions. Some of the literature focused on specific costs such as enforcement costs, direct costs, and error costs.[15] Other contributors analyzed the degree of precision of the rules of civil, criminal and administrative law as related to efficiency as well as the efficient number of statutory rules as opposed to judge-made rules.[16] Finally, legal precedents are analyzed where the body of legal precedents created by judicial decisions in prior periods is treated as capital stock that yields a flow of information services which depreciates over time as new conditions arise that were not foreseen by the framers of the existing precedents.[17]

Throughout much of this literature there exists a bias reflecting a preference for an expanded use of common law to shape the character of economic life. That is, the new law and economics' literature exhibits a strong predilection for the common law and antipathy for statute law. This has been observed by Frank I. Michelman who stated:

There is a categorical opposition, deep-rooted in our legal culture, between enacted ('positive') and common (judge-made) law. In this opposition it is common law that is usually perceived as the organic carrier of elemental, popular morality, the morality that goes without saying, whereas enacted law is taken to reflect specific dictates of deliberate policy or of particularistic formations of power. . . . It is preeminently the common law, the judge-made law, for which investigators claim to have documented an economic 'implicit logic' or 'basic character' which might in some way reflect an organic or consensual popular will. Far from expecting any economizing tendency in statute-based law, the theory offers reasons for *not* expecting any. . . . There is a realistic economic theory of legislator behavior paralleling that for judicial behavior but leading to the contrasting conclusion that there is no reason to expect pieces of legislation to be wealth maximizing. Legislators and judges are equally assumed (along with everyone else) to act as rational maximizers of their respective private ends; but the institutional environments conditioning the self-serving strategies for legislators are sharply distinguished from those for judges.[18]

In addition, throughout much of the literature assessing the efficiency of the common law there is a continuing tendency to shift from positive analysis to the normative advocacy of efficiency. Mark Tushnet states:

The most prominent school of post-realist positive analysis is associated with Chicago-style microeconomics and law. Actually, a substantial degree of ambivalence affects this school. Most of its adherents are standard American political conservatives, and are therefore at least deeply skeptical of, and more frequently very hostile to, governmental intervention in what they define as private affairs. These political attitudes support, and are supported by, a nearly exclusive focus on allocative efficiency as their subject of inquiry. Then, when faced with rules that depart from what their analysis shows would promote allocative efficiency, these scholars find it hard to resist the temptation to urge that the rules be altered.[19]

One of the leading advocates of the use of common law and the use of efficiency to describe its development is Richard A. Posner.[20] In 1977, in the second edition to his book entitled *Economic Analysis of Law,* Posner set forth the concept of "wealth maximization." He suggested that wealth maximization can be used to adequately describe the development of the common law and that it is an ethically attractive principle upon which to normatively base a theory of law.[21] It is to a discussion of wealth maximization that we now turn.

2. *Wealth Maximization*

Inasmuch as Posner's decision criterion of wealth maximization has been given much attention in the literature we will briefly explore it here. Posner normatively argues that the principle of wealth maximization can be used as a hypothesis in the positive, descriptive economic analysis of the common law. This is, of course, a perfectly legitimate procedure in positive analysis. That is, a normative choice may be involved in deciding on the hypothesis to be tested. Posner, for example, has chosen "wealth maximization;" someone else might choose "power;" and still others might choose "wealth equalization" as a hypothesis to explain the pattern of common law development. Notwithstanding the normative choice involved in formulating the hypothesis, the realm of a positive economic theory of law is to empirically test each and every hypothesis and see which hypotheses are supported and which are refuted by testing.

The process associated with the wealth maximization hypothesis can be briefly outlined to include the following: (1) the economic analyst treats the adopting of decision rules governing common law as a series of discrete judicial choices; (2) a decision rule (either one that prevails or is being proffered) is selected for analysis and is conceptually marked off from the remaining law; (3) it is assumed the remaining background law (i.e., the residual legal rules which in part determine the distribution of income) is held constant; (4) the decision rule is appraised by comparing it with one or more alternatives (those historically used or perhaps proposed); and (5) a decision rule is said to be efficient insofar as its anticipated resource allocation represents greatest total wealth as measured by total (estimated) willingness to pay.[22]

Thus wealth maximization is proffered by Posner as an attractive criterion by which the merits of various common law rules or entitlements can be compared. It can also be used to normatively choose one rule or entitlement over another. Recall, as explained in Chapter II, efficiency, regardless of the definition employed, is not decisive. That is, as a decision rule, efficiency is not able to unambiguously rank all states of the economy that result from different common law rules and entitlements. This is, of course, due to the fact that efficiency fails (and was never intended) to make distributional comparisons. In contrast, the criterion of wealth maximization, as articulated by Posner, seems to provide common law adjudication with a decision rule which unambiguously provides us with a way of comparing the outcomes associated with various common law rules and entitlements and a basis for selecting one as "best." How, why and whether wealth maximization is an unambiguous standard is the subject to which we now turn.

Posner offers wealth maximization as a preferred rule in part because of his dissatisfaction with efficiency (i.e., Pareto superiority) and the utilitarian imperative underlying the Pareto criterion.[23] He is in fact searching for a firmer basis for a normative theory of law (firmer than the standards of efficiency supply) in an attempt to establish the normative underpinnings of what he calls the positive economic analysis of law.[24]

As a deliberate attempt to avoid the use of the Pareto criterion and Benthamite utilitarianism, Posner adopts the more narrow maximand of "value" or what he calls "wealth." He defines it as follows:

> Wealth is the value in dollars or dollar equivalents . . . of everything in society. It is measured by what people are willing to pay for something or, if they already own it, what they demand in money to give it up. The only kind of preference that counts in a system of wealth maximization is thus one that is backed up by money—in other words, that is registered in a market.[25]

Elaborating on wealth maximization he states:

> It is consistent . . . with a desire, rooted in the principles of autonomy and consent, to minimize coercion. The system of wealth maximization . . . could be viewed as one of constrained utilitarianism. The constraint, which is not ad hoc but is supplied by the principle of consent, is that people may seek to promote their utility only through the market or institutions modeled on the market. As I have been at pains to stress, transactions that are consensual between the immediate parties may be coercive as to third parties. . . . The amount of coercion in a system of wealth maximization is easily exaggerated; where it is wealth maximizing to deny compensation ex post, ex ante the potentially affected parties may prefer that such compensation be denied.[26]

Posner employs the principles of autonomy and consent to provide the philosophical underpinnings of the concept of wealth maximization. That is, starting with the basic belief that systems that promote the exercise of liberty and autonomy are to be preferred to those that limit liberty and autonomy (a position which he ascribes to be broadly Kantian), Posner then suggests that the principle of consent is the ethically attractive basis for utilizing wealth maximization as a decision rule in common law adjudication.[27] The notion of consent employed by Posner is that of ex ante compensation. Posner equates the notions of ex ante compensation and consent by pointing out that individuals would consent to wealth maximization as a criterion for establishing common law rules for adjudication provided that there is a sufficient probability that the individuals will benefit in the long run from such rules, though they may be losers in the application of a particular rule.[28] In effect, this constitutes the Kaldor-Hicks criterion (i.e., potential Pareto superiority) which, unlike the Pareto superiority criterion that allows no one to be made worse off. Posner requires only that the increase in value be sufficiently large so that the losers could be fully compensated.[29]

It is not necessary to compensate, ex post, those who bear loses as a result of decisions of any wealth-maximizing legal institution.[30] Ex post compensation is uncalled for because, under wealth-maximizing legal institutions, individuals have garnered ex ante compensation. Posner's belief in the existence of this ex ante compensation rests on the hypothesis that wealth maximizing legal institutions are less costly than all others. Under institutions so structured, individuals who bear loses would neither expect nor have awarded to them ex post compensation since they have already received compensation in the form of these lower costs.[31]

a. Wealth Maximization and the Lack of a Theory of the Judiciary.

Much of the criticism leveled at Posner's concept of wealth maximization can be traced back to the fact that judicial behavior, as yet, is not well understood and, as such, is not yet amenable to the economic analysis of the common law, positive or normative.

Within the current literature it is clear that an explicit, plausible, causal explanation of the behavior of judges has not yet been established. That is, the linkage between (a) the behavior of individual participants in the legal-economic arena and (b) the incentives and thus the behavior and decisions of judges is not well developed. At one point in time Posner thought that perhaps an "implicit" theory would suffice and that an "explicit" theory as to the aspiration of judges was not even necessary.[32] He states:

An . . . important finding emerging from the recent law and economics research is that the legal system itself—its doctrines, procedures, and institutions—has been strongly influenced by a concern (*more often implicit than explicit*) with promoting economic efficiency.[33] (emphasis added)

Elsewhere he states:

The recent work on the sources of the efficiency bias in common law adjudication suggests that one need *not* posit a preference for efficiency on the part of the judges to explain how the common-law system *might* generate efficient rules. . . .

Among . . . objections to the efficiency theory of the common law that have been advanced are, first, the prevalence of noneconomic rhetoric in judicial decisions, and, second, the poor quality of much of the evidence—statistical data of the sort usually used to verify social scientific theories appear to be largely lacking with regard to the efficiency properties of common-law rules. The point about rhetoric ignores the fact that the major economizing doctrines of the common law preceded the development of an explicit economic thoery of law that might have made the specialized rhetoric of economics available for use in judicial decisions. Just as people were maximizing utility before the terms were invented by economists, judges *may* have been maximizing efficiency before the language of economics gained currency in judicial opinions (indeed, it still has not).[34] (emphasis added)

However, more recently Posner has seemingly indicated a need to establish formally a causal theory of judicial behavior. He states:

If we understood the incentives of judges—*if* we had a theory of judicial behavior— it might help us to understand how rules of law are made and changed and in turn would illuminate the question with which we began of whether law changes in response to changes in economic conditions. *The economic literature . . . which has sought to explain how the common law might come to consist largely of rules designed to promote efficiency, has tended to elide the issue of judicial incentives, preferences, behavior,* etc. by treating the judge as an essentially passive spectator of the combat between the litigants. There is no objection in principle to such an assumption. But *the literature erected on it cannot claim such great explanatory power* as to make uninteresting an attempt to develop a theory of the judicial process in which the behavior of judges is assumed to be an important factor in judicial rules and outcomes.[35] (emphasis added)

As a result of the lack of consistency evidenced in the above quotes, a tension surrounds the concept of wealth maximization as it is employed by Posner in the positive economic analysis of the common law. This is clearly revealed throughout the critical literature cited earlier.[36] As to the need for an explicit explanation of the behavior of judges as opposed to implicit assertions about their behavior, we join Michelman who stated:

In science, there may be some purely empirical hypotheses to which the data conform so clearly, so strikingly, so uniformly, that we are persuaded of their truth (in the pragmatic sense) although we haven't a clue to any causal mechanism that may be producing the phenomena we observe. In other instances the conformity of data to an empirical hypothesis, while detectible, is also irregular enough, the available measurements are lax enough, the general picture is murky enough, that a plausible causal explanation is required to make us believe in the theory. For me, the positive economic theory of the common law is definitely in the latter class.[37]

The lack of an explicit causal theory of judicial behavior has led critics, focusing on the implicit approach, to demonstrate that there is a fundamental flaw in Posner's logic which leads him to conclude that the common law is best explained as an effort to maximize wealth. The major thrust of this criticism is that mere observance of an efficient outcome does not necessarily mean that wealth maximization was employed in judicial decision making. This criticism can be rearticulated through the use of the following simple diagrams.

An efficient outcome is conditioned upon a set of givens, for example, demand, technology, among other things. Further, as depicted in Figure V.1, an efficient outcome (EO) is also conditioned upon the background law (L), which is comprised of the prevailing structure of property rights and working rules. L is partly a function of the decision rules (DR) employed by judges in common law adjudication. These rules may be chosen by a judge in a particular case because of their use in past decisions (after surveying rules employed in earlier similar cases) or the judge's belief that an entirely new rule (proffered by either legal scholars or the attorneys for a litigant) is preferable.

Figure V.1.

When some decision rule (e.g., DR_1) is chosen, it then serves to fashion the background law (L_1) which in turn conditions the efficient outcome (EO_1), see Figure V.2.[38] Some critics have argued, however, that any chosen decision rule, for example, DR_1, DR_2, DR_3, or DR_4, will create a structure of background law, L_1, L_2, L_3, and L_4, respectively and, in retrospect, will produce an efficient outcome, EO_1, EO_2, EO_3, and EO_4, respectively, see Figure V.3.

Figure V.2.

C. Edwin Baker has made this point clear:

An adequate positivist theory must have some predictive capacity. Posner tries to exhibit his economic theory's predictive power by looking at the historical development of common law principles and showing that they are, as the positivist economic theory would predict, 'efficient.' The problem is that one observes this efficiency from the perspective of the present in which the rules at issue have partly defined the 'given.' . . . From the judge's perspective, the efficiency or wealth-maximizing criterion is indeterminate—any of several proposed rules may create givens from which the chosen rule would then appear efficient. In fact, the normal, predictable effect of the choice of a particular rule is to create a distribution and generate preferences that increase the likelihood that the chosen rule will be efficient. Thus, the present efficiency of the rule does not show that the judge could have used efficiency criteria to choose the rule. To the extent that either choice will in retrospect appear efficient, the economic theory does not have explanatory power; thus, it is not even in contention as a positivist theory of the common law.[39]

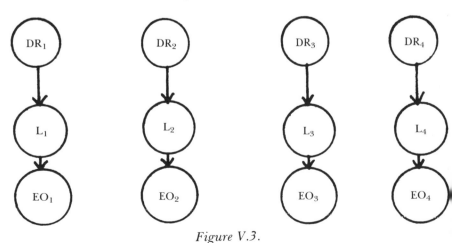

Figure V.3.

Hence, we can see the inherent flaw contained in Posner's implicit use of the wealth maximization hypothesis. Suppose an issue in property law arises where typically the dispute is over to whom property holdings initially will be assigned. For example, consider two doctrines governing the distribution of property in divorce cases. One doctrine, termed the "source doctrine," distributes property on the basis of which party had, in fact, acquired the property. The second doctrine, termed the "equitable distribution of property," distributes property on the basis of a variety of equity criteria, independent of the source.[40] Once property rights are assigned by the application of either doctrine, regardless of which doctrine is chosen, the parties will then engage in utility maximizing behavior from which an efficient outcome will emerge.

Thus, if in the course of the litigation the judge adopts decision rule DR_3 (e.g., the equitable distribution of property doctrine) to resolve the property dispute instead of DR_1 (e.g., the source doctrine) then we observe, along with Posner, efficient outcome EO_3. However, Posner then proceeds to claim that having observed an efficient outcome, the judge must have implicitly or unwittingly employed the notion of wealth maximization to adopt the decision rule. But, had the judge instead adopted decision rule DR_1, yielding efficient outcome EO_1, then Posner could have arrived at the same conclusion on having observed an efficient outcome, and so for any decision rule. The inherent problem is that there is no explicit theory of judicial behavior incorporated into the analysis to explain the choice of one rule over the other.[41] Posner's (and indeed society's) observation of an efficient outcome is not sufficient to conclude that the judge employed wealth maximization in choosing the decision rule to resolve a legal case. Any decision rule would generate a set of givens that would condition an efficient outcome. But the judge could have employed any criteria, perhaps one based on justice, or equity, or fairness, to choose the decision rule. To argue that the judge employed wealth maximization, because efficiency is observed, is without foundation.

b. The Shift from a Positive to a Normative Theory of Law.
If Posner were to argue, as indeed he appears to, that his wealth maximization standard will implicitly lead the judge to adopt DR_3 because EO_3 is superior (i.e., wealth maximizing) vis-à-vis EO_1, EO_2 and EO_4, then he opens the door to a variety of criticisms which point out the various normative intrusions and the ambiguities inherent in the concept of wealth maximization.[42] Returning to the property law dispute example, Posner suggests that the wealth maximization standard, implicitly employed by judges in common law, will provide an unambiguous answer (for example, a clear choice between the equitable distribution of property doctrine and the source doctrine or some other rule) as to which

decision rule the judge will, or perhaps *should,* adopt. It is here that the subtle shift from the positive to the normative analysis is observed. Now, Posner proffers wealth maximization as the standard by which judges can choose among the disputed initial assignment of rights in property law disputes. That the wealth maximization principle is claimed to have such scope is evidenced by his following statements:

> The principle itself ordains the creation of a system of exclusive rights, one that, ideally, will extend to all valued things that are scarce, not only real and personal property but the human body and even ideas. . . .

> Nor does the economist merely decree that exclusive rights be created and then fall silent as to where they should be vested. . . . If transaction costs are positive, the wealth-maximization principle requires the initial vesting of rights in those who are likely to value them the most.[43]

The issue now shifts from the hypothesis that wealth maximization explains the pattern of common law development to the proposition that the pursuit of efficiency by judges via wealth maximization is preferable to other criteria, say perhaps justice. Posner clearly thinks this to be the case:

> I believe . . . that the economic norm I shall call 'wealth maximization' provides a firmer basis for a normative theory of law than does utilitarianism. . . . The economist can provide conclusive normative directions to anyone for whom efficiency, or the particular concept of efficiency that the particular economist is advancing, happens to be the ruling value. While nowadays relatively few of the people in our society who think about these things consider wealth maximization or some other version of efficiency the paramount social value, few judge it a trivial one. . . . It seems to me that economic analysis has some claim to being regarded as a coherent and attractive basis for ethical judgments.[44]

3. Criticisms of Wealth Maximization

Posner's recommendation that judges adopt decision rules based on the wealth maximization standard has drawn various criticisms. Some of the critics have tried to uncover what, if any, additional normative premises underlie the use of wealth maximization while others have described the ambiguities and indeterminacies inherent in the concept of wealth maximization. Some of these criticisms will be reviewed briefly here.

a. Wealth Maximization as an Instrumental Value. When one is making recommendations as to standards judges should follow, one is really doing more. That is, the recommendation ultimately reaches to the entire judicial process and thus has implications for the character of economic life. In light of its potential consequences, wealth maximization as a value to be pursued by the judiciary must be clearly articulated and fully understood. As will be seen, this is not the case. There are various ways to conceive the concept of wealth maximization, all of which treat it as a value in the instrumental sense, i.e., instrumental in the corresponding pursuit of other values society adheres to. No one asserts that wealth is the only value in a society. Indeed Posner himself has stated that the judiciary's pursuit of wealth will instrumentally aid society to achieve other values:

> A society which aims at maximizing wealth, unlike a society which aims at maximizing utility (happiness), will produce an ethically attractive combination of happiness, of rights (to liberty and property), and of sharing with the less fortunate members of society.[45]

There are at least three ways of interpreting this instrumentalist pursuit of wealth maximization.[46] One way is to think of the achievement of wealth as the *cause* of achieving other values; such as, justice (J), fairness (F), happiness (H), equality (E), etc.

$$\uparrow W \text{ causes } \rightarrow \ \uparrow J, \ \uparrow F, \ \uparrow H, \ \uparrow E$$

Another way of conceiving of the instrumentalist claim is to think of wealth as an *ingredient* of other values; for example, the achievement of wealth can directly provide the resources necessary to enhance other values. A final perspective on the pursuit of wealth takes the position that it is a *surrogate target*. The idea suggests that there is a sufficiently high correlation between wealth and other values so as to legitimize the pursuit of wealth.

Whether Posner would embrace any of these instrumentalist conceptions of wealth maximization is unclear. In fact, notwithstanding his above quotation that appears instrumentalist in nature, Posner has also stated the judges have a general desire to "impose their preferences, tastes, values, etc. on society."[47] Why or whether judges would *necessarily* include wealth among their preferences and values remains unanswered. If Posner were to embrace any of the instrumentalist views of wealth maximization as formulated above, many questions remain. Three come to mind. First, are all of the increases in wealth directly (as opposed to inversely) related to changes in other values? For example, what is the basis for claiming that an increase in wealth (W) will correspondingly cause an increase in equality (E)? Furthermore, if, in fact, an increase in wealth (W) does cause an increase in happiness (H), one might ask whether all movements in other values (J, F, and E) also relate directly to increases in happiness (H). Before adopting the wealth maximization criterion one would have to establish unambiguously that all values (J, F, H and E) are all directly related to each other. Finally, if a society values J, F, H, and E along with W, in what sense is society any better off by having a judiciary pursue W as opposed to say, E, or some mixture of all?[48]

It would seem that before the modus operandi of the entire judiciary is altered to conform to the wealth maximization principle, these and other questions must be addressed and the basis of recommendations such as Posner's must be clearly articulated. Vague assertions cannot suffice.

b. ***Conflicts Between Gains in Wealth and Gains in Efficiency.*** The judiciary's reliance on the wealth maximization principle may lead to an inefficient allocation and an undesirable distribution of goods and resources. That is, allocative inefficiency and productive inefficiency may result from the use of wealth maximization. Ronald Dworkin has demonstrated the former inefficiency by the use of the following example. Two individuals, one poor and sick, the other rich and content, both desire to possess a book that is initially owned by the poor individual. The poor man must sell the book in order to buy medicine, though it is one of his few comforts, he is willing to sell it for $2 since he is desperate. The rich man is willing to buy it for $3, an insignificant portion of his wealth, on the off chance that he may read it someday. The wealth maximizing rule would call for the transfer of the book from the poor to the rich man with no compensation paid to the poor man. While wealth maximizing, the decision may well lead to a reduction in utility.[49] With respect to productive inefficiency, Lewis A. Kornhauser points out that monopoly production, by definition inefficient, may in fact lead to higher wealth, in a partial equilibrium setting, than in a competitive industry.[50] Given the possibility that judicial decisions that pursue wealth may result in allocative or productive inefficiencies, then in what sense can it be said that society is better off? This crucial question remains unanswered.

c. ***The Problem of Circularity: Rights and Prices.*** The normative application of the principle of wealth maximization attempts to deduce a structure of rights when in fact the structure of rights is needed to make such a deduction. This circularity has been observed by Cento G. Veljanovski:

> Rights must be assigned before trading can take place and the way they are assigned will determine the set of outcomes that are Pareto efficient [wealth maximizing]. Rights must be assigned before the wealth maximization principle can be used, and hence rights cannot be determined by it. If rights are to be assigned to mimic a perfect market outcome then we must know the right structure on which that outcome was based.[51]

Warren J. Samuels, commenting on the same problem, states:

> In both theory and practice the issue is which interest, and therefore which efficient result, is to count. Identifying which interests are to be given legal protection as a matter of right is the point at issue, and it is one on which the wealth maximization principle does not and cannot help. There is no independent test by which the law's solution can be said to be *the* efficient solution. Indeed, not only is there no independent test, but there cannot be: each legal solution points to a different efficient outcome. Posner is simply wrong in asserting that 'a system of rights could be deduced from the goal of wealth maximization itself'; different rights systems will produce many different wealth maximizations.[52]

Furthermore, as should be apparent, prices are crucial in calculating wealth. The choice as to "which prices" has brought forth two fundamental criticisms. The first criticism addresses the issue of which prices should be used to calculate wealth within the prevailing background law, and whether or not the decision rules that comprise that background law are presently wealth maximizing. The second criticism addresses the same issue of "which prices" but in this case some of the prevailing decision rules are, in fact, not wealth maximizing.

As to the first criticism, wealth maximization requires the use of status quo prices, since those are the only prices observable (especially to the judiciary). Furthermore, status quo prices are a function of the prevailing structure of background law, that is, partially a function of the decision rules employed in common law. In contemplating the adoption of a new rule, or a change in an existing one (or perhaps any change in the law), under the wealth maximization standard, the judiciary would have to rely on the use of status quo prices. But clearly, changes in the structure of the law could change prices. It is the set of prices that exist after the change in law that realistically indicates the change in wealth and therefore must be used to evaluate the new decision rule.[53] Since these latter prices are unknown, wealth would be calculated incorrectly using status quo prices and judicial decisions would be lead astray. As Coleman states:

> The problem is straightforward. Wealth maximization requires and affects prices. Prices must be fixed to employ the principle but employing the principle to recommend structural changes in the law affects prices.[54]

Posner recognizes this problem. He stated that ". . . it is difficult to compare the wealth of two states of society."[55] However, he goes on to assert that inasmuch as the common law typically involves cases whose resolution will have minor allocative impacts, then the change in prices will be minimal.[56] As a consequence, Posner believes that the status quo prices can serve as an adequate proxy in judicial rulemaking. Others argue that in landmark cases allocative impacts are significant and the change in prices will be large.[57] It is precisely in these cases that the application of Posner's wealth maximization criterion may misguide the judiciary. In the absence of empirical support for either position, this dispute persists.

The above criticism, which centers on the simultaneous determination of evolving law and prices, is legitimate whether the prevailing background law that has emerged over time is or is not wealth maximizing. However, as we will now see, if some of these prevailing rules are not wealth maximizing (the source of the second criticism), further problems with the wealth maximization standard become evident.

Recall, as developed earlier, that prevailing prices are a function of the prevailing background law (i.e., property rights and working rules). These property rights and working rules, in part, have emerged over time as a result of judicial decision making in the common law. Judicial decisions can be based on any number of decision rules that could reflect such values as justice, happiness, equality, and fairness or wealth. Consequently, it is possible (and quite probable) that some of the extant legal rules are not, in fact, wealth maximizing. If so, then the status quo prices will be different from the prices which would prevail if all legal rules were wealth maximizing. Given the possibility of the existence of some nonwealth maximizing (inefficient) rules, then Posner's recommendation that the judiciary apply the wealth maximization standard in resolving common law cases is suspect in that it involves the use of prices that are at variance with that standard.

Michelman and Richard A. Epstein have recognized this problem. Michelman states:

> There is the seemingly circular procedure of selecting pieces of law for investigation from a configuration arbitrarily defined by the very network of doctrinal formulations being investigated, and then appraising the efficiency of each piece on the assumption (which can only be provisional) that all the rest of law (which conditions the efficiency of the piece on the examination) is in a determinate and final state. Why, or in what sense, should one expect that the *corpus juris* resulting from a series of such piecemeal-efficient choices would be economically virtuous?[58]

Epstein further suggests:

> Posner's economic approach . . . makes it imperative that he undertake an exhaustive inquiry into the total complex of legal rules that govern any social problem before attempting to make efficiency pronouncements about a small subdivision of the applicable legal rules. . . . [Insofar as he does not undertake this, the] empirical substrate upon which his edifice rests is extensive, tenuous, and unexamined.[59]

Thus, the use of status quo prices in the calculation of wealth raises difficult questions that have yet to be resolved.

d. The Offer-Asking Price Dilemma. Posner's wealth maximization principle is equivalent to the Kaldor-Hicks criterion in welfare economics and, as established earlier, employs the concept of "willingness to pay."[60] This concept necessitates the use of prices but in situations where market prices are generally unavailable (perhaps because of high transactions costs). Given the unavailability of market prices, it then becomes extremely important to understand the valuation process through which proxy prices are generated.

Posner, in using "willingness to pay," has not made it clear whether offer or asking prices should be used in the calculation of wealth. An offer price is typically defined as what an individual is willing to pay in dollars for something, a right or an entitlement, if he does not own it; whereas, an asking price is defined as what an individual, if he already owns the right or entitlement, would demand in dollars to give it up.

It has been well established that these offer and asking prices may be different. This difference may occur because: the individual being questioned is richer with the entitlement to prevent an action than if he does not own the entitlement; people seem to have an enhanced concern for, and an attachment to, things as they are as compared to things as they could be; and the individual finds himself in the "no duty to act" paradox, i.e., people typically experience a much more intense duty to abstain from acts that cause suffering than to act affirmatively to prevent suffering.[61] Thus, one could expect a difference in offer versus asking prices.

Posner's lack of clarity as to the choice of offer versus asking prices has created confusion in the literature. For example, Lucian A. Bebchuk has stated:

> Posner's formulation of the WMC employs *offer* rather than asking prices—that is, the amount a party will be willing to pay for a given entitlement rather than the amount the party will be asking for the entitlement if it is initially assigned to him.[62] (emphasis added)

However, Baker has claimed, "When Posner says 'wealth is the value in dollars or dollar equivalents . . . of everything in society,' he must mean value to the person who possess the thing."[63] This would be an asking price.

Like many of the commentators, we remain confused as to what the calculation of wealth would actually entail. A reading of Posner leads one in two directions. In some cases, he appears to suggest that offer prices should be compared to asking prices in order to determine which state would be wealth maximizing.[64] It is unclear as to how this would be accomplished. In other cases, where the initial vesting of rights and rules is at issue, he appears to suggest that the offer prices of one party should be compared to the offer prices of another party (or several other parties). These offer prices would emerge through a conceptual, hypothetical auction that a judge would undertake.[65]

As to the latter case, that envisions the use of comparative offer prices, a variety of criticisms have been raised. First, many commentators have argued that the use of offer prices, as opposed to asking prices, to calculate wealth and thus assign rights creates a bias that favors the rich at the expense of the poor. The rich, by definition, have a greater ability to pay and therefore, under most circumstances, can offer more than the poor to get the right assigned to them.[66] Assuming this criticism is valid, it is of no minor importance inasmuch as the practitioners of the new law and economics claim to be concerned with both allocation and distribution. Second, the question has been raised, "Cannot wealth maximization be formulated so as to employ asking prices as opposed to offer prices and remain consistent with willingness to pay?" In lieu of the hypothetical auction used to determine offer prices (which requires that neither party originally own the right or entitlement), the judge could determine conceptually what each party would be willing to take in dollars to give up the right if they had owned it initially. That is, the judge estimates their asking prices and bases his decision on those estimates. As has been pointed out by Duncan Kennedy, adherence to the use of either offer or asking prices involves a necessity of choice.[67] The choice of one over the other to guide the judiciary is neither a correct nor an incorrect choice. The prices used by the judiciary to set initial rights and entitlements are a function of the specific value process employed (i.e., the choice of asking or offer prices). Adherence to one or the other involves subtle value judgments that have implications for the character of economic life and thus must be made known before judicial employment of the wealth maximization principle is begun.

As this review of the critics suggests, wealth maximization, as a normative principle, provides little foundation upon which to build a theory of law. Anthony T. Kronman's conclusion about the principle of wealth maximization best sums up what many of the critics have suggested:

> Wealth maximization is not a happy compromise between utilitarianism and Pareto superiority, a compromise which somehow retains the best and eliminates the worst features of these other two principles. If anything, just the opposite is true: wealth maximization exhibits the vices of both and the virtues of neither. Although an advocate of utilitarianism may be persuaded that people have rights that ought to constrain the pursuit of utility, this will not lead him to adopt wealth maximization as his ideal. Similarly, although someone who believes in autonomy and fundamental rights may be convinced that in extreme cases it is permissible to violate people's rights in order to secure a substantial increase in total happiness, this will not lead *him* to endorse wealth maximization as a normative principle either. I happen to believe that a combination of utilitarian and voluntarist principles best expresses our

moral judgments and best equips us to deal with the dilemmas of moral life. But whichever of these two elements one takes to be primary, wealth maximization is an absurd principle to adopt. Wealth maximization is not only an unsound ideal, it is an incoherent one which cannot be defended from any point of view.[68]

B. PUBLIC CHOICE THEORY

Public choice theory is defined as the economic analysis of nonmarket decision making.[69] Somewhat more narrowly, and perhaps more accurately, it is also defined as the application of economic analysis to political decision making, viewed in its broadest sense to include theories of the state, voting rules and voter behavior, party politics, log rolling, bureaucratic choice and regulation.[70] These two definitions move toward congruence the degree to which all nonmarket decisions (which would have to include analyses of religions, custom, non-profit organizations, etc.) are thought of as political decisions. The extent to which they are not, of course, causes difficulty in reconciling the two definitions. We will employ the more narrow definition of public choice theory, though the reader should be aware that public choice theory has been applied beyond political decision making.

The formal inception of public choice theory can be marked with the establishment of an economic journal in 1966 entitled *Papers on Non-Market Decision Making*. Two years later, the name was changed to *Public Choice*. In the interim, the Public Choice Society was formed. Actually, formal work in public choice theory began at least a decade prior to the establishment of the journal in 1966.[71] As it has developed, public choice theory is now made up of what is termed axiomatic social choice theory, the economic theories of bureaucracy, of legislatures, and of the state.

Before providing an overview of public choice theory, a distinction should be drawn between positive and normative public choice theory. In positive public choice theory, the attempt is to describe and explain political results in terms of rational, utility-maximizing behavior of the participants in the political process. Propositions derived from these models will find empirical support or refutation in the observable behavior of individuals in their capacities as participants in collective decision making processes.[72] The descriptive models of positive public choice theory attempt to analyze political outcomes in both direct and representative democracies.

In the analysis of direct democracy, the theory explores the properties and outcomes of various voting rules. Particular attention is paid to the outcomes of the unanimity rule and the simple majority rule, as well as to comparisons of these outcomes. In addition, several alternative rules have been proposed and their outcomes analyzed. These include the plurality rule, the Condorcet criterion, the Borda count, exhaustive voting, and approval voting.[73] It is recognized that, because of the problems caused by the existence of a large number of voters and issues, direct democracy has often given way to representative democracy.

In representative democracy, public choice theory assumes that the elected representatives, like voters in a direct democracy, are rational utility maximizers. Specifically, representatives are assumed to formulate campaign strategies and to make political decisions that maximize votes so that the representative or his political party will win elections. The positive public choice literature has focused on three aspects of representative democracy. These are: (1) the behavior of representatives and political parties both during the campaign and while in office, (2) the behavior of voters in choosing representatives, and (3) the outcomes that emerge under representative democracy.[74] In addition, the outcomes under representative democracy are compared to those of direct democracy.

Thus, in positive public choice theory, the attempt is to describe political outcomes under direct and representative democracy. In normative public choice theory, the attempt is to prescribe what political institutions (with an emphasis on their respective decision making processes) should be adopted. The contributors to this literature set forth basic postulates to structure the decision making processes of political institutions. These postulates reflect the values *believed* to be widely held and therefore are normatively chosen. In addition, normative public choice has proffered a variety of recommendations that attempt to improve upon existing political institutions.

1. Public Choice Theory—An Overview

Given the broad scope and diverse nature of what is emerging as public choice theory, in this section we will attempt to provide the reader with an overview of some of its major components. A description of the work on axiomatic social choice theory is followed by a description of what we are referring to as conventional public choice. With respect to the latter, the legislative and bureaucratic sectors are analyzed with a specific focus on the significance of the political rules for collective order. In Section 2 of this chapter we will analyze the contractarian approach to public choice theory.

a. Axiomatic Social Choice Theory. Axiomatic social choice theory (hereafter referred to as social choice theory) is an outgrowth of the theory of welfare economics and the literature on real valued social welfare functions. It should be noted that social choice theory is highly abstract and highly mathematical. As a result, it is often difficult to relate the theory to the specific activities of governments, politicians, and bureaucrats.[75]

Recall, the attempt in welfare economics is to identify states of the economy which correspond to the points of economic efficiency (i.e., Pareto optimal points) that are available to society. The locus of these Pareto optimal points comprises the grand utility possibility frontier, depicted in Figure V.4.

Within welfare economics, the duality theorem states that a perfectly functioning competitive market, barring externalities and public goods, will produce a Pareto optimal allocation of resources. That is, the purely competitive market, given an initial distribution of resources, will achieve an allocation of resources at one point on the grand utility possibility frontier, such as Point A in Figure V.4. An alternative initial distribution of resources will result in attaining some other point on the grand utility possibility frontier, such as B—and so forth for each initial

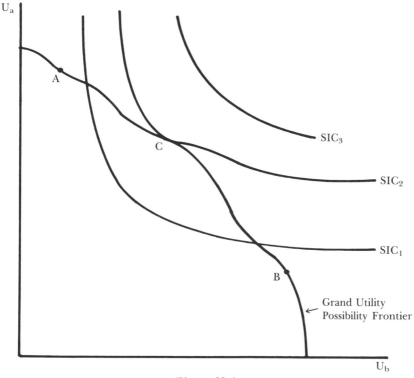

Figure V.4.

distribution. Normatively, each result is "good" in that each is Pareto optimal.

The logic of Pareto optimality alone does not allow us to find a unique point along the grand utility possibility frontier that is socially preferred. As a result, theorists have attempted to develop real valued social welfare functions to find that socially preferred point. The underlying presumption in this literature is that society has a consistent preference ordering since it is made up of individuals who individually have consistent preference orderings. The literature proceeds as if the preferences of individuals can be correctly aggregated. If, in fact, the values of the individuals in society can be translated into a social welfare function that yields social indifference curves (SIC_1, SIC_2, SIC_3 in Figure V.4) then the socially preferred point C can be determined. The attempt to make this translation has encountered great difficulties due to the apparent necessity of having to make cardinal, interpersonal utility comparisons.

Given the persistence of these difficulties in formulating a real valued social welfare function, social choice theory has emerged to shed light on social preferences and how they might be found. The methodology of social choice theory is: (1) to set forth various axioms which attempt to incorporate the value judgments of the society and which usually constrain society to choose from among the Pareto optimal set, and (2) to determine which collective choice processes (i.e., voting mechanisms in a democracy) satisfy the axioms.[76] The literature seems to imply that if a voting mechanism can be found which satisfies the axioms set forth and if society would endorse the axioms, then it can be concluded that the use of the specific voting mechanism will yield a solution which corresponds to a unique socially preferred point on the grant utility possibility frontier.[77]

Like much of the work on real valued social welfare functions, social choice theory has encountered many difficulties. Perhaps Allan M. Feldman has stated it best:

> Much of the analysis of social choice theory produces negative conclusions, conclusions of the type: Procedure X for determining when A is socially better than B has such-and-such a nasty characteristic. And all of these negative conclusions are drawn together in one important negative theorem, the most important single result of social choice theory, the Impossibility Theorem of Kenneth Arrow.[78]

b. Conventional Public Choice. In conventional public choice, there is a shift in emphasis away from the narrow search for *the* socially preferred solution that is undertaken in social choice theory. As will be elaborated upon shortly, the emphasis is more toward the incentives created by the political and bureaucratic decisions guided by the political rules of collective order (i.e., legislative and bureaucratic working rules). Further, unlike social choice theory, which is highly abstract, conventional public choice is more concerned with actual political processes and thus has more realistic applications. In addition, in marked contrast to neoclassical economics, the theory of public choice can be viewed in one sense as an "opening up" of neoclassical economics while at the same time as a movement towards "closure" with respect to the nature of the analysis. Each view deserves some elaboration.

Conventional public choice represents an "opening up" in the sense that the contributors perceive their approach as extending beyond the narrowly conceived limits of neoclassical economic theory and into an examination of the political, legal and social constraints which are typically taken as given in neoclassical economics.[79] The formal application of economic analysis to such subject matter as the theory of the state, voting rules and voter behavior, party politics, log rolling, bureaucratic choice, and regulation distinguishes conventional public choice from mainstream neoclassical economics.

At the same time, methodologically, conventional public choice represents a movement toward the analysis of closed systems.[80] In neoclassical economics, political decisions, and thus political decision makers, are often perceived as exogenous to economic activity; whereas in conventional public choice, they are endogenous. That is, rational, utility-maximizing individuals act not only in the marketplace but also participate in the political decision making processes to enhance their utility. Consequently, resources may be allocated either via the marketplace or via the political process by the same individuals acting in several separate capacities. James M. Buchanan has described this movement toward closure as follows:

> The critically important bridge between the behavior of persons who act in the marketplace and the behavior of persons who act in political process must be analyzed. The 'theory of public choice' can be interpreted as the construction of such a bridge. The approach requires only the simple assumption that the same individuals act in both relationships. Political decisions are not handed down from on high by omniscient beings who cannot err. Individuals behave in market interactions, in political–government interactions, in cooperative-nongovernmental interactions, and in other arrangements. Closure of the behavioral system, as I am using the term, means only that analysis must be extended to the actions of persons in their several separate capacities.[81]

Conventional public choice can be characterized by the diagram in Figure V.5, where the emphasis is on the political rules of collective order (hereafter referred to as the political rules). These political rules are the rules under which legislators and bureaucrats make political decisions. The rules provide both discretion for and constraint upon

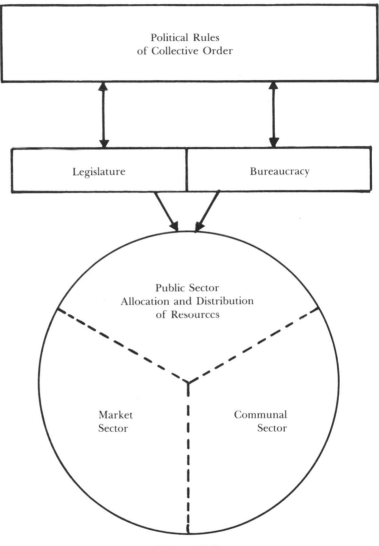

Figure V.5.

their choices. An understanding of: (1) the discretion and the constraints inherent in prevailing political rules as well as (2) what may be termed "political rule formulation" is important inasmuch as the political rules affect the public sector allocation and distribution of resources and ultimately the character of economic life.

i. Prevailing political rules. At any point in time, a set of political rules prevail. These prevailing rules provide legislators and bureaucrats with a range of discretion. This range can often be ambiguous in its scope, particularly in the bureaucracy in cases where the legislative mandate to the bureaucracy lacks specificity. On the other hand, the political rules can also provide various degrees of constraints upon the legislators and bureaucrats. The important point here is that the prevailing political rules establish both the range of discretion of and the degree of constraints upon the legislators and bureaucrats. As such, the rules serve to structure the incentives and therefore influence the behavior of the political decision makers in making their choices. These choices determine the public sector allocation and distribution of resources for the community at large.

Given the significance of the political rules, conventional public choice has examined the workings of the legislatures and bureaucracies in some detail. With respect to legislators, various models attempt to describe the behavior of politicians during the campaign to be elected and while in office, the impact of different voting rules, the role of party politics, and the behavior of voters in elections.[82] The models of bureaucracy attempt to describe the overall behavior of bureaucrats; the size of budgets; the interrelationships among the bureaucracy, special interest groups, and the legislature; and the problems relating to information with respect to costs and evaluation of output; among other things.[83]

All of these models share the common characteristic that they assume that legislators and bureaucrats are likely to seek utility from many sources and behave accordingly. Different models of legislators have postulated that such factors as votes, power, and political income enter the utility function of legislators.[84] (These factors are referred to as arguments in the utility function.) Similarly, various models of bureaucracy postulate that power, prestige, job security, perquisites, future salary, and working conditions enter the utility function of bureaucrats.[85] Thus, in a manner analogous to the economic analysis of "economic man" in the marketplace, these conventional public choice models postulate that legislators and bureaucrats act primarily out of self-interest. Furthermore, these models incorporate into the analysis the political rules of collective order which provide for discretion as well as for constraints upon the political decision makers. The attempt is to understand and explain the legislative and bureaucratic outcomes that can be expected to follow from the rational behavior of those engaged in legislative and bureaucratic choice under the prevailing political rules.

ii. Political rule formulation. Conventional public choice is not concerned only with analyzing the prevailing political rules. It is generally recognized that the rules of collective order are not given once and for all time but are subject to revision. This is accomplished through a complex process in which various parties may work to alter political rules in an attempt to foster their own interests. For example, legislative rules or bureaucratic rules may be altered as a result of the direct political activities of the community at large. These political activities are usually directed at the legislature as opposed to bureaucracies. Bureaucratic rules may be more often altered through political activities of specific interest groups (e.g., farm, labor, or education lobbies) and the bureaucrats themselves. In an attempt to maximize their utility, the parties of interest alter the political rules, which results in a broadening or narrowing of the range of discretion and the degree of constraint on the legislature and bureaucracy.

Before providing examples of this process, it is important to note two particular points with regard to conventional public choice as presented here. First, the political rules may be altered through the constitution (e.g., a constitutional amendment) which is not depicted in Figure V.5. In fact, conventional public choice has incorporated the analysis of constitutions into the literature.[86] Second, the political rules may be altered through the judicial and legal processes. These processes were largely the subject matter of Section A of this chapter, the new law and economics. Conceptually, it should be evident that we have come to the border between conventional public choice and the new law and economics with neither body of literature attempting to formally incorporate the other into its analysis.

In order to better understand political rule formulation, two examples will be presented. In the legislative sector, we will examine a legislative rule change from existing federal budget policy to a balanced budget rule. In the bureaucratic sector, we will examine a bureaucratic rule change focusing on the U.S. Army Corps of Engineers before and after passage of the 1972 Federal Amendments to the Clean Water Act.

Assume that a balanced budget rule has gained sufficient support from the community at large, various private and public interest groups, and bureaucrats and legislators, each seeking to maximize their respective utilities. Once in place, this rule has reduced the discretion of the legislature by providing an additional constraint on the budget process. Consequently, the incentives of the legislature have been altered. Specifically, the legislature may have a greater incentive and therefore act to increase taxes, to reduce expenditures, or some combination of the two. The actual choice they make depends upon the specific arguments in the legislators' utility functions as well as their perception of the preferences of the various parties of interest.[87] If, for instance, the legislature responds to the new incentives by eliminating the deficit through a reduction in expenditures, then we might expect reductions in the size of the public sector as well as possible changes in the composition of public expenditures. It is through this complex process that changes in the legislative rules can ultimately affect the public sector allocation and distribution of resources.

In the second example, assume that the legislature passes a law that mandates that a government bureau alter its scope of responsibility. For instance, in 1972 Congress passed the Federal Water Pollution Control Act Amendments. One of the major provisions of the Act was Section 404 which gave the U.S. Army Corps of Engineers the authority to regulate discharges of dredged and fill materials into waters of the U.S.. The effect of the Act was to alter the territorial scope and thus the responsibilities of the Corps (the "government bureau" in this example).[88]

For decades before the passage of the 1972 Act, the Corps, operating under previous statutes, engaged in intensive water resources development projects (for example, the construction of dams, flood control projects, etc.).[89] These projects were undertaken under the goals set forth by Congress to prevent impediments to navigation on the navigable waters of the U.S., the major mode of interstate commerce during much of this time. After passage of the 1972 Act, litigation ensued when the Corps, acting to maximize the arguments in its utility function, refused to acknowlege that the territorial scope of its jurisdiction and responsibilities to protect wetlands had been expanded by passage of provisions included in the Act (primarily Section 404). Specifically, the Corps attempted to utilize its past guidelines of "navigable waters of the U.S." to define its territorial scope. Under this definition the Corps would not have to provide for the protection of approximately 98% of the nation's stream-miles and 80% of the nation's wetlands. It could continue to exercise its discretion as the nation's water resources developer without the constraint brought on by having to protect the nation's wetlands.

As a result of the 1975 litigation, the court ordered the Corps to adopt new regulations which clearly recognized its full regulatory mandate and broad territorial responsibilities.[90] That is, the Corps was required to clearly focus on the water quality effects of hydrological modification projects. Water resources development projects could proceed under the direction and regulation of the Corps but, as of the 1975 litigation, the Corps also had to provide for the protection of estuaries and coastal wetlands to prevent water quality degradation, a constraint vis-à-vis its past practices.

It should be evident that the effect of the new bureaucratic rule (both legislatively and judicially determined) has been to alter the discretion of and constraints upon the Corps in both going forth with their own projects as well as regulating those of industry. Given the new rules, Edward Thompson described the anticipated change in the behavior of both the Corps as well as those regulated by the Corps. As to the Corps, he stated:

> The amendments establish a hierarchy of administrative mechanisms for the review of hydrologic modification. The detail of review, and hence the time consumed by the process, is tailored to the degree of water quality degradation that various categories of hydrologic modification may be expected to produce. To the extent that detailed regulatory review tends to have a chilling effect on the activity regulated, case-by-case scrutiny under section 404 of certain activities should continue to discourage hydrologic modification involving potentially severe water quality consequences in favor of environmentally less damaging alternatives.[91]

As to industry, he noted:

> Government regulation should not be deliberately burdensome. But 'much of the regulatory burden . . . with which industry claims it is saddled is self-inflicted. . . . The way for industry to ease the impacts of §404 regulation is by modifying its practices to respect the integrity of the aquatic ecosystem.'[92]

Thus, as in the case of the balanced budget legislative rule, Section 404 is illustrative of a bureaucratic rule change that, once in force, has the effect of altering the public sector allocation and distribution of resources as well as altering the borders between the public, market, and communal sectors (see Figure V.5).

The examples serve to illustrate the manner in which conventional public choice emphasizes the role of the individual decision maker as a utility maximizer. This approach is contrary to much of the pre-public choice approach where it is assumed (perhaps unconsciously) that the legislators and bureaucrats seek to maximize the public interest.[93] In addition, the examples serve to illustrate the significance in conventional public choice of the political rules of collective order and the role of the individuals who adopt them. As Buchanan has stated:

> The 'theory of public choice' rests instead on a single decision structure. It involves the explicit introduction of a 'democratic' model, one in which the rulers are also the ruled. The theory examines the behavior of persons as they participate variously in the formation of public or collective choices, by which is meant choices from among mutually exclusive alternative constraints which, once selected, must apply to all members of the community. In acting or behaving as a 'public choice' participant, the individual is presumed to be aware that he is, in part, selecting results which affect others than himself. He is making decisions for a public, of which he forms a part.[94]

2. *Contractarian Approach to Public Choice Theory*

Given the broad scope of conventional public choice as described here, we will not attempt to explore the entire body of literature. However, following the approach taken in Section A of this chapter, we will draw selectively from the literature to review that which we think best typifies one major thrust of conventional public choice theory—the contractarian approach. In doing so, we will concentrate much of our attention on the work of its major contributors, including James M. Buchanan, Gordon Tullock, Robert D. Tollison, and others. Within this review, it is recognized that: (1) some of the literature is dated as compared to the literature analyzed in Section A of this chapter, and (2) given the developments of public choice theory over the last decade, the contributors to this tradition may not all remain in agreement either with each other or certainly with our restatement of the contractarian approach to public choice theory.

We have chosen this facet of public choice inasmuch as it deals directly with and relates to the many difficult issues and questions that are raised in our model of Law and Economics. That is, just as the legal processes that are being studied in the new law and economics affect the law, rights, and working rules and consequently the character of economic life, so too do the constitutional and political processes studied in the contractarian approach to public choice theory alter the law, rights, and working rules and thereby affect the character of economic life.

Viewed from the perspective of our model of Law and Economics, the contractarian approach can be interpreted as one normative approach to organize political decision making processes. This approach seems to have been born out of a general dissatisfaction with past and present political and bureaucratic processes and outcomes.[95]

a. The Underlying Methodology of the Contractarian Approach.

The basic components of the contractarian approach to public choice theory include methodological individualism, consent requirements, and an emphasis on exchange in the political arena.

i. Methodological individualism.

Following the dictates of neoclassical economics, the contractarians employ methodological individualism as a postulate in formulating their theory. Methodological individualism is taken to mean either: (1) that group motivations which attempt to explain group behavior do not exist, or (2) even if they do exist, in principle, a more fruitful way of explaining group behavior is to isolate on the motivations of individuals.[96] Thus, the contractarians employ methodological individualism on the belief that no discernible social values exist apart from individual values. In keeping with their neoclassical economics predecessors, the contractarians believe that individual actions provide the only economic guide to evaluate collective choice. Buchanan expressed it succinctly:

> In my view, a consistent methodological position does not allow the introduction of non-individualistic norms in *either* allocation *or* distribution. . . . When non-individualistic norms are introduced, the domain of economics, *as I define the discipline*, is abandoned. This statement cannot be challenged.[97]

A public choice will be made through the political behavior of individuals acting upon their own preferences. Acceptance of a public choice is contingent upon it meeting the consent requirements embodied in the contractarian approach to public choice theory.

ii. Consent requirements.

[a.] The Unanimous Consent Requirement Inasmuch as the contractarians assert that social values do not exist apart from individual values in society, concensus or unanimity is the only test which can ensure that a change is beneficial. Buchanan and Tullock have indicated the significance of the unanimity rule in the contractarian approach:

> In political discussion . . . many scholars seem to have overlooked the central place that the unanimity rule must occupy in any normative theory of democratic government. We have witnessed an inversion whereby . . . majority rule has been elevated to the status which the unanimity rule should occupy.[98]

Thus, they have adopted the Pareto-Wicksellian group decision rule of unanimity.[99] Under this rule, a proferred legal change (i.e., a change in rights and rules related to specific policies or changes in rules at the constitutional level) would be adopted only if it commands unanimous consent.[100] Under the recognition that some individuals may be hurt by any policy change and thus vote against it, thereby preventing its adoption, the contractarians have adopted the compensation criterion.

[b.] Compensation Criterion The contractarians believe that the adoption of specific policies or constitutional rules may generate net gains to society. Hence, the possibility exists for part of those gains to be paid out as compensation to those hurt by the policy change in order to garner unanimous consent. Thus, the compensation requirement has become an integral part of the theory. Compensation is viewed as required to secure agreement by all parties to the proposed change.[101]

> Full compensation is essential, not in order to maintain any initial distribution on ethical grounds, but in order to decide which one from among the many possible social policy changes does, in fact, satisfy the genuine Pareto rule. Compensation is the only device available to the political economist for this purpose.[102]

The Pareto-Wicksellian compensation rule adopted by the contractarian theorists, in effect, states that if the prevailing social structure is to be modified by a legal rule change, taxes must be imposed on those who will gain from the proposed legal rule change and the compensation paid to those who will suffer a loss as a result of the change. The Pareto-Wicksellian compensation rule is confined to those changes that are "legitimately" classified as changes in the sanctioned legal structure. "Within the structure of existing law, no grounds for the payment of compensation exist."[103] This has raised the question of what constitutes a sanctioned legal structure. In answering this question, Buchanan has responded: "Compensation is required so long as the injured party previously was acting within the law."[104] He goes on to define the law as "a set of expectations, which include enforcement standards as traditionally observed, along with formal statute. A change in law, by my definition, involves an explicit modification of normal expectations."[105]

iii. An emphasis on exchange. Given the postulate of methodological individualism and the consent requirements, the general thrust of contractarian public choice theory is to structure a political process where values are revealed only through the political actions of individuals and concensus among individual members of the choosing group becomes the sole affirmation of social value. This normative approach to public choice theory focuses on the process of exchange and concentrates attention away from choice, the usual concern of economics.[106] In doing so, it stresses the potential for exchange in the political arena under the rule of unanimous consent and the compensation requirement. As a consequence, the political outcomes would conform to individual preferences analogous to the manner in which market outcomes conform to individual preferences. The theory is not, indeed need not be, concerned with the private-public mix.[107] As long as political institutions are structured around the common unifying principles of gains-from-trade and the unanimous consent requirement and are not subject to continuous redefinition, individuals will be led to voluntarily search for inclusive, complex trading or exchange agreements whereby prospects for mutual agreement to exploit a potentially realizable surplus are enhanced. Buchanan has described this as follows:

> I have argued that the contractarian or Paretian norm is relevant on the simple principle that 'we start from here.' But 'here,' the status quo is the existing set of legal institutions and rules. . . . I tried to argue that, to the extent that property rights are specified in advance, genuine 'trades' can emerge, with mutual gains to all parties. However, to the extent that existing rights are held to be subject to continuous redefinition by the State, no one has an incentive to organize and to initiate trades or agreements. This amounts to saying that once the body politic begins to get overly concerned about the distribution of the pie under existing property-rights assignments and legal rules, once we begin to think either about the personal gains from law-breaking, privately or publicly, or about disparities between existing

imputations and those estimated to be forthcoming under some idealized anarchy, we are necessarily precluding and forestalling the achievement of potential structural changes that might increase the size of the pie for *all*.[108]

Thus, the political arena is perceived merely as an instrument through which individuals attempt to carry out activities in order to secure common objectives. The contractarians believe that political activities should be structured in exchange terms, although they recognize that the political exchange process will be significantly more complex than market exchange, the central subject matter of orthodox economic theory.[109]

b. The Contractarian Calculus of Consent. One tenant of the contractarian approach is that the unanimous consent requirement is necessary to formulate the constitution itself. That is, the rules for making rules must be unanimously agreed upon. However, this does not imply that the voting rule governing a specific choice (i.e., one concerning a specific policy or legal change) must itself satisfy the unanimity requirement. Simply put, at the constitutional level *all* may agree that some voting rule other than unanimous consent may be required to adopt the specific policy or generally to implement a legal change. Buchanan and Tullock have observed:

> Moreover, since this calculus is possible for each individual, constitutional decisions to allow departures from unanimity at the level of specific collective choices may command unanimous consent.[110]

They recognize that outcomes associated with specific voting rules that require less than unanimous consent may, in the short run, run counter to the self interests of some individuals.

> Our basic analysis of the individual calculus that is involved in choosing among alternative organizational rules, in selecting a political constitution, has demonstrated that it will often be to the rational self-interest of the individual to select a particular rule that can be predicted to produce results on occasion that run counter to the self-interest of the individual calculated within a shorter time span. . . .
>
> Essential to the analysis is the presumption that the individual is *uncertain* as to what his own precise role will be in any one of the whole chain of later collective choices that will actually have to be made. For this reason he is considered not to have a particular and distinguishable interest separate and apart from his fellows. This is not to suggest that he will act contrary to his own interest; but the individual will not find it advantageous to vote for rules that may promote sectional, class, or group interests because, by presupposition, he is unable to predict the role that he will be playing in the actual collective decision-making process at any particular time in the future. He cannot predict with any degree of certainty whether he is more likely to be in a winning or losing coalition on any specific issue. Therefore, he will assume that occasionally he will be in one group and occasionally in the other. His own self-interest will lead him to choose rules that will maximize the utility of an individual in

a series of collective decisions with his own preferences on the separate issues being more or less randomly distributed.[111]

The calculus employed by the contractarians can be applied to direct democracy and to representative democracy. In direct democracy, the calculus can be used to determine the optimal voting rule (category specific) to be used in a referendum. In representative democracy, the calculus can be used to determine such issues as the number of representatives, the basis of representation, and the rules through which the legislature reach decisions.[112] The calculus that determines the optimal voting rule for each category of issues in direct democracy is depicted in Figure V.6.[113] If there are, say, 10 categories of issues confronting society, then the calculus would be conducted for each category.

In Figure V.6, D represents the expected decision-making costs; these costs typically will increase as the size of the group (hence the proportion of the population) required to agree on a collective decision increases. C represents the expected external costs of a collective decision. These costs represent the losses that an individual expects to bear as a result of a collective decision to which he is opposed. These costs typically will decrease as the proportion of the population required to agree on a collective decision increase. Clearly, the external costs on any one indi-

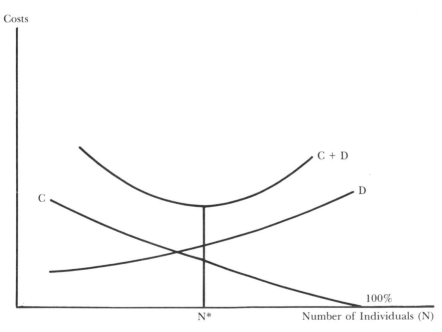

Figure V.6.

vidual will be zero when unanimous consent (i.e., 100% agreement) is the voting rule since any individual can vote down any issue to which he is opposed, thereby avoiding the external costs. The optimal voting rule is N* in Figure V.6, where C + D (the vertical addition of curves C and D) reaches a minimum.

For example, for some specific category of issues, N* may be determined to be, say, 60%. Any policy that garners the support of at least 60% of the voters would, of course, be adopted. It should be noted that, upon the adoption of the policy, some individuals may bear losses. Under the contractarian approach, these losses would not command compensation if the losses are part of individual's expected external cost function. The degree to which the external cost function reflects "traditional expectations," compensation would not be forthcoming. The reason for this is that the new policy does not constitute a change in the law inasmuch as it does not violate traditional expectations.[114]

It is unclear whether compensation would be required when a policy that was adopted under the 60% rule did constitute a change in law. Suppose that over 60% of the community voted to outlaw all smoke emitted from factory chimneys. Does this policy violate the traditional expectations of the factory owners? If not, compensation should not be forthcoming, as described above. If it does, compensation should be forthcoming. Buchanan suggests that the factory owners, in this case, should be compensated.[115] It is not clear to us how one can determine whether traditional expectations have been so violated as to command compensation. This seemingly raises a paradox.

A possible resolution to this paradox can be provided by carefully considering the contexts in which Pareto optimality is employed. In contrast to the contractarian approach, one could follow the solution proposed by the traditional welfare economists. That is, in the example, if analysis indicates that the gain of the families living adjacent to the smoke-creating plant is sufficiently large to compensate the factory owners for the losses incurred as a result of the adoption of the smoke abatement measures, then the policy is Pareto optimal and should be undertaken. The question of whether compensation must in fact be paid is left unanswered.

Instead of relying on the wisdom of the analysts to make the proper estimate of the gains and losses, the contractarians, at one level, suggest an alternative approach. In this approach, the political economist would offer specific policies, including schemes for side payments, to the voters or to the legislature as "presumed Pareto optimal."[116] Here, the political economist attempts to locate, from among many possible solutions, those solutions that would garner unanimous support. Side payments are crucial in this scheme. It is through the side payments made by the gainers to the losers that unanimous consent is secured. This "presumptive optimal" approach results in Pareto optimal outcomes inasmuch as it incorporates both unanimous consent and compensation in the form of side payments. However, as should be evident, this approach ignores the costs of decision making, D, to reach unanimous consent and need not consider external costs, C, inasmuch as they are zero under the unanimous consent rule.

It is through the formal inclusion of these costs that the contractarians begin to shift to a second level of analysis that purports to resolve the paradox described above. As discussed earlier, the formal inclusion of decision-making costs, when combined with the external costs, can lead to a less than unanimous voting rule, say 60%. It is clear that under such a rule some individuals may bear uncompensated losses consequent to the adoption of a policy. It appears that the application of this rule may result in a non Pareto optimal solution. However, as pointed out by Buchanan and Tullock, this conclusion rests on a narrow interpretation of Pareto optimality.[117]

> The welfare-political-economist approach indicates that a specific choice is Pareto-optimal only if all parties reach agreement. This suggests that even the most rationally constructed constitution will allow some decisions to be made that are 'nonoptimal' in the Pareto sense. This inference is correct if attention is centered on the level of specific collective decisions. The problem here lies in determining the appropriate level at which Pareto criteria should dominate.[118]

For Buchanan and Tullock, the appropriate level is the constitutional level for it is there that Pareto optimality (in the large) is attained by minimizing all costs involved in choosing the appropriate decision rule. Thus, it is at the constitutional level that less than unanimous consent rules can be seen to be consistent with the Pareto optimal criterion. As described by Buchanan and Tullock:

> 'Optimality' in the sense of choosing the single 'best' rule is something wholly distinct from 'optimality' in the allocation of resources within a given time span. . . . If the constitutional decision is a rational one, the external costs imposed by 'nonoptimal' choices because of the operation of a less-than-unanimity voting rule will be more than offset by the reduction in the expected costs of the decision making.[119]

It is now clear why losses suffered under a cost minimizing, less than unanimous consent voting rule will go uncompensated. The cost reductions inherent in such a rule are, in a sense, a form of ex ante compensation, thus no ex post compensation is required. Tullock stated:

> It should be noted, then, that the criteria that I have proposed would also indicate that some changes that are not Pareto optimal should be made. Suppose we consider

not an individual change but a policy for making changes in the future. Such a policy might well offer to every person a positive present discounted value *ex ante* while at the same time injure people in specific instances *ex post*. This type of Pareto optimality in the large was used as a foundation for *The Calculus of Consent* by James M. Buchanan and myself.[120]

It is in this manner that the paradox is purported to be resolved and the basic elements of the contractarian approach to public choice theory best understood.

c. *Fundamental Issues Raised by the Contractarian Approach.*

The contractarian approach to public choice theory is one normative method for organizing political and governmental activities. There are fundamental conceptual issues raised in contemplating its adoption and application. Some of these issues will be briefly explored here.

The first issue involves the question: "How do we get from here to there?" That is, what political mechanism should be used to determine if the contractarian approach should be adopted? The answer to this question is not clear in the contractarian approach. In one sense, it seems that the only legitimate method by which society could adopt the contractarian approach would be to rely on the unanimous consent rule. This method would conform to the logic underlying the contractarian approach. Alternatively, the contractarians might be content to use the existing constitutional and legislative processes to revise the existing constitution in order to adopt a contractarian constitution. This method also appears to conform to the logic underlying the contractarian approach, in that it utilizes the status quo structure of rights and rules as a starting point.[121] We are uncertain whether the use of the status quo (i.e., existing constitutional mechanisms) would be acceptable in that it does not require the use of the unanimous consent rule, thus a Pareto optimal outcome is not assured.

A second issue is raised once one conceptually adopts the contractarian approach. This issue concerns the normative intrusions into their analysis. They admit that their approach is normative to the extent to which it employs the unanimous consent requirement embodied in Pareto optimality:

> The choice among alternatives is made on the basis of some criteria; it is always possible to move one step up the hierarchy and to examine the choice of criteria; discussion stops only when we have carried the examination process back to ultimate 'values.'[122]

For Buchanan and Tullock, the discussion of values stops upon adoption of the unanimity rule. They claim that, "We do not propose to go beyond welfare judgments deducible from a rigorous application of the unanimity rule."[123]

However, this is not the case—they do go beyond the value judgments incorporated in the unanimity rule. Their reliance on the status quo is an additional normative facet of the contractarian approach, claims to the contrary notwithstanding. They argue that the status quo must be accepted ". . . for the simple reason that this is where he starts,"[124] and because it provides a basis from which ". . . genuine 'trades' can emerge, with mutual gains to all parties."[125] Clearly, *any* initial structure of rights can provide the starting point for subsequent public choices.[126] However, the ultimate character of economic life is, in part, dependent upon the starting point. Thus, a discussion of the values underlying the choice of a specific starting point can help unmask the options open to society.

NOTES AND REFERENCES

1. Editor, "Symposium on Efficiency as a Legal Concern," *Hofstra Law Review,* Vol. 18, No. 3 (Spring 1980), pp. 485–486 at 485.

2. As will become evident in this chapter, the notion of efficiency remains problematic in the new law and economics literature.

3. A similar definition is provided by Richard A. Epstein, "The Static Conception of the Common Law," *Journal of Legal Studies,* Vol. 9, No. 2 (March 1980), pp. 253–275 at 255.

4. Jules L. Coleman, "Efficiency, Utility, and Wealth Maximization," *Hofstra Law Review,* Vol. 8, No. 3 (Spring 1980), pp. 509–551 at 512.

5. Lewis A. Kornhauser, "A Guide to the Perplexed Claims of Efficiency in the Law," *Hofstra Law Review,* Vol. 8, No. 3 (Spring 1980), pp. 591–639 at 612. It is noted that throughout much of the literature the two notions of allocative and productive efficiency are often employed. Allocative efficiency can be best understood as the outcome associated with exhausting all gains-from-trade in utility space (i.e., a movement from off to on a contract curve in exchange space). Productive efficiency indicates that all factors of production have been realigned in production space such that no further realignments will increase output (i.e., a movement from off to on a contract curve in input space).

6. Richard A. Posner, "Some Uses and Abuses of Economics in Law," *University of Chicago Law Review,* Vol. 46, No. 2 (Winter 1979), pp. 281–306 at 294.

7. Ibid., pp. 288–289. See also Richard A. Posner, "An Economic Approach to Legal Procedure and Judicial Administration," *Journal of Legal Studies,* Vol. 2, No. 2 (June 1973), pp. 399–458.

8. William M. Landes, "An Economic Analysis of the Courts," *Journal of Law and Economics,* Vol. 14, No. 1 (April 1971), pp. 61–107.

9. Ibid.

10. The literature that analyzes and extends the basic trial settlement model includes: Richard A. Posner, "The Behavior of Administrative Agencies," *Journal of Legal Studies,* Vol. 1, No. 2 (June 1972), pp. 305–348; John P. Gould, "The Economics of Legal Conflicts," *Journal of Legal Studies,* Vol. 2, No. 1 (January 1973), pp. 279–300; and Steven Shavell, "Suit, Settlement, and Trial: A Theoretical Analysis Under Alternative Methods for the Allocation of Legal Costs," *Journal of Legal Studies,* Vol. 11, No. 1 (January 1982), pp. 55–82.

11. Paul H. Rubin, "Why is the Common Law Efficient?" *Journal of Legal Studies*, Vol. 6, No. 1 (January 1977), pp. 51–64 at 51.

12. Ibid., p. 55. See also George L. Priest, "The Common Law Process and the Selection of Efficient Rules," *Journal of Legal Studies*, Vol. 5, No. 1 (January 1977), pp. 65–82.

13. John C. Goodman, "An Economic Theory of the Evolution of Common Law," *Journal of Legal Studies*, Vol. 7, No. 2 (June 1978), pp. 393–406.

14. Ibid., pp. 394–395.

15. Posner, "An Economic Approach to Legal Procedure and Judicial Administration," pp. 399–458. Warren F. Schwartz and Gordon Tullock, "The Costs of a Legal System," *Journal of Legal Studies*, Vol. 4, No. 1 (January 1975), pp. 75–82.

16. Isaac Ehrlich and Richard A. Posner, "An Economic Analysis of Legal Rulemaking," *Journal of Legal Studies*, Vol. 3, No. 1 (January 1974), pp. 257–286.

17. William Landes and Richard A. Posner, "Legal Precedent: A Theoretical and Empirical Analysis," *Journal of Law and Economics*, Vol. 19, No. 2 (August 1976), pp. 249–307. Other literature pertaining to evolutionary theories of the common law include: William M. Landes and Richard A. Posner, "Adjudication as a Private Good," *Journal of Legal Studies*, Vol. 8, No. 2 (March 1979), pp. 235–284; Robert Cooter and Lewis Kornhauser, "Can Litigation Improve the Law Without the Help of Judges?" *Journal of Legal Studies*, Vol. 9, No. 1 (January 1980), pp. 139–163; Epstein, "The Static Conception of the Common Law," pp. 253–289; Paul H. Rubin, "Common Law and Statute Law," *Journal of Legal Studies*, Vol. 11, No. 2 (June 1982), pp. 205–223; and Jack Hirschleifer, et al., *Research in Law and Economics*, (Evolutionary Models in Economics and Law), Vol. 4 (1982).

18. Frank I. Michelman, "Constitutions, Statutes, and the Theory of Efficient Adjudication," *Journal of Legal Studies*, Vol. 9, No. 3 (June 1980), pp. 431–461 at 432–433, 440–441. Michelman's comments are directed at such statements as this:

> Although the correlation is far from perfect, judge-made rules tend to be efficiency promoting while those made by legislatures tend to be efficiency reducing.

Richard A. Posner, *Economic Analysis of Law*, 2nd ed., (Boston: Little, Brown and Company, 1977), p. 404.

19. Mark Tushnet, "Post-Realist Legal Scholarship," *Wisconsin Law Review*, Vol. 1980, No. 6 (1980), pp. 1383–1401 at 1388–1389.

20. See Richard A. Posner, *Economic Analysis of Law* (Boston: Little, Brown and Co., 1973). In addition see the following reviews and comments on the efficiency analysis of the common law: C. Edwin Baker, "The Ideology of the Economic Analysis of Law," *Philosophy and Public Affairs*, Vol. 5, No. 1 (Fall 1975), pp. 3–48; James M. Buchanan, "Good Economics—Bad Law," *Virginia Law Review*, Vol. 60, No. 3 (March 1974), pp. 483–492; Kent Greenawalt, "Policy, Rights, and Judicial Decision," *Georgia Law Review*, Vol. 11, No. 5 (September 1977), pp. 991–1053; James E. Krier, "Review of Economic Analysis of Law, by Richard A. Posner," *University of Pennsylvania Law Review*, Vol. 122, No. 6 (June 1974), pp. 1664–1705; Arthur Allen Leff, "Economic Analysis of Law: Some Realism About Nominalism," *Virginia Law Review*, Vol. 60, No. 3 (March 1974), pp. 451–482; H. H. Liebhafsky, "Price Theory as Jurisprudence: Law and Economics, Chicago Style," *Journal of Economic Issues*, Vol. 10, No. 1 (March 1976), pp. 23–40; Richard S. Markovits, "A Basic Structure for Microeconomic Policy Analysis in Our Worse-Than-Second-Best World: A Proposal and Related Critique of the Chicago Approach to the Study of Law and Economics," *Wisconsin Law Review*, Vol. 1975, No. 4 (1975), pp. 950–1080; A. Mitchell Polinsky,

"Economic Analysis as a Potentially Defective Product: A Buyer's Guide to Posner's Economic Analysis of Law," *Harvard Law Review*, Vol. 87, No. 8 (1974), pp. 1655–1681; Warren J. Samuels, "The Chicago School of Political Economy: A Constructive Critique," and "Chicago Doctrine as Explanation and Justification," and "Further Limits to Chicago School Doctrine," in Warren J. Samuels, Ed., *The Chicago School of Political Economy* (East Lansing: Division of Research, Graduate School of Business Administration, Michigan State University, 1976), pp. 1–18, and pp. 363–457.

21. For those interested in understanding the intellectual origins, the philosophical issues and the political and economic ramifications surrounding the use of wealth maximization as proffered by Posner see the following line of literature: Posner, "Some Uses and Abuses of Economics in Law," pp. 281–306; Frank I. Michelman, "A Comment on Some Uses and Abuses of Economics in Law," *The University of Chicago Law Review*, Vol. 45, No. 2 (Winter 1979), pp. 307–315; Richard A. Posner "Utilitarianism, Economics, and Legal Theory," *Journal of Legal Studies*, Vol. 8, No. 1 (January 1979), pp. 103–140; Ronald M. Dworkin, "Is Wealth a Value?" *Journal of Legal Studies*, Vol. 9, No. 2 (March 1980), pp. 227–242; Anthony T. Kronman, "Wealth Maximization as a Normative Principle," *Journal of Legal Studies*, Vol. 9, No. 2 (March 1980), pp. 227–242; Richard A. Posner, "The Value of Wealth: A Comment on Dworkin and Kronman," *Journal of Legal Studies*, Vol. 9, No. 2 (March 1980), pp. 243–252; Richard A. Posner, "The Ethical and Political Basis of the Efficiency Norm in Common Law Adjudication," *Hofstra Law Review*, Vol. 8, No. 3 (Spring 1980), pp. 487–507; Jules L. Coleman, "Efficiency, Exchange, and Auction: Philosophic Aspects of the Economic Approach to Law, *California Law Review*, Vol. 68, No. 2 (March 1980), pp. 221–249; Coleman, "Efficiency, Utility, and Wealth Maximization," pp. 509–551; Kornhauser, "A Guide to the Perplexed Claims of Efficiency in Law," pp. 591–639; Mario J. Rizzo, "The Mirage of Efficiency," *Hofstra Law Review*, Vol. 8, No. 3 (Spring 1980), pp. 641–658; Lucian A. Bebchuk, "The Pursuit of a Bigger Pie: Can Everyone Expect a Bigger Slice?" *Hofstra Law Review*, Vol. 8, No. 3 (Spring 1980), pp. 671–709; Donald Keenan, "Value Maximization and Welfare Theory," *Journal of Legal Studies*, Vol. 10, No. 2 (June 1981), pp. 409–419; Frank I. Michelman, "Norms and Normativity in the Economic Theory of Law," *Minnesota Law Review*, Vol. 62, No. 6 (July 1978), pp. 1015–1048; Gary T. Schwartz, "Economics, Wealth Distribution, and Justice," *Wisconsin Law Review*, Vol. 1979, No. 3 (1979), pp. 799–813; Mark Kelman, "Choice and Utility," *Wisconsin Law Review*, Vol. 1979, No. 3 (1979), pp. 769–797; Ernest J. Weinrib, "Utilitarianism, Economics, and Legal Theory," *University of Toronto Law Journal*, Vol. 30, No. 3 (Summer 1980), pp. 307–332. See also Richard S. Markovits, "Legal Analysis and the Economic Analysis of Allocative Efficiency," Morton J. Horowitz, "Law and Economics: Science or Politics?" Lawrence G. Sager, "Pareto Superiority, Consent, and Justice," C. Edwin Baker, "Starting Points in the Economic Analysis of Law," all in *Hofstra Law Review*, Vol. 8, No. 4 (Summer 1980). Warren J. Samuels, "Book Review - Maximization of Wealth as Justice: An Essay on Posnerian Law and Economics as Policy Analysis," *Texas Law Review*, Vol. 60, No. 1 (December 1981), pp. 147–172.

22. This is drawn largely from Michelman's description of the methodology of Posner's wealth maximization criterion. Michelman, "Constitutions, Statutes, and the Theory of Efficient Adjudication," pp. 433–434.

23. Posner's early work employed utility-based notions of economic efficiency, see Posner, *Economic Analysis of Law*. His current views are reflected in these works: Posner, "Some Uses and Abuses of Economics in Law," pp. 286, 287, 291; Posner, "Utilitarianism, Economics, and Legal Theory," pp. 103–127 and Posner, "The Ethical and Political Basis of the Efficiency Norm in Common Law Adjudication," pp. 487–497. His objection to the use of utilitarianism rests on three arguments: (1) the problems of measurement (how is one to measure subjective satisfaction objectively?); (2) the boundary problem (whose

satisfactions are to count?) and (3) the problem of moral monstrousness (how do we weigh the satisfactions of the criminal and the unproductive?). On these points see Posner, "The Value of Wealth: A Comment on Dworkin and Kronman," p. 251.

24. Posner, "Utilitarianism, Economics, and Legal Theory," p. 103. See also Kronman, "Wealth Maximization as a Normative Principle," pp. 227–229.

25. Posner, "Utilitarianism, Economics, and Legal Theory," p. 119.

26. Posner, "The Ethical and Political Basis of the Efficiency Norm in Common Law Adjudication," p. 497.

27. Ibid., pp. 489–491.

28. Ibid., p. 492 at footnote 13.

29. Ibid., p. 491. See also the following two articles by Coleman, "Efficiency, Exchange and Auction: Philosophical Aspects of the Economic Approach to Law," pp. 221–249, and "Efficiency, Utility and Wealth Maximization,"pp. 512–526.

30. Comparisons of outcomes associated with (1) the market, (2) legal change with compensation, and (3) wealth maximization are given by Kronman, "Wealth Maximization as Normative Principle," pp. 229–232 and Coleman, "Efficiency, Utility and Wealth Maximization," pp. 532–540.

31. This point is elaborated on by Coleman:

> The argument appears to be this: wealth-maximizing institutions by hypothesis are less costly than nonwealth-maximizing ones. A system in which compensation is paid and accepted ex post - that which is Pareto superior - is more costly than one in which compensation is not paid. The initial costs of wealth-maximizing, Kaldor-Hicks-based institutions are, therefore, lower. The difference in initial entrance costs constitutes a kind of ex ante compensation. So possible losers who engage in such activities consent by their acceptance of the lower entrance fee. They give their consent by accepting ex ante compensation in the form of lower costs.
>
> The general argument can be illustrated by example. Suppose, as Posner does, that the negligence system is less costly than a system of strict liability. One way in which strict liability and negligence differ concerns the likelihood of a victim recovering damages. In strict liability a victim is more likely to recover than in negligence where the conditions of liability are more demanding. For example, victims can recover in strict liability in cases in which the injurer is not at fault, whereas in negligence liability the victim will not recover unless the injurer is at fault.
>
> Posner apparently believes that in strict liability a victim's acceptance of compensation ex post constitutes consent to the activity that caused the harm. In negligence liability the lower costs of the system, as exemplified in insurance premiums, constitute a form of ex ante compensation, the acceptance of which constitutes for each victim consent to an uncompensated loss.

Ibid., p. 535.

32. The critical literature employs the use of the word "implicit" to capture the notion that judges may unwittingly be deciding cases on the basis of wealth maximization standard, while "explicit" is used to convey the idea that judges know and understand economics, efficiency analysis, wealth maximization . . . etc. and consciously employ these concepts to decide common law disputes.

33. Richard A. Posner, "The Economic Approach to Law," *Texas Law Review*, Vol. 53, No, 4 (May 1975), pp. 757–782 at 763–764. See also Posner, "The Value of Wealth: A Comment on Dworkin and Kronman," pp. 249–250.

34. Posner, "Some Uses and Abuses of Economics in Law," p. 292. That a judge "can hardly fail" or will "probably" incorporate economic criterion into his decision rule for resolving common law cases is asserted by Posner:

> The typical common law case involves a dispute between two parties over which one should bear a loss. In searching for a reasonably objective and impartial standard, as the traditions of the bench require him to do, *the judge can hardly fail* to consider whether the loss was the product of wasteful, uneconomical resource use. (emphasis added)

Posner, *Economic Analysis of Law,* 2nd ed., p. 181. Elsewhere, Posner states:

> To say what the common law is not is not to say what it is, but that too can be derived from the preceding analysis. There are numerous politically effective groups in the society; the question is what their rational objectives are likely to be in areas regulated by common law methods. *Probably their self-interest is promoted* by supporting the efficiency norm in those areas. By doing so they increase the wealth of the society; they will get a share of that increased wealth; and there is no alternative norm that would yield a larger share. (emphasis added)

Posner, "The Ethical and Political Basis of the Efficiency Norm in Common Law Adjudication," p. 505. For synoptic critiques see Michelman, "A Comment on Some Uses and Abuses of Economics in Law," pp. 307–315, and Epstein, "The Static Conception of the Common Law," pp. 271–273.

35. Richard A. Posner, "Legal Change, Judicial Behavior, and the Diversity Jurisdiction," *Journal of Legal Studies,* Vol. 9, No. 2 (March 1980), pp. 367–386 at 368.

36. See footnote 21 (this chapter).

37. Michelman, "A Comment on Some Uses and Abuses of Economics in Law," p. 312.

38. The question immediately arises as to why background law that emerges from the application of a specific decision rule will ultimately yield an efficient outcome. One answer to this question is provided by the evolutionary theories of the common law, reviewed earlier in this chapter.

39. Baker, "Starting Points in the Economic Analysis of Law," p. 967.

40. For a discussion of the doctrine of the equitable distribution of property and the criteria that will be taken into account in its application see *Painter v. Painter,* 65 N. J. Supreme 196 (1974) Supreme Court of New Jersey.

41. With respect to "fundamental rights" the issue is not resolved by either supporting or rejecting judicial intervention in the judicial review of such doctrines. Active or inactive review courts both decide on the legitimacy of decision rules. The point here is that regardless of the choice, an efficient outcome will still be observed. See Paul Brest, "The Fundamental Rights Controversy: The Essential Contradictions of Normative Constitutional Scholarship," *The Yale Law Journal,* Vol. 90, No. 5 (April 1981), pp. 1063–1109.

42. Posner's normative choice of a "best" structure of rights based on his wealth maximization principle is also recognized in Kornhauser, "A Guide to the Perplexed Claims of Efficiency in the Law," p. 595.

43. Posner, "Utilitarianism, Economics, and Legal Theory," p. 125.

44. Ibid., pp. 103, 110.

45. Posner, "The Ethical and Political Basis of the Efficiency Norm in Common Law Adjudication," p. 487.

46. The following conceptions of the instrumentalist pursuit of wealth maximization is drawn from Dworkin, "Is Wealth a Value," p. 195.

47. Posner, *Economic Analysis of Law*, 2nd ed., p. 416.

48. On this latter question see Coleman, "Efficiency, Utility, and Wealth Maximization," pp. 528–530.

49. Dworkin, "Is Wealth a Value?" pp. 199–201.

50. Kornhauser, "A Guide to the Perplexed Claims of Efficiency in the Law," pp. 597–603.

51. Cento J. Veljanovski, "Wealth Maximization, Law and Ethics—On the Limits of Economic Efficiency," *International Review of Law and Economics*, Vol. 1, No. 1 (June 1981), pp. 5–28 at 20.

52. Samuels, "Book Review–Maximization of Wealth as Justice: An Essay on Posnerian Law and Economics as Policy Analysis," p. 155.

53. Alan Randall suggests the use of status quo prices will always result in a bias in favor of the status quo. Alan Randall, "Property Rights and Social Microeconomics," *Natural Resources Journal*, Vol. 15, No. 4 (October 1975), pp. 729–747 at 739–740.

54. Coleman, "Efficiency, Utility, and Wealth Maximization," p. 526.

55. Posner, "The Ethical and Political Bias of the Efficiency Norm in Common Law Adjudication," p. 501.

56. Posner, *Economic Analysis of Law*, 2nd ed., pp. 61–62. See also Posner, Utilitarianism, Economics, and Legal Theory," pp. 108–109.

57. Coleman, "Efficiency, Utility, and Wealth Maximization," pp. 525–526.

58. Michelman, "Constitutions, Statutes, and the Theory of Efficient Adjudication," p. 434.

59. Richard A. Epstein, "Privacy, Property Rights, and Misrepresentations," *Georgia Law Review*, Vol. 12, No. 3 (September 1978), pp. 455–474 at 462.

60. See text at footnote 25 (this chapter).

61. These are reviewed by Duncan Kennedy, "Cost-Benefit Analysis of Entitlement Problems: A Critique," *Stanford Law Review*, Vol. 33, No. 3 (February 1981), pp. 387–445 at 401–402.

62. Bebchuk, "The Pursuit of a Bigger Pie: Can Everyone Expect a Bigger Slice?" p. 679.

63. Baker, "Starting Points in the Economic Analysis of Law," p. 949.

64. Posner, "Utilitarianism, Economics, and Legal Theory," p. 121.

65. As Coleman has pointed out, Posner's rule does not actually involve an auction but instead assigns rights and entitlements as if they were being auctioned; Coleman, "Efficiency, Exchange and Auction: Philosophic Aspects of the Economic Approach to Law," p. 241 at footnote 25. See also Kronman, "Wealth Maximization as a Normative Principle," pp. 240–242.

66. On this point see Bebchuk, "The Pursuit of a Bigger Pie: Can Everyone Expect a Bigger Slice?" pp. 678–681 and Baker, "The Ideology of the Economic Analysis of Law," pp. 3–48.

67. Kennedy, "Cost-Benefit Analysis of Entitlement Problems: A Critique," pp. 401–421.

68. Kronman, "Wealth Maximization as a Normative Principle," pp. 228–229. Morton J. Horowitz goes as far as any of the critics suggesting that Posner's foray into normative law and economics is "a dramatic sign that the scientific pretensions of the economic analysis of the law are rapidly crumbling." See Horowitz, "Law and Economics: Science or Politics?" p. 905.

69. Dennis C. Mueller, *Public Choice* (Cambridge: Cambridge University Press, 1979), p. 1.

70. Ibid.

71. Two seminal works in this area are Anthony Downs, *An Economic Theory of Democ-*

racy (New York: Harper and Row, 1957), and Duncan Black, *The Theory of Committees and Elections* (Cambridge: Cambridge University Press, 1958).

72. Mueller has suggested the validity of propositions derived from public choice models are contingent upon a favorable comparison with non-economic models which attempt to explain the same phenomena. He states:

> It is common practice in economics to 'test' a hypothesis by checking whether the results are 'consistent' with it without exploring whether they are also consistent with other, conflicting hypotheses. While it is perhaps unfair to hold public choice to higher standards than the other branches of economics, I do not think that this methodology suffices here. To demonstrate that public choice has something useful to contribute to the existing empirical literature on public finance and public policy, its models must be tested against the existing models, which ignore public choice considerations. Unless public choice derived models can out-perform the 'traditional, ad hoc' models against which it competes, the practical relevance of its theories must remain somewhat in doubt. Mueller, *Public Choice*, p. 111.

73. These voting rules are reviewed in Ibid., pp. 19–67.

74. Ibid., pp. 97–124.

75. William C. Mitchell, "Textbook Public Choice: A Review Essay," *Public Choice*, Vol. 38, No. 1 (1982), pp. 97–112 at 98–101, and Mueller, *Public Choice*, p. 207.

76. The most often referred to set of axioms are set forth in Kenneth J. Arrow, *Social Choice and Individual Values* (New York: John Wiley and Sons, Inc. 1951). For reviews of Arrow's work see Mueller, *Public Choice*, pp. 184–206 and Allan M. Feldman, *Welfare Economics and Social Choice Theory* (Boston: Martinus Nijhoff Publishing, 1980), pp. 178–196.

77. Typically Pareto optimality is incorporated into the axioms. It is unclear to us (1) whether a particular voting mechanism which satisfies the axioms could yield more than one socially preferred point, and (2) whether two or more voting rules, each of which satisfies the axioms, will yield separate socially preferred points.

78. Feldman, *Welfare Economics and Social Choice Theory*, p. 6.

79. A notable contribution to relaxing the typical neoclassical constraints by someone not located in the public choice tradition is Gary Becker, *The Economic Approach to Human Behavior* (Chicago: University of Chicago Press, 1976).

80. The methodological movement toward closure has its origins in the works of the European public finance scholars. For a review of the thrust of their work and a description of the movement toward closure see James M. Buchanan, "Toward Analysis of Closed Behaviorial Systems," in James M. Buchanan and Robert D. Tollison, Eds., *Theory of Public Choice* (Ann Arbor: The University of Michigan Press, 1972), pp. 11–23 and James M. Buchanan, "Public Finance and Public Choice," *National Tax Journal*, Vol. 28, No. 4 (December 1975), pp. 383–394 at 384–385.

81. Buchanan, "Toward Analysis of Closed Behaviorial Systems," p. 12.

82. These are reviewed in Mueller, *Public Choice*, pp. 97–147.

83. Important contributions to this area include William A. Niskanen, *Bureaucracy and Representative Government* (Chicago: Aldine-Atherton, 1970). Gordon Tullock, *The Politics of Bureaucracy* (Washington, D.C.: Public Affairs Press, 1965). Anthony Downs, *Inside Bureaucracy* (Boston: Little, Brown and Co., 1967).

84. Downs, *An Economic Theory of Democracy*. Robert Abrams, *Foundations of Political Analysis* (New York: Columbia University Press, 1980). William Riker and Peter Ordeshook, *An Introduction to Positive Political Theory* (Englewood Cliffs: Prentice-Hall, Inc., 1973).

85. See sources at footnote 83 (this chapter).

86. A seminal work in this area is James M. Buchanan and Gordon Tullock, *The Calculus of Consent: Logical Foundations of Constitutional Democracy* (Ann Arbor: The University of Michigan Press, 1965).

87. This assumes the legislator has correctly perceived the preferences of the parties of interest. Within limits he may be able to make choices contrary to these known preferences. Further, it is possible that he may have incorrectly perceived the preferences. In either case beyond some point, if his political choices do not coincide with the actual preferences of the parties of interest, they may lobby to alter his choice or replace him with someone who will better serve their interests.

88. For an in depth historical review of Section 404 and its impact on the U.S. Army Corps of Engineers see Edward Thompson, Jr., "Section 404 of the Federal Water Pollution Control Act Amendments of 1977: Hydrologic Modification, Wetlands Protection and the Physical Integrity of the Nation's Waters," *Harvard Environmental Law Review*, Vol. 2 (1977), pp. 264–287. The facts in the text describing this rule change borrows heavily from the Thompson article.

89. Principally the *Rivers and Harbors Act of 1899*.

90. *National Resources Defense Council, Inc. v. Callaway*, 392 F. Supp. 685 (D.D.C. 1975).

91. Thompson, "Section 404 of the Federal Water Pollution Control Act Amendments," pp. 279–280. These comments were directed at the 1977 Act which preserved intact the major thrust of Section 404 of the 1972 Act. Thus, they remain applicable here.

92. Ibid., pp. 279–280 at footnote 87.

93. Roland N. McKean, "Divergences Between Individual and Total Costs Within Government," in Ryan C. Amacher, et al., Eds., *The Economic Approach to Public Policy* (Ithaca: Cornell University Press, 1976), pp. 362–368 at 363.

94. Buchanan, "Toward Analysis of Closed Behavioral Systems," p. 14.

95. The dissatisfaction with the prevailing political and bureaucratic processes is illustrated in the following quotes. With respect to the political processes Buchanan has stated:

> If the behavior of politicians in seeking and securing 'political income' while holding elective office does nothing but create some slack between the working of practical government and an idealized drawing-board model, there would be no cause for concern here. But if this behavior of politicians biases results consistently in the direction of larger governments, it becomes relevant for our purpose. The presence of such biases seems clearly established.

James M. Buchanan, "Why Does Government Grow?" in Thomas Borcherding, Ed., *Budgets and Bureaucrats: The Sources of Government Growth* (Durham: Duke University Press, 1977), pp. 3–18 at 13. With respect to the bureaucracy the following has been pointed out:

> As the public sector has grown during the last several decades, charges of bureaucratic inefficiency and unresponsiveness have become increasingly widespread. In the past, criticism of bureaucratic decision-making arose primarily from sources seeking to reduce the size of government. However, in recent years, advocates of public sector action have often been at the forefront of those charging that the bureaucracy has failed to carry out legislative intent and has been insensitive to the needs of the average citizen.

James D. Gwartney and Richard Stroup, *Microeconomics: Private and Public Choice*, 2nd ed., (New York: Academic Press, 1980), p. 451.

96. For a detailed discussion of methodological individualism see May Brodbeck,

"Methodological Individualism: Definition and Reduction," *Philosophy of Science*, Vol. 25, No. 1 (January 1958), pp. 1–22.

97. James M. Buchanan, "What Kind of Redistribution Do We Want?" *Economica*, Vol. 35, No. 138 (May 1968), pp. 185–204 at 188.

98. Buchanan and Tullock, *The Calculus of Consent*, p. 96.

99. See footnote 5, Chapter IV.

100. Variations to the unanimity rule are incorporated into their analysis and will be taken up shortly.

101. James M. Buchanan, "Positive Economics, Welfare Economics, and Political Economy," *Journal of Law and Economics*, Vol. 2 (October 1959), pp. 124–138 at 128–133. James M. Buchanan, "The Coase Theorem and the Theory of the State," *Natural Resources Journal*, Vol. 13, No. 4 (October 1973), pp. 579–593 at 583–584.

102. Buchanan, "Positive Economics, Welfare Economics, and Political Economy," p. 129.

103. Ibid., p. 131.

104. Victor P. Goldberg, "Public Choice—Property Rights," *Journal of Economic Issues*, Vol. 8, No. 3 (September 1974), pp. 555–579 at 562. (Goldberg's account of Buchanan's position is a synthesis of Buchanan's writing and personal correspondence between them.)

105. Ibid., p. 563. (Private correspondence from James M. Buchanan to Goldberg, dated November 1, 1973.)

106. James M. Buchanan, "What Should Economists Do?" *Southern Economic Journal*, Vol. 30, No. 3 (January 1964), pp. 213–222 at 217. This notion of "political exchange" is described in Buchanan and Tullock, *The Calculus of Consent*, pp. 250–253. See also James M. Buchanan, "Before Public Choice," in Gordon Tullock, Ed., *Explorations in the Theory of Anarchy* (Blacksburg: Center for the Study of Public Choice, 1972), pp. 27–37.

107. Buchanan and Tullock, *The Calculus of Consent*, p. 210.

108. Buchanan, "Before Public Choice," p. 36. Elsewhere Buchanan states:

> There is an explicit prejudice in favor of previously existing rights, not because this structure possesses some intrinsic ethical attributes, and not because change itself is undesirable, but for the much more elementary reason that only such a prejudice offers incentives for the emergence of voluntary negotiated settlements among the parties themselves.

James M. Buchanan, "Politics, Property, and the Law: An Alternative Interpretation of Miller et al. v. Schoene," *Journal of Law and Economics*, Vol. 15, No. 2 (October 1972), pp. 439–452 at 452.

109. Buchanan, "The Coase Theorem and the Theory of the State," p. 583.

110. Buchanan and Tullock, *The Calculus of Consent*, p. 95.

111. Ibid., pp. 78, 314.

112. Ibid., pp. 211–231.

113. Ibid., pp. 63–84.

114. See text circa footnotes 102 and 103 (this chapter).

115. Buchanan, "Positive Economics, Welfare Economics, and Political Economy," pp. 130–131.

116. Ibid., pp. 126–128.

117. Buchanan and Tullock, *The Calculus of Consent*, pp. 92–96. See also James M. Buchanan, "The Relevance of Pareto Optimality," *Journal of Conflict Resoluton*, Vol. 6, No. 4 (1962), pp. 341–354 at 351–354.

118. Buchanan and Tullock, *The Calculus of Consent*, p. 94.

119. Ibid., pp. 94–95.

120. Gordon Tullock, *The Logic of the Law* (New York: Basic Books, Inc., 1971), p. 8.

121. The significant role of the status quo structure of rights and rules within the contractarian approach is discussed in footnote 108 and text circa footnote 108 of this chapter.

122. Buchanan and Tullock, *The Calculus of Consent,* p. 341.

123. Ibid., p. 14. See also text circa footnotes 11 through 20 of Chapter IV.

124. Buchanan and Tollison, *Theory of Public Choice,* p. 5.

125. Buchanan, "Before Public Choice," p. 36.

126. See James M. Buchanan and Warren J. Samuels, "On Some Fundamental Issues in Political Economy: An Exchange of Correspondence," *Journal of Economic Issues,* Vol. 9, No. 1 (March 1975), pp. 15–38.

Chapter VI

Summary

Surely one might have grounds other than comparative efficiency for choosing among regimes. A regime might be preferred for the sake of its expected distributional outcomes, or because it conforms to extraeconomic conceptions of rights. Such concerns might immediately dictate the choice among regimes without regard to efficiency comparisons; or efficiency comparisons might be relevant but not necessarily controlling, given some 'social welfare function' that specifies the form and rate of exchange among efficiency and other concerns.[1] (Michelman, 1982)

The attempt has been to present a descriptive model of Law and Economics that can serve as a basis for a comparative institutional approach to study the various points of intersection between law and economics. The model, essentially neoinstitutional in its origin, brings together the most prominent legal-economic schools of thought under an umbrella framework. Within this framework, we have explored the basic components of the new law and economics, the economics of property rights, public choice theory and the necessary and valuable critiques of the neoinstitutionalists and the critical legal studies group. As such, our attempt has been to provide an integrated approach to Law and Economics that focuses on the common unifying elements of the various schools of thought as opposed to one more book of readings.[2] We recognize that the comparative institutional approach embodied in our model of Law and Economics is only one normative way of analyzing the interrelations between the economic and legal arenas. In the market place of ideas, we would hope that there will be alternative attempts to integrate these various schools of thought from perspectives different from our own.

The purpose of the comparative institutional approach to Law and Economics is to better understand the world we live in, concentrating on the interaction between law and economics and the role played by the legal-economic institutions in determining the character of economic life. This approach is amenable not only to the study of the prevailing legal-economic institutions and legal relations governing society but also to the study of alternative legal-economic institutions and legal relations. We believe that this approach helps to unmask the options open to society as well as to highlight the necessity of choice involved throughout Law and Economics.

In an attempt to provide a better understanding of our model of Law and Economics, we will briefly discuss the major issues highlighted in Chapters III, IV, and V as we review the basic components of the model. Recall, the legal institutions (which include legislatures, judiciaries, executive offices, government commissions, bureaucratic agencies, and custom) are at center stage and are treated as endogenous decision-making units. Thus, the prevailing legal institutions are not given immutably by nature but are themselves a response to economic needs and are flexible in response to changes in those needs. The legal-economic participants are rational, utility maximizing individuals who not only act in the market place but also participate in the legal and political decision-making processes to enhance their utility. It is recognized that any action of the legal-economic participants to alter working rules or rights carries with it an opportunity cost. The participants will endeavor to structure or revise: (1) the constitution, (2) the working rules of institutions, and (3) the property, status, and communal rights in the private, public, and communal sectors, respectively, in an attempt to achieve an allocation and distribution of resources that enhance their individual welfares. See Figure VI.1.

At the constitutional stage of choice, the contractarian approach to public choice theory provides one normative theory of constitutions. It is a Pareto optimal, efficiency-based scheme by which a constitution can be structured and revised. Axiomatic social choice attempts to provide an alternative approach to structure constitutions, although, as described earlier, the results are of questionable value. Regardless of the manner in which constitutions are formulated and revised, the constitution partially structures the legal institutions and thus affects, though perhaps subtly, the character of economic life.

In order to better understand the interrelationship between the institutional stage of choice and the economic impact stage of choice, we will briefly review the theories of Law and Economics that were taken up in the previous chapters. The public choice contractarian approach provides a Pareto optimal, efficiency-based method for organizing political and governmental activities. Within the context of our model, it provides one normative set of rules by which legal institutions can operate in formulating the legal relations governing society. In conventional public choice theory, the political rules of collective order (i.e., the working

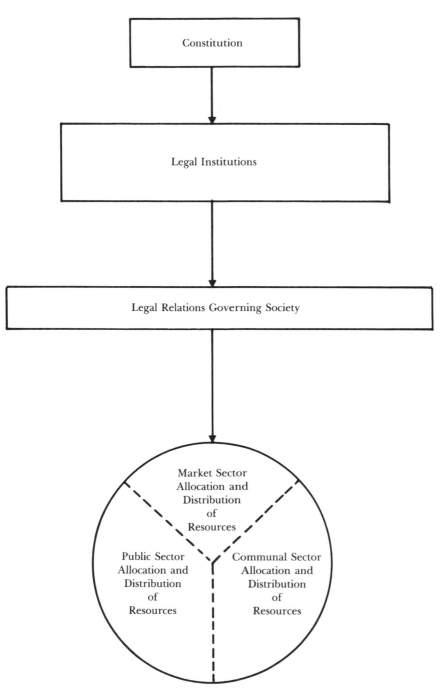

Figure VI.1.

rules) that guide the behavior of legislatures and bureaucratic agencies are analyzed. In this work, the attempt is to provide a better understanding of the choices of legislatures and bureaucracies concerning the property rights, status rights, and communal rights that comprise the legal relations governing society. The literature includes pure descriptive empirical work, positive efficiency-based analysis, and normative analysis that relies heavily on efficiency criteria.

With respect to the new law and economics some of the contributors have attempted to assess the efficiency of the legal relations that emerge from the entire common law process by use of trial settlement models and various evolutionary models of the common law. Further, contributors to the new law and economics have offered several decision rules to guide the judiciary in deciding cases. Richard A. Posner has advanced his decision rule of wealth maximization. Wealth maximization is a normative criteria that may be adopted by the judiciary to guide it in common law adjudication. As formulated by Posner, wealth maximization is equivalent to the Kaldor-Hicks efficiency criterion. Other decision rules include justice, fairness, happiness, and equality. Clearly, these decision rules are not efficiency based. However, it is evident that a choice of any one decision rule over another will impact on the legal relations governing society and ultimately the character of economic life. The discussion of the taking issue was used to highlight the interaction between the judiciary and those governmental units that have police power or eminent domain authority. Once a government action is accomplished under the police power or the power of eminent domain and a party of interest claims that a taking has occurred, the judge must then decide whether or not the government action constitutes a taking. There are various decision rules that the court could employ to resolve these cases. In deciding these cases, the courts establish, in part, the rights that comprise the legal relations governing society.

Some contributors to the new law and economics, together with some of those who write on the economics of property rights, have studied liability rules in the area of tort law. Various negligence standards, strict liability standards, and other rules for assigning liability have been analyzed from an efficiency standpoint. Typically, the concern is whether the various liability rules and consequent assignments of liability are efficient in the sense that they minimize interaction damage costs. Liability rules and consequent assignments of liability based on justice or fairness are also set forth. The court in adopting, or perhaps the legislature in promulgating, one liability rule over another will structure the set of rights that comprise the legal relations governing society.

Contributors to the economics of property rights have also explored the concept of the attenuation of property rights in the market sector.

Here, the various decision rules used by the judicial and political institutions determine the degree of attenuation of rights to effective commodities and resources that ultimately affect the prevailing legal relations governing society.

The above brief review is intended to emphasize that the working rules of institutions—the political rules of collective order; judicial decision rules to guide the judiciary: wealth maximization, justice, fairness, happiness, and equality; decision rules in taking issue litigation: the harm-benefit rule, the fair compensation test, and the critical natural features test; the liability rules of tort law; and the decision rules that determine the attenuation of property rights—establish the legal relations governing society. Additionally, these legal relations establish the property rights, status rights, and the communal rights. These rights determine the scope and content of the market, public, and communal sectors. These sectors, as means of social control, allocate and distribute resources and thereby affect the character of economic life.

Given our perspective of the legal economic system and our conception of Law and Economics, we suggest the scope of legal-economic analysis should include the following fundamental elements:

1. Start the analysis with the situation approximating that which actually exists, recognizing that prevailing benefits and costs are partially a function of the prevailing structure of working rules and property rights. In this context, prevailing "side effects" or "externalities" may be viewed as merely economic impacts consequent to the prevailing structure of working rules and property rights.

2. Describe the behavior of the legal-economic participants as they are engaged in constitutional, institutional, and economic impact stages of choices in order to gain better understanding of the prevailing legal-economic processes. While our model poses individual utility maximization as the primary motivational force of the legal-economic participants, other models might use group motivation, public interest, power, etc.

3. Examine the full array of consequences of altering: (a) the constitution, (b) the working rules of the legal institutions, or (c) the prevailing structures of private property, status and communal rights governing the allocation and distribution of resources between and within the market, public and communal sectors.

Accomplishing this task involves the following fundamental problems that have yet to be worked out in Law and Economics:

First, with respect to a specific legal-economic problem confronting society, it is unclear at which level the analysis should be conducted. It is observed that practitioners of Law and Economics, for example, have analyzed the issue of interaction damage costs at various levels of choice. Specifically, James M. Buchanan and Gordon Tullock analyze the issue at the constitutional stage of choice, Posner analyzes it at the institutional stage of choice, and Ronald H. Coase analyzes it at the economic-impact stage of choice. In general, it is unclear if there is an "appropriate" level at which to conduct the analysis.

Inasmuch as the distribution of resources is an important component of Law and Economics, policies incorporating legal change that are sanctioned on the basis of the compensation principle should stipulate whether or not actual compensation will be forthcoming. If actual compensation is mandated, one distribution of resources will result, whereas, if compensation is not mandated, an alternative distribution of resources will result. The full array of consequences can be known only if the question of compensation is explicitly addressed.

A third problem involved in examining the economic consequences of altering the legal relations governing society concerns the necessary use of status quo prices. Alan Randall describes this methodological problem as follows:

> Positive empirical efficiency analysis of alternative structures of rights suffers an almost intractable difficulty. If prices generated under an existing structure of rights are used to evaluate that output expected under an alternative structure of rights, an inexorable bias in favor of the status quo is introduced into the analysis. This principle is best grasped when considering two alternative sets of nonattenuated rights. Each is efficient on its own terms. Each is suboptimal, in terms of the value of output generated, when evaluated according to prices generated by the other set of rights. Thus, an efficiency analysis comparing two sets of nonattenuated rights, one of which is the status quo, will always favor the status quo set.[3]

Furthermore, in situations where prices are not observable, practioners of Law and Economics are forced to use "some" prices in order to assess the allocative consequences of a change in the legal relations governing society. One can use offer prices, asking prices, or some other set of proxy prices. The implications of this normative choice among these alternatives must be made clear.

Finally, it must be recognized that society faces a continuing necessity of choice at each stage of choice, the resolution of which will ultimately determine the character of economic life in society. As Victor P. Goldberg puts it "this requires that we must to at least some extent 'play God.' But given the ungodly alternative, play we must."[4]

NOTES AND REFERENCES

1. Frank I. Michelman, "Ethics, Economics, and the Law of Property," in J. Roland Pennock and John W. Chapman, Eds., *Ethics, Economics, and the Law: Nomos XXIV* (New York: York University Press, 1982), pp. 3–40 at 6, 7.

2. Three recent books (not collections of readings) in law and economics are: Roger Bowles, *Law and the Economy* (Oxford: Martin Robertson, 1982); A. Mitchell Polinsky, *An Introduction to Law and Economics* (Boston: Little, Brown and Co., 1983); and Cento G. Veljanovski, *The New Law -and- Economics* (Oxford: Centre for Socio - Legal Studies, 1982).

3. Alan Randall, "Property Rights and Social Microeconomics," *Natural Resources Journal,* Vol. 15, No. 4 (October 1975), pp. 729–747 at 739–740.

4. Victor P. Goldberg, "Public Choice—Property Rights," *Journal of Economic Issues,* Vol. 8, No. 3 (September 1974), pp. 555–579 at 573.

Acknowledgments

The following chapters contain reprinted material from the various journals and books indicated.

Chapter I

Theoretical Welfare Economics, copyright © 1975 by Cambridge University
   Press. Reprinted with permission.
Introduction to General Equilibrium Theory and Welfare Economics, copyright
   © 1968 by McGraw Hill Book Co. Reprinted with permission.
The Economic Approach to Public Policy, copyright © 1976 by Cornell Uni-
   versity Press. Reprinted with permission.
Economic Foundations of Property Law, copyright © 1975 by Little, Brown
   and Co. Reprinted with permission.

Chapter II

A Theory of Justice, copyright © 1971 by The Bellnap Press. Reprinted
   with permission.
Law and Economics: An Introductory Analysis, copyright © 1979 by Academic Press. Reprinted with permission.
The Calculus of Consent: Logical Foundations of Constitutional Democracy,
   copyright © 1965 by the University of Michigan Press. Reprinted
   with permission.
The Economics of Property Rights, copyright © 1974 by Ballinger Publishing Co. Reprinted with permission.

"Interrelations Between Legal and Economic Processes," Vol. 14, No. 2, copyright © 1971 (October) by the *Journal of Law and Economics.* Reprinted with permission.

"Economics as a Moral Science," Vol. 37, No. 2, copyright © 1974 (October) by the *Review of Social Economy.* Reprinted with permission.

Essays in Positive Economics, copyright © 1953 by the University of Chicago Press. Reprinted with permission.

"The Problem of Social Cost," Vol. 3, copyright © 1960 (Spring) by the *Journal of Law and Economics.* Reprinted with permission.

Chapter III

The Economics of Welfare, copyright © 1952 by Macmillan and Co. Reprinted with permission.

"Property Rules, Liability Rules, and Inalienability: One View of the Cathedral," Vol. 85, No. 6, copyright © 1972 (April) by *Harvard Law Review.* Reprinted with permission.

Property, Power, and Public Choice: An Inquiry into Law and Economics, copyright © 1978 by Praeger Publishers. Reprinted with permission.

"Transaction Costs, Resource Allocation, and Liability Rules—A Comment." Vol. 11, copyright © 1968 (April) by the *Journal of Law and Economics.* Reprinted with permission.

"The Problem of Externality," Vol. 22, No. 1, copyright © 1979 (April) by the *Journal of Law and Economics.* Reprinted with permission.

Chapter IV

"Property Rights and Economic Theory," Vol. 10, No. 4, copyright © 1972 (December) by the *Journal of Economic Literature.* Reprinted with permission.

Redistribution Through Public Choice, copyright © 1974 by Columbia University Press. Reprinted with permission.

Theory of Public Choice, copyright © 1972 by The University of Michigan Press. Reprinted with permission.

"Takings and the Police Power," Vol. 74, No. 1, copyright © 1964 (November) by the *Yale Law Journal.* Reprinted with permission.

"In Defense of a Positive Approach to Government as an Economic Variable," Vol. 15, No. 2, copyright © 1972 (October) by the *Journal of Law and Economics.* Reprinted with permission.

"Fairness and Utility in Tort Theory," Vol. 85, No. 3, copyright © 1972 (January) by the *Harvard Law Review.* Reprinted with permission.

"Property Rules, Liability Rules, and Inalienability: One View of the Cathedral," Vol. 85, No. 6, copyright © 1972 (April) by the *Harvard Law Review*. Reprinted with permission.

"The Problem of Social Cost," Vol. 3, copyright © 1960 (Spring) by the *Journal of Law and Economics*. Reprinted with permission.

Economic Analysis of Law, 2nd ed., copyright © 1977 by Little, Brown and Company. Reprinted with permission.

Chapter V

"Symposium on Efficiency as a Legal Concern," Vol. 18, No. 3, copyright © 1980 (Spring) by the *Hofstra Law Review*. Reprinted with permission.

"Some Uses and Abuses of Economics in Law," Vol. 46, No. 2, copyright © 1979 (Winter) by the *University of Chicago Law Review*. Reprinted with permission.

"Why is the Common Law Efficient?" Vol. 6, No. 1, copyright © 1977 (January) by the *Journal of Legal Studies*. Reprinted with permission.

"An Economic Theory of the Evolution of Common Law," Vol. 7, No. 2, copyright © 1978 (June) by the *Journal of Legal Studies*. Reprinted with permission.

"Constitutions, Statutes, and the Theory of Efficient Adjudication," Vol. 9, No. 3, copyright © 1980 (June) by the *Journal of Legal Studies*. Reprinted with permission.

"Post-Realist Legal Scholarship," Vol. 1980, No. 6, copyright © 1980 by the *Wisconsin Law Review*. Reprinted with permission.

"The Ethical and Political Basis of the Efficiency Norm in Common Law Adjudication," Vol. 8, No. 3, copyright © 1980 (Spring) by the *Hofstra Law Review*. Reprinted with permission.

"Efficiency, Utility, and Wealth Maximization," Vol. 8, No. 3, copyright © 1980 (Spring) by the *Hofstra Law Review*. Reprinted with permission.

"Legal Change, Judicial Behavior, and the Diversity Jurisdiction," Vol. 9, No. 2, copyright © 1980 (March) by the *Journal of Legal Studies*. Reprinted with permission.

"A Comment on Some Uses and Abuses of Economics in Law," Vol. 45, No. 2, copyright © 1979 (Winter) by the *University of Chicago Law Review*. Reprinted with permission.

"Starting Points in the Economic Analysis of Law," Vol. 8, No. 4, copyright © 1980 (Summer) by the *Hofstra Law Review*. Reprinted with permission.

Chapter VI

Author Index

Abel, Richard A., 10n, 42n
Abrams, Robert, 161n
Ackerman, Bruce A., 9, 10n, 12n
Alchian, Armen A., 24, 41n
Alstyne, Arvo Van, 113n, 115n
Amacher, Ryan C., 10n, 11n, 12n, 59, 67n, 162n
Arrow, Kenneth J., 12n, 140, 161n
Auerbach, Carl A., 40n
Ayers, Clarence E., 2, 29, 42n

Baden, John, 42n
Baker, C. Edwin, 128, 135, 156n, 157n, 159n, 160n
Balbus, Isaac D., 10n, 40n
Banta, John, 114n, 115n, 116n
Barlowe, Raleigh, 41n, 113n
Barone, E., 109n
Bator, Francis M., 65n
Baumol, William J., 66n
Bebchuk, Lucian A., 135, 157n, 160n
Becker, Gary, 161n
Berger, Lawrence, 115n
Berolzheimer, Fritz, 1, 10n
Beuscher, J. H., 114n

Birmingham, Robert L., 65n
Black, Duncan, 161n
Blaug, Mark, 5, 8, 12n
Borcherding, Thomas, 162n
Bosselman, Fred, 114n, 115n, 116n
Boulding, Kenneth E., 65n
Bowles, Roger, 171n
Breit, William, x
Brest, Paul, 10n, 159n
Brodbeck, May, 162n
Brown, John P., 98, 111n, 113n
Buchanan, James M., 1, 11n, 19, 36, 40n, 41n, 42n, 65n, 66n, 74, 75, 110n, 141, 146, 147, 148, 149, 150, 153, 154, 156, 161n, 162n, 163n, 164n, 170
Burrows, Paul, 10n, 11n, 113n

Calabresi, Guido, 1, 59, 61, 67n, 68n, 79, 80, 85, 86, 87, 96, 97, 98, 106, 111n, 112n, 113n, 115n
Calles, David, 114n, 115n, 116n
Carter, Allan M., 66n
Chapman, John W., 170n

Cheung, Steven N. S., 6, 12n, 67n
Chipman, John S., 108n
Clark, John M., 67n
Coase, Ronald H., 1, 10n, 39, 42n, 56, 57, 58, 59, 60, 61, 62, 63, 64, 66n, 67n, 68n, 81, 82, 83, 84, 85, 106, 111n, 112n, 115n, 170
Cochran, Kendall P., 11n, 36, 42n
Coleman, Jules L., 109n, 118, 133, 155n, 157n, 158n, 160n
Conybeare, John A. C., 112n
Cooter, Robert, 67n, 156n
Costonis, John J., 114n, 115n

Dahlman, Carl J., 11n, 43, 62, 64, 65n, 68n
Demsetz, Harold, 24, 41n, 58, 60, 61, 62, 63, 65n, 67n, 68n
Dick, Daniel T., 66n
Downs, Anthony, 160n, 161n
Dunham, Allison, 114n
Dworkin, Ronald, 132, 157n, 158n, 159n, 160n

Ehrlich, Isaac, 156n
Ellickson, Robert C., 115n
Elzinga, Kenneth, x
Englard, Izhak, 110n, 111n
Epstein, Richard A., 78, 79, 111n, 112n, 113n, 134, 155n, 156n, 159n, 160n

Feldman, Allan M., 41n, 140, 161n
Ferguson, C. E., 65n
Fletcher, George P., 76, 78, 79, 110n, 111n, 112n, 113n
Foley, Duncan K., 11n

Friedman, Milton, 11n, 12n, 38, 42n
Frisch, Ragnar, 11n
Fulham, John F., 114n
Furubotn, Eirik G., 1, 24, 27, 41n, 65n, 110n

Galbraith, John Kenneth, 66n
Gibson, W. L., Jr., 12n, 40n, 108n
Goldberg, Victor P., 110n, 163n, 170, 171n
Goodman, John C., 121, 156n
Gould, John P., 65n, 155n
Graaff, J. de V., 4, 11n, 12n, 109n
Grant, J. A. C., 114n
Greenawalt, Kent, 156n
Gregory, Charles O., 113n
Gruchy, Allan G., 10n
Gwartney, James D., 162n

Hagman, Donald G., 114n
Hand, Learned, 92
Hardin, Garrett, 42n
Hayek, F. A., 109n
Henderson, James M., 11n
Herber, Bernard, 43, 65n
Hicks, J. R., 109n
Hirsch, Werner Z., 10n, 14, 40n, 68n, 112n
Hirschleifer, Jack, 65n, 156n
Hirschoff, Jon T., 80, 96, 97, 98, 111n
Hochman, Harold H., 11n, 73, 110n
Holmes, Oliver W., 103
Horowitz, Morton J., 10n, 157n, 160n

Johnson, George W., 114n
Johnson, Harry G., 40n
Johnston, John D., Jr., 114n

Kahn, Alfred E., 66n
Kaldor, Nicholas, 11n, 109n
Keenan, Donald, 157n
Kelman, Mark, 2, 67n, 157n
Kennedy, Duncan, 2, 10n, 113n,
    115n, 136, 160n
Klappholz, Kurt, 11n
Klare, Karl, 2, 10n
Klevorick, Alvin K., 10n
Kloten, Norbert, 12n
Koopmans, Tjalling C., 11n
Kornhauser, Lewis A., 118, 132,
    155n, 156n, 157n, 159n,
    160n
Krier, James E., 156n
Kronman, Anthony T., 136,
    157n, 158n, 160n

Lancaster, Kelvin, 53, 54, 66n
Landes, William M., 155n, 156n
Larsen, Wendy V., 114n
Leff, Arthur A., 42n, 66n, 156n
Lekachman, Robert, 10n
Liebhafsky, H. H., 2, 42n, 156n
Lipsey, Richard G., 53, 54, 66n
Little, I. M. D., 11n
Lovett, William A., 10n

Manne, Henry G., 10n, 40n
Markovits, Richard S., 12n, 156n,
    157n
McConnell, Campbell R., 65n
McKean, Roland N., 162n
McKenzie, Richard, 40n
Meade, James E., 65n
Melamed, A. Douglas, 59, 67n,
    79, 85, 86, 87, 96, 98,
    111n, 112n, 113n, 115n
Mercuro, Nicholas, 110n, 115n,
    116n
Michelman, Frank I., 115n, 122,
    126, 134, 156n, 157n,
    159n, 160n, 165, 170n

Miliband, Ralph, 42n
Mills, Edwin S., 66n
Mishan, Ezra J., 11n, 12n, 54, 64,
    65n, 68n
Mitchell, William C., 161n
Moore, James C., 108n
Morgenstern, Oskar, 11n, 12n
Mueller, Dennis C., 40n, 160n,
    161n
Musgrave, Richard, 66n, 109n,
    110n
Myrdal, Gunner, 2

Nath, S. K., 5, 11n, 12n, 41n,
    109n
Nelson, Robert H., 115n
Netherton, Ross D., 114n, 115n
Niskanen, William A., 161n

Oates, Wallace E., 66n
Ordeshook, Peter, 161n

Pareto, Vilfredo, 12n
Peacock, Alan T., 11, 40n, 54,
    66n, 109n
Pejovich, Svetozar, 1, 15, 24, 27,
    40n, 41n, 65n, 110n
Pennock, J., Roland, 170n
Peterson, George E., 110n
Pigou, Arthur C., 55, 56, 60, 61,
    66n
Polinsky, A. Mitchell, 87, 113n,
    156n, 171n
Posner, Richard A., 1, 10n, 40n,
    80, 82, 90, 111n, 112n,
    113n, 118, 121, 123, 124,
    125, 126, 127, 128, 129,
    130, 131, 132, 133, 134,
    135, 156n, 157n, 158n,
    159n, 160n, 168
Priest, George L., 121, 156n

Quandt, Richard E., 11n
Quirk, James, 5, 6, 11n

Radomysler, A., 8, 12n
Randall, Alan, 21, 24, 25, 26, 27, 40n, 41n, 160n, 170, 171n
Rawls, John, 13, 39n, 76
Regan, Donald H., 67n
Riker, William, 161n
Riley, John G., 65n
Rizzo, Mario J., 111n, 112n, 157n
Robbins, Lionel C., 8, 12n, 70, 108n
Rodgers, James D., 11n, 110n
Rosenberry, Marvin B., 89
Rothbard, Murry N., 60, 68n
Rothenberg, J., 11n
Rowley, Charles K., 11, 40n, 54, 66n
Rubin, Paul H., 111n, 121, 156n
Ryan, Timothy P., 110n, 116n

Sager, Lawrence G., 157n
Samuels, Warren J., 2, 10n, 12n, 26, 36, 40n, 41n, 42n, 75, 110n, 115n, 133, 157n, 160n, 164n
Samuelson, Paul, 66n
Sandler, Ross, 114n
Saposnik, Rubin, 5, 6, 11n
Savage, Donald T., 72, 110n
Sax, Joseph L., 75, 102, 110n, 114n
Scharf, Stephen, 114n
Scherer, Fredrick M., 53, 66n
Schmid, A. Allan, 2, 40n, 60, 67n
Schwartz, Alan, 65n
Schwartz, Gary T., 157n
Schwartz, Louis B., 66n
Schwartz, Warren F., 156n
Scitovsky, Tibor, 11n, 12n, 65n, 109n
Seneca, Joseph J., 66n
Shavell, Steven, 98, 113n, 155n

Shepherd, William G., 66n
Siegan, Bernard H., 10n, 42n, 115n
Siemon, Charles L., 114n
Smith, Adam, 29, 41n
Steiner, Joseph M., 67n, 78, 111n, 113n
Stigler, George J., 10n, 65n
Stroup, Richard, 162n
Stubblebine, William C., 65n

Taussig, Michael K., 66n
Taylor, John F. A., 40n
Thompson, Edward, 145, 162n
Tideman, T. Nicolaus, 69, 108n
Tollison, Robert D., 10n, 74, 110n, 147, 161n, 164n
Tullock, Gordon, 1, 19, 40n, 41n, 147, 148, 150, 153, 154, 156n, 161n, 162n, 163n, 164n, 170
Tushnet, Mark, 2, 40n, 122, 156n

Varian, Hal R., 71, 109n
Vejanovski, Cento G., 10n, 67n, 78, 110n, 111n, 132, 160n, 171n
Viner, Jacob, 65n

Wallis, W. Allen, 10n
Weinrib, Ernest J., 157n
Wicksell, Knute, 109n
Wilcox, Clair, 66n
Wilde, Louis L., 65n
Willet, Thomas D., 10n
Williams, Alan, 10n
Wonnacott, Paul, 65n
Wonnacott, Ronald, 65n
Wunderlich, Gene, 12n, 40n, 108n

Subject Index

Accomodation power, 104
Administrative law, 118
Allocative efficiency, 132, 155n
Anarchy, 17, 18
Antitrust, 55
Asking prices, 135, 136
Attenuation of property rights
    (*See* Nonattenuation of
    property rights)
Autonomy, principle of, 125, 136

Background law, 123, 127, 128,
    133, 134, 159n
Background risks, 76, 77, 88, 89
Bureaucracy, theories of, 137,
    140–146, 162n

Calculus of consent, 150–155
Closed behavioral systems, 141,
    161n
Coase/Demsetz treatment of ex-
    ternalities, 60–62
Coase Theorem, 56–58, 82, 83
Common law, 84, 85, 87, 89,
    112n, 117–124
Common property resource, 50,
    51, 55

Communal rights, 14, 15, 127,
    128, 134, 146, 166, 169
Communal sector, 22, 30–32, 37,
    39, 166
Comparative institutional ap-
    proach, ix, x, 13, 14, 37–
    39, 60–62, 165, 169
Compensation, ex ante, 125, 153,
    154, 158n
Compensation, ex post, 125, 149,
    152, 153, 158n
Consent, principle of, 125
Constitutional stage of choice,
    16–21, 35, 41n, 150–155,
    166, 169
Contract law, 117, 118
Contractarian approach to public
    choice theory, 146–155,
    166
Corrective justice approach to
    tort law, 80, 81, 106
Costs of collective decisions, 151,
    152
    expected decision making costs,
    151, 152
    expected external costs, 151,
    152

Criminal law, 118
Critical legal studies, ix, 1, 2, 10n,
    165

Damage remedies, 87
Decision rules in common law,
    123, 127–129, 133, 134
Democracy
    direct, 137, 138, 151
    representative, 137, 138, 151
Duality theorem, 45, 139

Economic approach to tort law,
    77, 78, 88–90
Economic compensation princi-
    ple, 8, 9, 12n, 69–76, 106–
    108, 109n, 115n, 148, 170
Economic impact stage of choice,
    16, 17, 22–35, 168–170
Economic performance, 14
Economics of property rights, ix,
    1, 65n, 165, 168
Effective commodities, 24, 41n,
    76, 107
Effective resources, 24, 41n, 76,
    107
Efficiency analysis of the com-
    mon law, 112n, 118–123
Eminent domain, 41n, 69, 99,
    100–102, 108, 168
Endogenous decision making
    units, 4, 15, 37, 56, 62, 63,
    141, 166
Endogenous economic variables,
    3
Enforcement, 28, 29, 51–53
Environmental economics, 55
Evolutionary theory of the com-
    mon law, 119–123
Exchange in the political arena,
    149, 150
Exogenous economic variables, 3,
    4

Externality, 43, 44, 51, 56–59,
    62–64, 65n, 169

Federal Water Pollution Control
    Act Amendments, 1972,
    145, 146
Fifth Amendment of the U.S.
    Constitution, 100, 101,
    114n

Gains from trade, 23, 119, 149
Governmental regulation (collec-
    tive fiat), 59, 80, 81, 102,
    103, 106–108, 112n
Grand utility possibility frontier,
    139, 140

Impossibility theorem, 140
Information, 51, 52
Injunction, 87
Institutional stage of choice, 16,
    17, 21, 22, 33, 35, 166,
    169, 170
Interaction damage costs, 90–92,
    106, 107, 168, 170

Justice-fairness approach to tort
    law, 77–80

Kaldor-Hicks criterion, 8, 70,
    109n, 118, 125, 135, 168
Kohler Act, 103

Law and Economics, ix, 1, 13, 15,
    37, 117, 147, 165
Learned Hand rule, 79, 92
Legal-economic arena, 31–35
Legal institutions, ix, 13, 15, 16,
    21, 29, 32, 37, 62, 63, 119,
    165, 166
Legal relations governing society,
    16, 23, 25, 29, 32, 33, 166,
    168, 169

Legislatures, theories of, 137, 140–146, 162n
Liability rules, 56, 57, 69, 76–99, 118, 168
  Hand formula with contributory negligence-version, 1, 2, 94, 95
  least cost avoider liability rule, 96–99
  simple Learned Hand, 93
  strict liability with contributory negligence-version, 1, 2, 95, 96

Market failure, 47–53
Market sector, 14, 22–29, 31, 32, 37, 39, 44–47, 146, 166
Methodological individualism, 7, 147, 148
Monopolistic competition, 50
Monopsony, 48, 49, 54, 55

Necessity of choice, 35–37, 73, 90, 136, 170
Negligence standards, 77, 87–90, 168
Neoclassical economics, 2, 3, 5, 15, 25, 43, 44
Neoinstitutionalist economic theory, ix, 1, 2, 165
New law and economics, ix, 1, 117–137, 144, 147, 165, 168
Nonattenuated property rights, 24–28, 41n, 107, 108, 168, 169
Normative economic analysis, 3, 5–7, 9, 11n–12n, 38, 74, 122–124, 129, 130, 136–138, 149, 154, 155

Offer prices, 135, 136
Old law and economics, ix, 1

Oligopoly, 50
Opportunity cost, 18, 40n, 47

Pareto optimality, 5, 7–9, 12n, 25, 26, 37, 38, 45–47, 52, 57, 59, 65n, 118, 127–129, 139–140, 152, 153, 166
Pareto optimality in the large, 154
Pareto superiority, 118, 124
Pareto-Wicksellian criterion, 8, 70, 75, 109n, 148, 149
Pigovian treatment of externalities, 55, 56, 59, 60
Police power, 41n, 69, 99–102, 107, 108, 168
Political rules of collective order, 140–146, 166–169
  prevailing, 142, 143
  formulation, 143–146
Positive economic analysis, 3, 5–7, 9, 11n–12n, 38, 70, 74, 118, 122–124, 129, 130, 137, 138
Potential Pareto superiority, 8, 70, 71, 125
Presumed Pareto optimality, 152, 153
Private property rights, 14, 22–25, 28, 33–35, 40n, 127, 128, 134, 166, 169
Productive efficiency, 118, 132, 155n
Property law, 117, 118
Property rules, 85, 86
Public choice theory, ix, 1, 117, 137–155, 161n, 165–168
  axiomatic social choice theory, 138–140, 166
  contractarian public choice theory, 146–155, 166
  conventional public choice theory, 140–146, 166–168

Public goods, 54
Public sector, 22, 29–32, 37, 39, 143, 145, 146, 166
Public utility regulation, 55
Pure competition, 43, 44
Pure monopoly, 50

Real valued social welfare functions, 138–140

Social contract theory, 18, 19
Social indifference curves, 139, 140
Social welfare, 26
State, theory of, 137
Status quo prices, 132–134, 170
Status quo structure of rights and rules, 72–75, 149, 154, 155
Status rights, 14, 15, 30, 127, 128, 134, 166, 169
Strict liability rules, 77, 87, 88, 90, 168

Taking issue, 69, 99–108
  categorization of taking issue cases, 104–106
Taking issue decisional rules, 99, 104
  critical natural features rule, 104, 169
  fair compensation rule, 104, 169
  harm-benefit rule, 104, 169
Theory of the second best, 53, 54, 66n

Tort law, 69, 76–99, 117, 118
Transactions costs, 56–59, 66n, 83–85
Trial settlement models, 119–121

Unanimous consent requirement, 8, 148–150, 154, 155
U.S. Army Corps of Engineers, 144–146
Utility, 7, 17, 70, 140, 143

Veil of ignorance, 19, 20, 150, 151

Wealth maximization, 118, 123–137, 166, 169
  criticisms of wealth maximization
    conflicts between gains in wealth and gains in efficiency, 132
    the offer-asking price dilemma, 135–137
    the problem of circularity: rights and prices, 132–134
    wealth maximization as an instrumental value, 130–132
  judicial behavior, 125–129
Welfare economics, 4–9, 11n, 139
Willingness to pay, 124, 135
Working rules, 14, 33–35, 127, 128, 134, 141, 166–169